in freedom we trust:
an atheist guide to
religious liberty

in freedom we trust:
an atheist guide to
religious liberty

Edward M. Buckner and Michael E. Buckner

 **Prometheus Books**

59 John Glenn Drive
Amherst, New York 14228-2119

Published 2012 by Prometheus Books

Cover design by Grace M. Conti-Zilsberger

Inquiries should be addressed to
Prometheus Books
59 John Glenn Drive
Amherst, New York 14228–2119
VOICE: 716–691–0133
FAX: 716–691–0137
WWW.PROMETHEUSBOOKS.COM

16 15 14 13 12   5 4 3 2 1

Library of Congress Cataloging-in-Publication Data

Buckner, Ed.
    In freedom we trust : an atheist guide to religious liberty / by Edward M. Buckner and Michael E. Buckner.
      p. cm.
    Includes bibliographical references and index.
    ISBN 978–1–61614–644–3 (pbk. : alk. paper)
    ISBN 978–1–61614–645–0 (ebook)
    1. Liberty—Religious aspects. 2. United States—Religion. 3. Religion and politics—United States. 4. Religious tolerance—United States. I. Buckner, Michael E. II. Title.

BL2525.B843 2012
323.44'20973—dc23

                           2012025636

Printed in the United States of America on acid-free paper

For Diane

Contents

Introduction

Is there "Nothing New Under the Sun"? That could almost have served as the title of this book. Consider:

- The president of the United States is attacked by political opponents for not being a real Christian, first as a candidate, then as president.
- That same president is heavily criticized for engaging in war against Libyans without a congressional declaration of war.
- The United States and Americans are violently attacked by Muslim extremists.
- Bitter political arguments and angry fights erupt over whether the United States is or should be a Christian nation and whether our government is based on Christian principles.
- Legislators in the Virginia House of Delegates wrangle over proposed laws alleged to protect religious expression.
- Political hay is made—or at least sought—over American "exceptionalism," over whether this nation was established by acts of God and therefore set aside for divine purposes and approval.
- Middle Easterners rise up in arms over what forms their own governments should take, with religious differences often at the heart of the emotions running high; Tripoli is frequently in the news.

All of the above come straight from current or recent news stories. But all also describe events or stories from many years earlier in American history, and the parallels are not just coincidences. Nor are any of these merely matters of abstract, theoretical, or academic interest—lives are changed, even lost, in the conflicts; freedom and perhaps even national survival are also imperiled or strengthened by sectarian strife.

President Barack Obama, like President Thomas Jefferson before him, and like other 2012 presidential candidates, has struggled politically with his ability to counter claims that he is not a good Christian.[1] (More on Obama and other current political leaders in chapter 3.) In the election of 1800, according to James F. Simon,

> Federalists charged that a Jefferson presidency threatened to destroy America's soul. Voters had only to ask one question of themselves, suggested the leading Federalist newspaper, the *Gazette of the United States*: "Shall I continue in allegiance to God—and a religious President, or impiously declare for Jefferson—and no God!"[2]

Simon went on to discuss Federalist attacks predicting moral chaos or worse in the nation if Jefferson were to be elected. Edward J. Larson described the election in detail in his book *A Magnificent Catastrophe: The Tumultuous Election of 1800, America's First Presidential Campaign.* As Larson noted, "Hamilton and the Federalists repeatedly warned that Republican [roughly the equivalent then of today's Democrats; Jeffersonians] rule might lead to . . . attacks on churches in America."[3]

Robert Bentley, who became governor of Alabama in January 2011, caused an uproar—and eventually apologized—because he declared not long after he was inaugurated that "anybody . . . who has not accepted Jesus Christ as their savior, I'm telling you, you're not my brother and you're not my sister."[4]

Local elected officials across America entangled their religion with their elections—or paid a political price for not doing so. A judge in Bowie County (Texarkana), Texas, proclaimed (at his inauguration in early 2011) that he did officially "hereby dedicate to the Lordship of Jesus Christ Bowie County Texas and the civil government thereof."[5]

Texas is not the only part of the United States where leaders assume that fundamentalist Christianity ought to be promoted by elected officials, but it certainly is a state where the idea, including the idea that the whole nation should be dedicated to Christ, is widespread. And Texas has helped "contribute" these bogus ideas to the whole nation, through President George W. Bush and others—and threatens to do so again. Recently Texas governor Rick Perry (candidate, for a while, for the 2012 Republican nomination for president) declared that "Right now, America is in crisis: we have been besieged by financial debt, terrorism, and a multitude of natural disasters. As a nation, we must come together and call upon Jesus to guide us through unprecedented struggles, and thank Him for the blessings of freedom we so richly enjoy."[6] As governor, Perry also issued calls to pray for rain[7] and asked national and state leaders to come to a 2011 meeting in Houston. Since Perry's asked-for "day of prayer" was in addition to a "National Day of Prayer" (called in early May every year by religious leaders described in detail in Jeff Sharlet's books), it seemed likely at the time that the event in Houston was actually intended to be a "National Day of Perry." In his call for that meeting (quoted above), Perry also asserted that "there is hope for America. It lies in heaven, and we will find it on our knees."[8] (For more on Rick Perry and his entanglement with fundamentalist Christianity, see chapter 3, "Religion and Politics Now.") Perry, like many others who are accepted—elected, in fact, to high office—by thousands of Americans, has no apparent understanding of or respect for the logic and history of American secularism.

The constitutional guarantee that "no religious test shall ever be required as a qualification to any office or public trust under the United States" (Article VI) failed to prevent the political tests any of these leaders faced or invited. As Ray Suarez noted, "Voting for the most religious candidate on Election Day or counting a less publicly religious posture against a candidate when making one's decision may make an individual voter feel better, while saddling the entire community with an elected official who is religious, and incompetent."[9]

Violent attacks on Americans by men claiming to act on behalf of Allah plagued us—as well as Muslims in general—in the 1790s as surely as in 2001. A treaty agreed to while George Washington was still president and ratified after John Adams succeeded him reassured an Islamic nation that our government is not based on Christianity and that Muslims were safe from religious-based wars with the United States (see chapter 8, "From the Shores of Tripoli . . . ," for details).

Sarah Palin declared on Fox News[10] that it is "mind-boggling" to declare that "America is not a Christian nation" and went on to assert that our Constitution acknowledges that Americans' rights "don't come from man; they come from God." Similarly, former US Speaker of the House Newt Gingrich insisted (in June 2009) that, "I am not a citizen of the world. I am a citizen of the United States, because only in the United States does citizenship start with our creator."[11] In his tellingly subtitled 2010 book, *To Save America: Stopping Obama's Secular-Socialist Machine*,

Gingrich asserted that "America . . . was founded on Judeo-Christian principles,"[12] though he never made clear what principles he meant. The argument Palin and Gingrich make started before either of them—or the United States itself—was born. (More on the careless declarations of recent American national candidates, including Palin and Gingrich, in chapter 3. Still more on Gingrich in chapter 4.)

As the preparations for commemorating the tenth anniversary of the September 11, 2001, attacks on the United States neared completion, the mayor of New York was roundly criticized for *not* turning the ceremony into a religious event. Richard Land of the Southern Baptist Convention, for example, asserted that "We're not France. Mr. Bloomberg is pretending we're a secular society, and we are not."[13] Land, like many others, does not know American history or understand secularism, and he apparently does not even know the policies of his own group—see our "History Is Not on the Side of the Angels," chapter 5, for more on the Southern Baptists.

Many popular pundits have loudly argued throughout most of our history that America is a Christian nation and that those who declare otherwise are engaging in a great deception. For example, Michael Medved identified this "deception" in *The 10 Big Lies about America: Combating Destructive Distortions about Our Nation*. Medved's third chapter is "Big Lie #3: The Founders Intended a Secular, Not Christian, Nation."[14] John A. Stormer (of *None Dare Call It Treason* [1964] fame) asserts that "a careful search shows that the Declaration's life, liberty, and happiness are in the Bible. The rights spelled out in the Constitution's Bill of Rights can be found there also."[15] Medved insisted on a distinction between a Christian or Judeo-Christian nation (which he said the United States is) and a "Christian government" (which he admitted the United States does not have). But he thereby ignores the facts: the government is *the* instrument that "We the People" use for making, interpreting, and administering laws and is therefore crucial to American identity and society. He and others like him also ignore the fact that the specified and preferred form of government in the Bible is theocratic, not democratic. (See "The Unchristian Roots of the Fourth of July," chapter 6, and "The Unchristian Nature of the US Constitution," chapter 7, for more on this.) The twisted "logic" that Medved and Stormer and many others employ can be entertaining but is utterly unpersuasive.

There are more credible and serious proponents of a much vaguer, more general connection between Christianity and Western society—suggested for example by the dust-jacket description of *The World Turned Upside Down* by Melanie Phillips: "We tell ourselves that religion and reason are incompatible, but in fact the opposite is the case. It was Christianity and the Hebrew Bible that gave us our concepts of reason, progress and an orderly world—the foundations of science and modernity."[16] But, except in the most tenuous sense, these proponents are also unpersuasive. And, even if they were correct about sources, secularism is the only way forward now.

Not all Christians, of course, make the kind of false claims alluded to above, nor do all Christians fail to realize that secularism is in their best interests. The Baptist Joint Committee for Religious Liberty maintains an excellent website (http://www.bjcpa.org) on secularism (on church and state), and publishes useful materials. And authors like John Fea, *Was America Founded as a Christian Nation*, and Mark Weldon Whitten, *The Myth of Christian America*, defend church-state separation with solid logic, mostly accurate historical facts and interpretation, and mostly reasonable discourse. Whitten's book is especially good on the subject, even if he did significantly misrepresent our secularist friend and scholar Tom Flynn as having "evidenced a radical and hostile view of church-state separation" and mischaracterized Flynn's views as "extreme and idiosyncratic."[17]

Thomas Paine wrote, "my country is the world, and my religion is to do good."[18] Thomas Jefferson himself, the primary author of the Declaration of Independence in 1776, wrote in 1782, "The legitimate powers of government extend to such acts only as are injurious to others. But it does me no injury for my neighbor to say there are twenty gods, or no god. It neither picks my pocket nor breaks my leg."[19] The US Constitution—our governing charter—nowhere even hints that our rights "come from God," as Gingrich and Palin and many others have asserted. The primary author of that document, James Madison, wrote in a letter in 1819 of the positive effects of the "total separation of the church from the State."[20]

In discussions leading up to the 2012 elections (see chapter 3 for more), politicians, as in many earlier elections, often suggested that American exceptionalism, based on our founding as a Christian (or, sometimes, as a Judeo-Christian) nation gives the United States special rights and power in the world—and derided an American leader like Barack Obama for daring to say, as he did in 2009, that other nations also see themselves as exceptional. Sarah Palin devoted an entire chapter on American exceptionalism, including attacks on Obama, in her recent book, *America by Heart* (2010). Newt Gingrich declared that Obama is part of "a radical left-wing elite that does not believe . . . in American exceptionalism."[21] We argue that America does have a fair claim to being "exceptional" in an important, international sense (see chapter 7, "The Unchristian Nature of the US Constitution"), but not in a way Gingrich or Palin would appreciate.

The heavily religious/antisecular overtones and the attendant problems of the contemporary connotations of this exceptionalism were made especially clear in an essay by Richard Cohen.[22] For more on this, including more on what Cohen wrote, see chapter 3.

Arguments during the constitutional ratification process (1787–1789) often included complaints that the US Constitution improperly omitted any invocation of any gods. John Adams (who later became the second president) wrote in a 1787–1788 publication that "it will never be pretended that any persons employed in that service [writing the Constitution] had interviews with the gods, or were in any degree under the influence of Heaven." (This quotation is even better in context and is quoted at much greater length in our general chapter on history, chapter 5, which we recommend reading for more.)

What Christian-nation supporters need to do, but never do and cannot do, is connect *any* principle of our government to genuine Christian sources. Our Constitution is justifiably famous for important and valuable ideas—such as individual freedom, separation of powers, freedom of religion, free speech, civilian control of the military, freedom of the press, and democratic elections—but *none* of these are Christian. Some—religious liberty and democratic elections, for example—are even directly opposed to biblical principles.

Turmoil in the Middle East and beyond—most recently in Tunisia, Egypt, Bahrain, Yemen, Libya, Jordan, Algeria, Mali, and Iran—has been close to ubiquitous for centuries. The conflicts that have torn the area have involved territory, opposition to dictatorships, outrages rooted in race and ethnicity, and more—but almost always with major exacerbation from religious differences. These religious differences have been within

Islam (Shia versus Sunni) and between Islam and Christianity or between Islam and Judaism. The United States has been affected by and entangled with these wars and disputes since the earliest days of our existence.

President Obama has been criticized for moving against Libya without proper congressional authorization.[23] President Jefferson, who like Obama before his election was thought by his critics to be too soft on military options, possibly even a pacifist (see the first chapter in Joseph Wheelan's *Jefferson's War*), engaged in an undeclared war—one of America's first—after Jefferson began the path to making the United States a world-class military power by building our first real US Navy. Under Jefferson the United States launched the first attack against Libya (then just known as Tripoli). Obama followed steps in 2011 that paralleled, in a sense, those taken over two centuries before.

An example of American history that showed incredible violations of the American secular ideal—and of politics suffused with religious bigotry that resulted from the violations—came in the short and unsuccessful 1928 campaign of Democratic presidential nominee Al Smith. Smith biographer Robert A. Slayton reported that

> feelings were so strong that they swirled into a hurricane of abuse, a crescendo of fear and hate blasting through eight weeks. The school board of Daytona Beach, Fla., sent a note home with every student. It read simply, "We must prevent the election of Alfred E. Smith to the Presidency. If he is elected President, you will not be allowed to have or read a Bible." Fliers informed voters that if Smith took the White House, all Protestant marriages would be annulled, their offspring rendered illegitimate on the spot.[24]

Another example from twentieth-century American history: in 1941 Lyndon Baines Johnson, who became president in 1963 when John F. Kennedy was assassinated, ran for the US Senate. His chief rival for the Democratic nomination (then tantamount to election in Texas and other Southern states) managed to edge Johnson out in an election that may not have been entirely legitimate. According to the Austin, Texas, LBJ Library museum caption on a 1941 election campaign photo, LBJ's

> major opponent is colorful and folksy Governor W. Lee O'Daniel, who calls himself "Pappy." LBJ's campaign emphasizes his support of Presi-

dent Roosevelt, in contrast with O'Daniel's pledge of "one hundred percent approval of the Lord God Jehovah, widows, orphans, low taxes, the Ten Commandments, and the Golden Rule."[25]

Quite similar sweeping political statements heavy with pious religious declarations have been common from the early days of the republic right up until today. The more recent candidates who have held forth in this way have been more likely to be Republicans rather than Democrats like O'Daniel, but they have been common in all American mainstream political parties.

All the above examples—the historical and the current political ones—show why a defense of secularism is necessary. The case for that defense is the purpose of this book. The resistance to secularism, then and now, is at base a resistance to accepting and even celebrating tentativeness and skepticism. Secularism requires everyone to admit that ultimate religious truth, if it exists at all, is not within the grasp of human beings. It opposes what our friend Chris Snider once called an attitude of "Yahweh or the highway."[26] Secularism is not the same thing as science, but it shares with science a crucial requirement that tentativeness and doubt be embraced, not opposed or merely accepted. It also shares not merely an acceptance of healthy skepticism but also a view of skepticism as both positive and necessary. Cullen Murphy has eloquently extolled the great virtues of doubt and has tied those virtues to the wisdom of secularism and the foolishness of declaring America a Christian nation or of deeming certain religions and beliefs intolerable.[27]

The United States is a free country, not a Christian nation. The United States *ought* to be a free country, not a Christian nation. This does not mean that the government of the United States ought to be actively opposed to the Christian religion or to persecute Christians. The Founding Fathers did not intend—and we do not here advocate for—an anti-theistic government or even an atheistic government except in the narrow sense that government should not be based on or dependent on religious ideas, or anyone's conclusion of what any god is like or wants us to do. Secular means "not religious"—it does not necessarily mean "antireligious." That the United States is not a Christian nation does not mean that the majority of its citizens are not Christians in one sense or another—after all, a majority of Americans are considered to be white, but almost no one thinks we should call ourselves or think of ourselves as a "white nation." A majority of us are women, but this isn't a "female nation." And to advocate that the United States remain a free country rather than being a Christian nation is not necessarily an attempt to persuade the majority of Americans to abandon their Christian beliefs. Of course "Christian beliefs," including beliefs about whether our nation is or should be Christian, vary quite widely in the United States. According to J. Gordon Melton, "By the end of the twentieth century, there were more than 2,000 denominations in the United States; by that time, however, only about half were Christians."[28] And there are assuredly wide variations in belief even within most Christian denominations.

There are now—and to great extent, have been throughout our history—prominent leaders like 2008 VP candidate Sarah Palin or 2011 Alabama governor Robert Bentley or Judge Sterling Lacy in Bowie County, Texas, who say or act as if being a good Christian is a requirement for official power in this nation. Demagogues like Newt Gingrich (it is impossible to prove he knows what he is spewing is false; given his background in academia, it is equally difficult to believe he does not know it) write books—one of Gingrich's is titled *Rediscovering God in America*, another is *To Save America*—allegedly proving that the United States is based on Christian ideas and principles. Our take on Speaker Gingrich is not new: historian Robert S. Alley wrote of Gingrich in 1995—not long after Gingrich became Speaker—that Gingrich "operates under the banner of a Ph.D. in history," that he "simply lied to the Congress and the American people," and that "facts hold no charm for the Republican leader."[29] There are additional details on Gingrich in chapter 3, and he is "honored" with a chapter all his own immediately following that (as a prime example of the sort of "leader" who seems to work hard to undermine secularism, or at least to use a false representation of secularism to gain political power for himself).

As this book will show, those who claim that the United States is or can be or should be *both* free and Christian as a nation are wrong. Those who insist that the United States is a free country *because* it is Christian are profoundly mistaken.

Fundamentally, *all* citizens of the United States are free (and Christian only if as individuals they choose to be Christian) because the Constitution of the United States, the supreme law of the land, establishes precisely that. As the Constitution is the legal foundational document of the United States, for the United States to be a Christian nation (or a Buddhist nation, or a Masonic nation, or a monarchy), it would have to be declared in the Constitution. But not only does the Constitution fail to establish the United States as a Christian nation, it specifically avows that "under the United States," "no religious test" is allowed (Article VI), and it guarantees equal religious liberty to all, with only a few exceptions (if your religion tells you that it is desirable to harm someone else, you will not be free to do that in this country)—it establishes the United States as a free country right from the start.

The framers of the Constitution certainly understood that religious liberty depends directly on preventing the central government from making any religious choices for its citizens, and the framers gave us both the history and the logic that undergird our case.

We—father (Ed) and son (Michael)—are freethinkers, secular humanists, and atheists (for our definitions, see the glossary), and this book is written from that viewpoint, which we suppose makes us "avowed" atheists. We nevertheless firmly believe, and argue throughout this book, that a secular nation, governed without preference for any religious or irreligious view, is best for all Americans. There are other books, including some fine, valuable, well-argued, and carefully documented works, that make parts of the case we want to make. (A list of many of these can be found in the bibliography of this book.) But this book will feature arguments, details, and an organization not found elsewhere, and it can serve as a reference for anyone interested in the subject.

This is not, except indirectly, a book that makes the case for atheism versus Christianity or other theisms; many of the books that have done that (or that at least have seriously challenged orthodox theism) in recent years—books by Dan Barker, Robert Collins, Richard Dawkins, Daniel Dennett, Bart D. Ehrman, David Eller, Annie Laurie Gaylor, Sam Harris, Guy P. Harrison, Christopher Hitchens, Edwin Kagin, Russ Kick, Paul Kurtz, Michael Martin, Dale McGowan, David Mills, Keith Parsons, John Allen Paulos, Darrel Ray, George H. Smith, Victor J. Stenger, and Frank Zindler, especially—are listed in the bibliography of this book.

The basic logical argument for secularism (see glossary for precise definition) is presented in the first chapter, "Why Secularism?" in sufficient detail to persuade any reasonable person but concisely enough to be readily used in debates, summarized in letters to the editor, or explained to the aggressively proselytizing religious coworker in the next cubicle. The Founding Fathers (and the times were indeed sexist enough that few "Founding Mothers" can be identified) of this country gave many eloquent arguments for the wisdom and justice of maintaining the "wall of separation between church and state," and human history, both before and since the founding of our nation, gives many woeful examples of the folly and injustice of founding nations upon religious beliefs.

Religion, by its nature, can never produce uniformity of opinion—as believers often delight in pointing out, religion is a matter of "faith," not of certain knowledge. To seek to give official preference to the beliefs of some, even a majority, over the beliefs of others, even a few, in matters that (to quote Jefferson again) "neither pick my pocket nor break my leg," produces neither justice nor peace. To permit everyone the liberty of making up his or her own mind on religion, and of peacefully espousing whatever conclusions he or she comes to, has demonstrably produced a society where both liberty and order flourish. Religious establishments and the entanglement of law and religion have demonstrably produced oppression, disorder, and strife. In the basic "Why Secularism?" chapter, we will make clear why "free country" and "Christian nation" are necessarily opposed concepts.

A brief chapter, "Atheists Are Not Un-American," puts atheism, freethinking, religious unorthodoxy, religious dissent of all sorts, and support for a thorough secularism into context as a legitimate and persistent feature of American life since the beginning of the republic—and decidedly not as an aberration.

Another chapter follows on religion and politics now, providing an overview of the current political status of the long-standing debate on whether this is or should be a Christian nation, primarily in the context of the 2012 presidential election. That is followed by our chapter "honoring" Speaker Newt Gingrich.

The next four chapters summarize, again without getting bogged down with every possible relevant detail, the history, in general, that favors secularism and the secular nature of the US Constitution. The second and fourth of these chapters are essays on key specific documents (the Declaration of Independence and an obscure treaty) that support the need for a strict separation of government and religion. There are examples from history alleged to support both our claim and the opposite, but the counterexamples will be seen, in context, to be superficial exceptions to the overall pattern, or in some cases examples of efforts by those who *lost* the fight against a secular government. In these chapters, beginning with the general history chapter, readers will learn, for example, that Republican presidents have been among the fiercest supporters of a strict separation of religion and government—in the last half of the nineteenth century—and that the NRA (*not* the gun-rights organization—the National Reform Association) lobbied hard but unsuccessfully for officially declaring the United States to be a Christian nation. Also noted will be the increased religious diversity in America that led Barack Obama to write in 2006 that "whatever we once were, we are no longer just a Christian nation; we are also a Jewish nation, a Muslim nation, a Buddhist nation, a Hindu nation, and a nation of nonbelievers."[30] Obama famously said something quite similar in his inaugural address in 2009: "For we know that our patchwork heritage is a strength, not a weakness. We are a nation of Christians and Muslims, Jews and Hindus, and non-believers."[31]

The specific chapter focused on the unchristian roots of the Fourth of July is followed with one on the nature of (and only incidentally on the history of) the Constitution, then one on an otherwise minor treaty from 1796/1797 ("From the Shores of Tripoli . . ."). Although the words of America's Declaration of Independence are often quoted by those who would seek to claim our free country as a Christian nation, in fact the philosophy of the Declaration of Independence, while by no means atheistic, was radically unbiblical and in opposition to many centuries of Bible-based Christian political thought and traditions. Indeed, a fair and open-minded consideration of the political values of the Bible or of pre-Enlightenment Christian traditions and of the political values of the United States (in its Declaration of Independence and in its Constitution) shows a vast gulf between Christian and American values. For example, where the various authors of the Bible express opinions that can be described as political, those ideas are anti-democratic and opposed to individual rights.

Despite the deistic language of the American Declaration of Independence, American values are fundamentally humanistic and have been since the founding of the United States—a revolutionary break with the earlier theocratic underpinnings of many of the colonies and of European nations. Like most revolutions, this transformation was well under way before the outbreak of actual fighting in the Revolutionary War and continued to be worked out long after the shooting stopped. Even those attempts by nineteenth-century would-be theocrats to amend the Constitution to make the United States into a Christian nation[32] bore witness to the fact that it was not already so. Our non-Christian Constitution and history have been repeatedly reaffirmed by our legal system and our courts, including by the Supreme Court of the United States.

A short chapter, "Tolerance, Toleration, and Liberty," then follows on the historical and logical debate between tolerance or toleration (decried in the early days of American independence by Baptist preacher John Leland, by President George Washington, by "father of the Constitution" James Madison, by framer and second president John Adams, *and* by deist Thomas Paine) and liberty. We show that Leland, Madison, Washington, Paine, and all of us are right to prefer individual tolerance with overall liberty to governmental toleration and that this is at the heart of the importance of secularism.

The persistent problems and false claims regarding the public schools and church-state separation are addressed in "Secular Schooling," chapter 11. Here can be found succinct discussions of "Intelligent Design," government-sponsored school prayer, and lies about children disciplined for saying grace in the school lunchroom.

In "He Who Is Not with Me Is against Me," chapter 13, secularism (and the separation of church and state) is then shown, despite repeated false and hysterical claims to the contrary, *not* to be anti-Christian, in intent or necessarily in effect. The idea of a "Christian Nation" is an obvious threat to those of us who are not Christians, but it is also a trap for those who are. In a "Christian Nation," even Christians will not be free; their faith will become a political question, and their consciences will be subject to the dictates of those who hold political power. A free country—where each citizen is free to follow his or her conscience on questions of religion, and the state must remain secular—allows both Christians and non-Christians to follow their consciences. In one of the great apparent paradoxes of American history, this freedom has demonstrably benefited rather than harmed the flourishing of religion even as it has afforded liberty to people who are not persuaded by any religion.

A "Christian Nation" is hostile to Christianity, if Christianity is understood to be a religion of individual conscience and free commitment, while the United States as a free country has demonstrably allowed Christianity to flourish as a faith freely chosen by millions of Americans. The apparent paradox—that a non-Christian nation can actually be good for the Christian religion—is partially resolved in terms of a religion's ability to do well, or at least survive, without the government's help. Neutrality by the state in matters of religion is not Christian but does allow any religion to compete freely in the public sphere. Brief discussions are also presented in this chapter on the relationship of houses of worship to governments and on whether Christians are persecuted in our secular society.

In another chapter, "The Naked Public Square?" the pernicious and misleading claim that separationists or atheists or the courts are denying or trying to deny Christians or other religious believers access to the public square is addressed. This issue, closely related to the topic of neutrality covered in the preceding chapter, is crucial but more complex than it seems on first consideration.

Religion as the reputed basis for, or at least an indispensable support for, morality, as often alleged by modern Christian-nation advocates (and Islamic proponents in other contexts), is then demonstrated to be a false and misleading argument in "The Big Lie," chapter 15. This false idea was in fact sometimes supported by early US leaders like Jefferson or Franklin, but the Founding Fathers should not be accepted as authorities on everything, even where their "original intentions" are known.

Sarah Palin and Newt Gingrich and minor officials in Oklahoma join forces to inspire a chapter called "God's Law: Sharia and the Ten Commandments versus the Constitution." The clear alternatives—secularism versus any specific religious alternative—show why secularism is the only reasonable choice for Americans committed to liberty. We really must choose either secularism or some specific set of religious ideas to adopt as our guiding principle(s), and this chapter briefly examines the major religious choices on offer. (An earlier chapter on the Ten Commandments includes discussion of the Decalogue and its posting in courthouses and public-school classrooms as a political gimmick.)

There are also chapters on holidays (chapter 12, "Holy Days and Holidays in a Secular Society") in a secular society and on religious language (chapter 18, "What in the Name of God?") in the Pledge of Allegiance and the national motto. Though blasphemy and heresy are discussed in a number of places (in historical discussions and in chapter 16, the "God's Law" chapter), a discussion of the problems with any laws about blasphemy and heresy in a secular society can be found in chapter 17, "Blasphemy and Heresy."

In the remaining chapter preceding the conclusion, chapter 19, "Questions," we present a number of repeatedly declared specific claims (in the form of questions considered unanswerable by some) that allegedly support the value of the United States being a Christian nation—and we show in each case why the questions are wrongly framed or wrongly answered (or both) by the Christian-nation advocates. This "frequently asked questions" section includes concrete details and references throughout.

We then conclude—though by that point it will certainly be redundant for our wise readers—with a concise but comprehensive summary of the reasons that the United States of America is and should always remain a free country and not a Christian nation. Part of this conclusion will also be prescriptive: we recommend actions, primarily educational efforts and support of worthy organizations, that Americans should undertake to protect our religious liberty.

Our notes for each chapter are in every case intended to document facts or cite specific sources, not to extend arguments. The Bible quotations included in several chapters are from the *New International Version*.[33] The various sections of the appendix provide tools for those who want more details or who just want to find quickly the facts we have provided: a good index, a list of key dates, a glossary that sets forth what we mean by various key terms, and a list of other fine writing (and some writing that is interesting because it is so bizarrely bad, too) on subjects related to the one presented here.

Chapter 1.

Why Secularism?
The Basic Logical and Philosophical Argument

Thile United States is and ought to be a free country, *not* a Christian nation. Whatever anyone says or thinks, it cannot be both. Nations, including the United States, have to choose either to endorse and support a religion or to be free. We are going to explain here exactly why the choice is necessary and why the only defensible choice is to be free. Everyone, including deeply religious Christians, should agree with us. And that is not arrogance on our part, nor is it foolish one-sidedness—so let us first explain our optimism: Why should readers—some of you are probably Christians, maybe even fundamentalists—why should you listen to a pair of atheists, much less decide that we are right? (After all, there are far more Christians in the United States than there are atheists.) You should agree with us on this for two reasons: first, you rightly pride yourselves, we are sure, on being bright and open-minded, sincere searchers for the truth, as well as strong, freedom-loving, patriotic Americans (readers from Canada and elsewhere are hereby invited to be patriotic to their own "exceptional" nation); and second, we really are right about this.

American history supports this view (see next chapters) and shows conclusively that we are not a Christian nation. And, as many well-documented quotations demonstrate, America's founders supported religious liberty and understood that government support of any religion undermines religious freedom.

There are many "myths"—false things many people think they know about separation of religion and government—that need to be countered. (See chapter 19, "Questions," for specific replies to most of these.) But anyone who wants to claim that our government should support Christianity (or any other religion) must explain away American history, contradict our decidedly unchristian form of government, and, finally and most crucially, demonstrate that separation of church and state is not in everyone's best interest.

This point about everyone's self-interest is the ". . . and ought to be" part of our argument. Anyone who disagrees would have to show why any of four very basic points don't hold up:

1. Americans do not all agree on religion.
2. *Human* judgement is imperfect.
3. Religious truth cannot be determined by force or by majority vote.
4. Religious liberty is worth defending.

These four statements, all true, are the bedrock reasons that separation of religion and government is necessary and desirable for all. We will return to an analysis and defense of these four later in this chapter.

Our history and the documented words of the founders and of our governing documents clearly show that American government was not designed to be Christian. But perhaps even more difficult for those who claim that the United States is a Christian nation is the severe conflict between biblical Christianity and our government and society as it is now organized.

Not only was the Declaration of Independence politically radical, it was radical in religious terms as well. (See chapter 6, "The Unchristian Roots of the Fourth of July," for more detail.) The Declaration explicitly denied the old doctrines of "Divine Right of Kings" and aristocracy:

> That to secure these rights, governments are instituted among men, deriving their just powers from the consent of the governed. That whenever any form of government becomes destructive of these ends, it is the right of the people to alter or to abolish it, and to institute new government, laying its foundation on such principles and organizing its powers in such form, as to them shall seem most likely to effect their safety and happiness.[1]

These words weren't just a challenge to the power of kings; they also went against the plain text of the Bible:

> Let everyone be subject to the governing authorities, for there is no authority except that which God has established. The authorities that exist have been established by God. Consequently, whoever rebels against the authority is rebelling against what God has instituted, and those who do so will bring judgment on themselves. For rulers hold no terror for those who do right, but for those who do wrong. Do you want to be free from fear of the one in authority? Then do what is right and you will be commended. For the one in authority is God's servant for your good. But if you do wrong, be afraid, for rulers do not bear the sword for no reason. They are God's servants, agents of wrath to bring punishment on the wrongdoer. Therefore, it is necessary to submit to the authorities, not only because of possible punishment but also as a matter of conscience. This is also why you pay taxes, for the authorities are God's servants, who give their full time to governing. Give to everyone what you owe them: If you owe taxes, pay taxes; if revenue, then revenue; if respect, then respect; if honor, then honor. (Romans 13:1–7)

And the First Amendment's proclamation that there be no law abridging the free exercise of religion is a far cry from the demands of biblical law:

> If your very own brother, or your son or daughter, or the wife you love, or your closest friend secretly entices you, saying, "Let us go and worship other gods" (gods that neither you nor your ancestors have known, gods of the peoples around you, whether near or far, from one end of the land to the other), do not yield to them or listen to them. Show them no pity. Do not spare them or shield them. You must certainly put them to death. Your hand must be the first in putting them to death, and then the hands of all the people. Stone them to death, because they tried to turn you away from the LORD your God, who brought you out of Egypt, out of the land of slavery. Then all Israel will hear and be afraid, and no one among you will do such an evil thing again. (Deuteronomy 13:6–11)

The First Amendment—which says you may worship whatever god or gods you believe in, in whatever manner your conscience demands, or believe in and worship no gods of any sort, if that's where your reason guides you—stands in stark contrast to the First Commandment's dictate of "No other gods before me." Of course Christians (and Jews) are still free to follow the First Commandment as a matter of individual conscience; but biblical laws (or qur'anic ones) that would enforce one view of God over all others on pain of death can never be implemented in the United States—as long as we safeguard the unbiblical heritage of liberty bequeathed to us by the Founding Fathers.

Theists in America frequently assert that our rights come from the Judeo-Christian God, that the founders knew this and built that knowledge into our governing documents, and that we must all agree that our rights are God-given or must instead conclude that they come from government officials. The false choice that is thus set up is then used in debates to attack the logic of secularism and American history that supports it. The governing documents the founders created demonstrate that they did not see government and God as the only possible sources of our rights and that they plainly did not rely on either source.

Not only does our Constitution assert in its preamble that the source of authority is "We the People," and not any god or allegedly sacred text, but also the document includes explicit procedures for changing anything in that charter. If the framers had wanted to tie rights set forth in the document to God as expressed in the Bible or in any other sacred text, they certainly had many precedents for doing that. But the procedures set forth for changing what counts as a right makes no reference to any religious source. And it is worth noting that theists generally insist that "sacred" or "God-given" rights cannot ever be changed. There is, after all, no procedure for amending the Qur'an or the Book of Deuteronomy.

That our rights can actually be changed is not mere abstract and technical fact. We know they can be changed because they have been. Women, eighteen-year-old citizens, members of racial minorities, all "natural-born" citizens, and others have gained rights as a result of amendments to the Constitution. Slavery has been abolished in this way; rights related to drinking or selling alcoholic beverages have been changed and then changed back by constitutional amendment.

Imagine (we trust that this can happen *only* in imagination) that someone in the United States decided that men in the United States do not deserve to be able to vote or hold public office, that only women should be so empowered. Could that happen? What would it take to make it happen? If a preacher found a biblical passage (s)he interpreted as requiring that, could the president or the US Supreme Court make the necessary changes to our laws? Consider this argument:

Why We Don't Want Men to Vote

- Because man's place is in the army.
- Because no really manly man wants to settle any question other-wise than by fighting about it.
- Because if men should adopt peaceable methods, women will no longer look up to them.
- Because men will lose their charm if they step out of their natural sphere and interest themselves in other matters than feats of arms, uniforms, and drums.
- Because men are too emotional to vote. Their conduct at baseball games and political conventions shows this, while their innate tendency to appeal to force renders them unfit for government.

What would it take to implement the changes preferred by this feminist writer? There are two explicit limits agreed to in the original 1787 document as to what can be amended in the Constitution, regarding abolishing the slave trade and the votes each state is entitled to in the US Senate,[2] so the founders clearly *did* consider how much amendment freedom they were willing to grant to future citizens. But no protection for the rights of male citizens was incorporated.

The answers to this thought experiment are revealing. Men *could* lose their citizenship rights, but not by decree of any religious or political authority. And it could happen even if *all* the citizens most directly affected by it—men—were opposed to it. If a minority of US citizens—every woman in three-fourths of the states—thirty-eight states—was fully committed to the project, the US Constitution could, in time, be amended to take away citizenship from all men in all fifty states. And women are in the majority right now in forty-three of the fifty states.[3] These determined women would have to elect state legislators and US congressional representatives and senators who would do their bidding, but then it could happen. The fact that every citizen reading this, man or woman, no doubt finds the idea virtually unthinkable and would not even briefly entertain it is what will keep it from happening. And the "argument" quoted above—written by Alice Duer Miller in 1915[4]—was almost certainly presented only as satire, as a parody of the case then being put forth against giving women the vote. All this demonstrates conclusively that the rights protected in the US Constitution are protected not by God or government administrators or judges but only by "We the People." Our strong consensus, often developed at great cost and over many years, has changed rights with previous amendments. Our nearly universal consensus against seriously eroding or eliminating citizens' rights is what protects those rights.

The United States, with its refusal to have an official religion or accept any national definition of or belief in any god, didn't start out very biblical, and it has gotten less biblical as time has gone on—which is a good thing in the view of nearly all Americans. One of the greatest blots on our history was the shameful legacy of some 250 years of treating other human beings as property, from colonial Jamestown right up until our bloodiest war, the Civil War. But after four years of bloodshed, we finally proclaimed as a nation in the Thirteenth Amendment that "neither slavery nor involuntary servitude, except as a punishment for crime whereof the party shall have been duly convicted, shall exist within the United States, or any place subject to their jurisdiction."[5] More generations of struggles allowed us to finally make good on the promises of equal rights for all Americans that were made after the Civil War. But ending slavery certainly wasn't the biblical thing to do. The Bible never condemns slavery itself, in either the Old Testament or the New; at most, the Bible calls for masters to treat their slaves kindly (Ephesians 6:9)—while calling for slaves to humbly obey their masters, as they would God himself (Ephesians 6:5–8). As for actually *freeing* all the slaves:

> Your male and female slaves are to come from the nations around you; from them you may buy slaves. You may also buy some of the temporary residents living among you and members of their clans born in your country, and they will become your property. You can bequeath them to your children as inherited property and can make them slaves for life, but you must not rule over your fellow Israelites ruthlessly. (Leviticus 25:44–46)

By the twentieth century we had also finally become a nation that acknowledged, in the Nineteenth Amendment, that men and women should be equal citizens; "the right of citizens of the United States to vote shall not be denied or abridged by the United States or by any State on account of sex."[6] We have women as governors, as senators and representatives, as secretaries of state and ambassadors, and as CEOs and corporate executives. Most Americans probably accept as a matter of course that someday our president will be a woman. But the Bible says that "A woman should learn in quietness and full submission. I do not permit a woman to teach or to assume authority over a man; she must be quiet" (1 Timothy 2:11–12). So much for Madeleine Albright, Condoleezza Rice—and Ann Coulter!

History makes clear that many of the claims made by theists related to separation of government and religion are false, as addressed throughout this book. Hundreds of documents and quotations from the founders of American government that will be cited throughout this work support the idea that the framers quite deliberately established a secular government. But whatever the history or the opinions of the framers, why should anyone support freedom instead of one's own religious beliefs? Were the founders right to create a free country instead of a Christian nation?

More needs to be said about the four basic principles mentioned above and the crucial importance of them:

First: *Not all American citizens hold the same opinions on religion.*
Second: *Human judgement is imperfect.*
Third: *Religious truth cannot be determined by votes or by force.*
And fourth and finally: *Freedom, especially religious liberty, is worth having and protecting.*

Anyone who wants to claim that the United States is a Christian nation, that the American government should support any religion, must show you why any of these four very basic points do not stand. If he defeats *any* of these four closely related claims, convinces you that any of the four does not hold up, then and only then can he begin to build a case that this ought to be a Christian nation.

If we all agreed on religion—a state that has probably never existed even in the most closed society and certainly not in the United States—there would be no need to resolve religious conflicts. If human decision making could be considered consistent or reliable, even close to perfect, then legislators and majorities could be trusted to promote the "right" religious ideas. If it is possible to arrive at religious truth via an election or through force, then electoral or even military means might reasonably be employed to reach that truth. If liberty can be seen as inherently worth protecting, as nearly all Americans accept, and if religious liberty is correctly seen as primary to liberty more generally, then threats to religious liberty must be thwarted. Secularism—separation of religion and government, of church/mosque/temple and nation/state/city/county—needs to be understood and defended by all.

Not all American citizens hold the same opinions on religion and on important matters related to religion (like whether or not there is a god and, if so, what its nature is; or how or when or whether to worship God; or what God says to us about how to live). This is not related to the question of whether you think your own religious ideas are the right ones—presumably everyone thinks he or she is right when it comes to religion. But clearly not all citizens have the *same* beliefs on important religious matters.

Human judgement is imperfect. For Catholics, the pope is sometimes an exception, with regards to official matters of doctrine, but even Catholics, like all the rest of us, *do not* believe that human voters and human legislators always know what God wants us to do. The Bible is quite clear on this point: "Do not judge, or you too will be judged," as it says in the beginning of Matthew, chapter 7, and there are dozens of other biblical passages that make it clear that human judgement is not always reliable. Please keep in mind, whether or not you believe in God, this is not a declaration about whether *God's judgement* is perfect—only whether man's is.

Religious truth cannot be determined by votes or by force. In America, as in other genuinely free nations, neither a majority of citizens nor the government acting on the majority's behalf can make religious decisions for individuals. If you think you might disagree with idea number 3, ask yourself, if a nationwide vote were taken this fall and 99 percent of American voters disagreed with you on a religious matter, would that change your mind? If 99 percent of the citizens wanted this country to adopt Catholicism or Methodism or Islam or atheism as the "right" religious point of view, would you accept their decision, would that convince you? And it's not just voting, it's the law itself, the power of government, that we're talking about here. Remember Abdul Rahman, the poor citizen in Afghanistan who was arrested a few years ago, faced the danger of being executed and finally had to flee to another country, all for the crime of changing his religious beliefs (from Muslim to Christian).[7] Would you change your beliefs *or* be kept from changing them—could you even change what you really believe—if the law required you to?

There really is no middle ground here: either governments have the power to make religious decisions for citizens, or governments lack that power. In 1785 James Madison, later to act as "the father of the Constitution," wrote a petition against using Virginia taxpayer money to support Christians of all denominations. In that petition—signed by enough Virginians to get the legislation killed—Madison wrote,

> Who does not see that the same authority which can establish Christianity in exclusion of all other religions may establish, with the same ease, any particular sect of Christians in exclusion of all other sects? That the same authority which can force a citizen to contribute threepence only of his property for the support of any one establishment may force him to conform to any other establishment in all cases whatsoever?[8]

Freedom, especially religious liberty, is worth having and protecting. This seems self-evident to most of us, regardless of which religious beliefs we hold. As Thomas Jefferson wrote to Benjamin Rush in 1803, "It behooves every man who values liberty of conscience for himself, to resist invasions of it in the case of others; or their case may, by change of circumstances, become his own."[9] As James Madison wrote to a friend in 1774, "Religious bondage shackles and debilitates the mind and unfits it for every noble enterprise every expanded prospect."[10] A generation or two later, another prominent American also put into words the apparent difficulty human beings seem to have with religious liberty for people who disagree with them. As Robert E. Lee wrote to his wife in 1856 (in a letter more famous for revealing his opinions on slavery), "Is it not strange that the descendants of those pilgrim fathers who Crossed the Atlantic to preserve their own freedom of opinion have always proved themselves intolerant of the Spiritual liberty of others?"[11]

It should by now be clear that the heart of argument, the crux of everything that matters that is presented in this book, is summed up in these four principles. If all four of these ideas are correct, there is no doubt that we need to keep church and state separate, that we have to insist, as the framers of the Constitution did, that religion is far too important to mix it up with government power. If governments, any governments, get to control religious decisions for any of us, religious liberty cannot be guaranteed for anyone. We do not devote much space or energy to defending the idea that religious liberty is worth preserving, but only because we trust that most will agree on that central idea.

If you thought that America is or ought to be a Christian nation, we are convinced—and expect this book to convince you—that what you thought was wrong. The reason it is not and ought not be can be summed up in one sentence: To guarantee your own religious liberty, you have to help protect everyone else's, too.

Chapter 2.

Atheists Are Not Un-American
Atheists Are,
Despite Congressman Rabaut,
American Through and Through

"An atheistic American is a contradiction in terms."

—Rev. George Docherty, quoted by Congressman Louis Rabaut, sponsor of the bill to amend the Pledge of Allegiance to insert "under God" (Rev. Docherty in his sermon also called atheists "spiritual parasites"—but he assured his listeners he meant by this "no term of abuse"![1])

It is often asserted that Docherty's bigoted statement from the 1950s is in keeping with the ideals of this country's founders. Such notions were indeed rife in the era of McCarthy, which saw both the addition of "under God" to the Pledge of Allegiance and the formal adoption of "In God We Trust" as the "national motto." And surely they can also be traced back to the founding of the nation—the man who wrote that our rights are endowed by our Creator was clearly a devout Christian and would agree that an atheist (who believes in no Creator) cannot be truly moral and cannot really be considered a true American—right?

Of course, Thomas Jefferson's views of "true Christianity" did not include belief in the Trinity, the Resurrection, or that Jesus was the Son of God (see chapter 6, "The Unchristian Roots of the Fourth of July"). As to the morality of atheists, Jefferson said

If we did a good act merely from the love of God and a belief that it is pleasing to Him, whence arises the morality of the Atheist? It is idle to say, as some do, that no such being exists. We have the same evidence of the fact as of most of those we act on, to-wit: their own affirmations, and their reasonings in support of them. I have observed, indeed, generally, that while in protestant countries the defections from the Platonic Christianity of the priests is to Deism, in catholic countries they are to Atheism. Diderot, D'Alembert, D'Holbach, Condorcet, are known to have been among the most virtuous of men. Their virtue, then, must have had some other foundation than the love of God.[2]

In a request for craftsmen to do some work at Mount Vernon (not, one might think, an occasion for lofty political or theological theorizing), George Washington wrote:

If they are good workmen, they may be of Assia [*sic*], Africa, or Europe. They may be Mahometans [Muslims], Jews, or Christian of any Sect— or they may be Athiests [*sic*]—I would however prefer middle aged, to young men and those who have good countenances & good characters on ship board.[3]

(See chapter 15, "The Big Lie," for more on the founders and morality.) George Washington also wrote to the members of Touro Synagogue in Newport, Rhode Island, "For happily the Government of the United States, which gives to bigotry no sanction, to persecution no assistance requires only that they who live under its protection should demean themselves as good citizens, in giving it on all occasions their effectual support."[4] As we note in "Tolerance, Toleration, and Liberty" (chapter 10), this letter was an important rejection of the notion of official "toleration" of religious "dissenters" in favor of freedom of religion for all; Washington's words also show the possibility of a definition of "good citizenship" free of any sectarian baggage. To Washington, to be a good citizen was a secular matter, a question of the acts one did in this world, not of one's beliefs about the next world.

The founders not only accepted atheists as civil and moral equals, at times they even advocated bold questioning of the most central tenets of religion, including the very existence of God:

Religion: . . . shake off all the fears & servile prejudices under which weak minds are servilely crouched. Fix reason firmly in her seat, and call to her tribunal every fact, every opinion. Question with boldness even the existence of a god; because, if there be one, he must more approve of the homage of reason, than that of blindfolded fear.[5]

While not atheistic per se, the sort of freethinking advocated by Jefferson has been fundamental in the formation of modern atheist thought. This freethinking tradition has been an ever-present aspect of the American character. Thomas Paine, the famous patriot pamphleteer of the American Revolution, later wrote *The Age of Reason*, a scathing critique of the Bible and revealed Christianity (prompting Teddy Roosevelt, quite unfairly, to label the deist Paine a "filthy little atheist"[6]).

In the nineteenth century, the openly nonreligious "Great Agnostic," Robert G. Ingersoll, delivered speeches to enormous crowds and played a major role in the mainstream politics of the day,[7] even delivering the nominating speech for a candidate for the party nomination for president of the United States—at the *Republican* National Convention.

Our Constitution has always prohibited religious tests as qualifications for the holding of "any office or public trust under the United States." After the Civil War, "citizen of the United States" was given an explicit and nationwide definition for the first time in the pivotal Fourteenth Amendment to the Constitution:

> All persons born or naturalized in the United States, and subject to the jurisdiction thereof, are citizens of the United States and of the State wherein they reside. No State shall make or enforce any law which shall abridge the privileges or immunities of citizens of the United States; nor shall any State deprive any person of life, liberty, or property, without due process of law; nor deny to any person within its jurisdiction the equal protection of the laws.

Thus, to be an American, in constitutional terms, is entirely separated from one's beliefs about religion.

As for the Pledge of Allegiance—Congress had to vote to add the words "under God" to the pledge because, of course, those words weren't originally there. The pledge, as originally written in 1892 by Francis Bellamy, a Baptist minister and "Christian Socialist," was as godless as our Constitution.

Many people object to the very idea of pledging allegiance to the flag, and they certainly ought not be forced to do so if they believe a pledge of allegiance to a flag is an inappropriate expression of patriotism or if they have some philosophical objection to the whole idea of patriotism (because they believe only God deserves that sort of reverence or because they believe our loyalty ought to be to the whole human race). The pledge is certainly open to criticism on the grounds that, in a free society, even an expression of loyalty to America and belief in "liberty and justice for all" is not something that can be compelled, since "freedom to differ is not limited to things which do not matter much" as the Supreme Court noted in its 1943 decision *West Virginia Board of Education v. Barnette*, striking down laws that made recitation of the (pre–"under God") pledge by public-school students compulsory. The pledge can also be criticized as a very easy and by the same token ultimately pretty meaningless act of patriotism, too easily substituted for real service to one's country or for the thoughtful dissent on which a free republic thrives.

However, another objection to the pledge as it stands is that it excludes patriotic citizens who don't believe in God but who do want to participate in this simple little patriotic ritual from doing so without lying about their beliefs. The pledge ought to be restored to its pre-McCarthyite form so that all Americans who want to can engage in this civic ritual without having to choose between their patriotism and their religious convictions. We wouldn't tell Jews "Oh, you can just leave out the 'under Jesus Christ' bit when everyone is saying the pledge," and we certainly wouldn't consider it acceptable to say, "Oh, if you Jews don't like saying 'one nation under Jesus Christ,' well, you don't have to say the pledge—I mean, if you don't want to pledge allegiance to this great nation, suit yourself."

The other bit of Cold War atheist-bashing rhetoric, the proclamation of "In God We Trust" as the national motto, either means that atheists are not part of the "we"—and to hell with the Fourteenth Amendment to the Constitution—or else it's a lie, since manifestly we *don't* all trust in God (and even those of us who do don't all trust in the same God). (For more on the pledge and the national motto, see chapter 18, "What in the Name of God?")

Another common canard is the claim that "there are no atheists in foxholes!" To be sure, this declaration is sometimes no more than an observation that people in fear of imminent death may turn (or return) to religion and is not necessarily intended as a slander on those without religion. However, it is all too often taken seriously to literally mean that there are no atheists in foxholes—either *everyone* who serves in combat (or simply finds himself or herself in a situation where his or her life is in immediate danger) converts, or worse yet, that atheists, by their nature, are too cowardly and self-centered to ever risk their lives for a country or for a cause or for their fellow human beings.

However it is meant, the old saw simply is not true. Undoubtedly there are many who have responded to the horrors of war with a renewed commitment to the religions they learned as children. There probably have been some, genuinely atheists to begin with, who have sought solace in the comforts of religion. On the other hand, atheists have certainly gone off to war, including in the service of the United States, and had their skepticism about the existence of a just and loving and all-powerful god reinforced by what they've seen and experienced on the battlefield. And some believers have *lost* their faith and *become* atheists in foxholes in response to death and suffering and the sheer randomness of war.

Pat Tillman was an American professional football player who, in the wake of the September 11 terrorist attacks (by fanatic religionists), gave up a successful career as a professional athlete, with a multimillion-dollar contract, to enlist in the US Army and fight al Qaeda and the Taliban in Afghanistan. He was killed on April 22, 2004, in a tragic "friendly fire" incident. The US military named a base in Afghanistan "Forward Operating Base Tillman" in his honor.[8]

According to his friends and family, Pat Tillman was an atheist when he walked away from the possibility of wealth and fame in order to do what he saw as his duty, and he never "found God" in Afghanistan. Although someone somewhere will claim that just about any atheist who dies has made a deathbed conversion, there is every reason to believe Pat Tillman was a nonbeliever to his dying breath.

Though the circumstances of Pat Tillman's life brought him greater notice, before and after his death, he is only one example of the many atheists who have risked or given their lives in service to this country, in war or in peace (for example, as law-enforcement officers, emergency medical technicians, or firefighters).

American ideals aren't dependent on any religion. No religion or point of view about God is "un-American," except for those points of view that oppose our basic ideals of freedom of speech and religion, liberty, and justice for all. The beliefs of a Stalinist, being opposed to basic American ideas of freedom, justice, and fairness, are un-American, but atheism per se is not. Indeed, freethought is as American as apple pie. Forming one's own conclusions, independent of any authority, is an American ideal as old as the republic itself.

In fact, it is the doctrines of the Christianists and other theocrats that are un-American, not the beliefs of the vast majority of Americans calling themselves freethinkers, secular humanists, or nonbelievers of many stripes.

Chapter 3.

Religion and Politics Now

The Political State of the Arguments over Secularism in the Context of a Presidential Election

Virtually every American election, at every level throughout our history, has involved at least some tension over religion. Many, all the way back at least to Jefferson's presidential elections in 1800 and 1804, featured virulent attacks on candidates for being insufficiently religious or too unorthodox. For a balanced and comprehensive analysis of this through the 2004 election, see Ray Suarez's *The Holy Vote*. Future elections seem certain to continue this trend, at the highest levels and in many other races; the 2012 election campaign certainly did. Barack Obama was steadily pummeled for even suggesting tolerance for religious diversity, and a significant portion of the electorate apparently accepts that he is of no faith or of one different from his firm declarations. Republican nominee Mitt Romney fought against religiously oriented attacks in both the Republican primaries and in the general election campaign. Republican vice presidential candidate for 2012 Paul Ryan had to contend with at least some criticism related to religion. Though a Catholic, Ryan had a history of admiration of Ayn Rand, the objectivist/atheist.[1] Ryan and Democratic vice-presidential candidate Joe Biden, both Catholics, drew some critical comments related to their common religion and to the apparent support of the Catholic hierarchy for Romney, as hinted at by the presence of Cardinal Timothy M. Dolan at the Republican National Convention, though that was later countered by Dolan's agreeing to perform the same ritual at the Democratic convention.[2] The political involvement of the Catholic Church in the 2012 election is discussed in more detail later in this chapter. All the other Republican candidates contributed to or suffered from—or both—religion-based attacks and innuendos, many detailed in this chapter. Many Americans simultaneously want political candidates to be deeply and predictably religious but also to keep their religion private, to avoid "wearing it on their sleeves." There is also evidence that an increasing number of voters would rather see less religious talk by candidates. One survey found in 2012 that a plurality of voters (38 percent) think candidates have talked "too much" about religion, with smaller numbers responding with "right amount" or "too little"—and this was the first time religious talk scored so poorly with poll respondents.[3] And voters most often want candidates perceived as agreeing with their own specific religious beliefs, even when those beliefs are held by only a small proportion of the voters.

In recent national election campaigns, including 2012, the Republicans appear to have worked hard to be worthy of the nickname "God's Own Party," though, according to Amy Sullivan (*The Party Faithful*), the Democrats are now struggling to compete. As we demonstrate elsewhere in the book, Republicans in the last half of the nineteenth century were consistently the strongest proponents of secularism, often making declarations in favor of a quite strict separation of church and state, including urging Congress to tax church property. In the last one hundred years or more, the Democratic Party—along with the media—is more often seen as antireligious. Conservative columnist Cal Thomas summed up a pretty extreme example of this sort of perception:

> Evidence of big media's bias against religion that doesn't advance the secular and liberal agenda of the Democratic Party is beyond dispute. Any faith attached to a conservative agenda is to be ridiculed, stereotyped, and misrepresented. Islam is a notable exception. The media appear to bend over backward not to offend Muslims.[4]

It seems safe to say that most American Muslims would not share Thomas's conclusion about anyone's eagerness to avoid offending them, and it also seems most unlikely that many in the media or the Democratic Party would agree with what Thomas claims is "beyond dispute"— but his views are probably common enough among conservatives.

Given that the US Constitution explicitly prohibits any "religious test" for holding office, it is fair to wonder about the persistence of conflict along these lines. The correct explanations are nuanced and complex, but the most basic answers are:

- Voters, of whatever religious persuasion themselves, interpret their freedom to vote as the freedom to choose whom to vote for on whatever grounds they see fit.
- Being of the "correct" religious persuasion—or, especially, being religious at all—has throughout our history been presumed to correlate well with morality and character or even to be synonymous with morality and character (see chapter 15, "The Big Lie," for more detail)—and of course candidates seek to be seen as moral and to say or imply that their opponents are not.
- Sincere religious beliefs and status are difficult if not impossible to verify—and hence easy to impugn or mislead others about, directly or by gossip and innuendo.

There seems to be little doubt that misunderstanding and misrepresentation of the religious motives and preferences of American voters contributes to conflicts between secular principles and voting behavior. Anthropology professor T. M. Luhrmann has analyzed the different bases for votes between Democrats and evangelicals, and he has argued that better understanding could help both groups achieve their goals.[5] Politics and religion remain key ingredients for controversy in the United States and seem destined to continue to be, even if understanding of all voters is improved.

In 2008, Barack Obama was famously politically attacked for things his preacher (Jeremiah Wright) had preached[6] and eventually disavowed what Wright had said and distanced himself from his former pastor. Obama was slated, apparently, as being a target connected to Rev. Wright again in 2012 in a "Super-PAC" ad, though the idea was dropped after significant publicity on it.[7] Though the Super-PAC ad never went into production, Romney did state that Obama is engaged in trying to "make America a less Christian nation." And it was related to this that Romney uttered his now-infamous declaration that "I'm not familiar precisely with what I said, but I'll stand by what I said, whatever it was."[8] Rev. Wright and others associated with what is known as "liberation theology" were still being attacked by conservatives in 2012.[9] Obama was not alone in this sort of thing in 2008: Republican nominee John McCain was also criticized for statements preacher supporters—like Rev. John Hagee, who called the Catholic Church "the great whore"—made.[10] McCain also flatly claimed at one point in 2007,

> I would probably have to say yes, that the Constitution established the United States of America as a Christian nation. But I say that in the broadest sense. The lady that holds her lamp beside the golden door doesn't say, "I only welcome Christians." We welcome the poor, the tired, the huddled masses. But when they come here they know that they are in a nation founded on Christian principles.[11]

As this book demonstrates beyond any reasonable doubt, McCain was mistaken about the Constitution and also about the nation being founded on Christian principles. But many of the candidates for 2012 made similar false claims.

As the 2012 election got under way, columnist Richard Cohen of the *Washington Post* summed up perhaps the core attack on secularism that candidates launched:

> The term "American exceptionalism" has been invoked by Mitt Romney, Mike Pence, Newt Gingrich, Rick Santorum, and, of course, Sarah Palin . . . [After Cohen explained that the phrase has had different historical meanings]. Now, though, it is infused with religious meaning, which makes it impervious to analysis. Once you say God likes something, who can quibble? . . .
>
> The huge role of religion in American politics is nothing new but always a matter for concern nevertheless. In the years preceding the Civil War, both sides of the slavery issue claimed the endorsement of God. . . . Therein lies the danger of American exceptionalism. It discourages compromise, for what God has made exceptional, man must not alter. And yet clearly America must change fundamentally or continue to decline. It could begin by junking a phrase that reeks of arrogance and discourages compromise. American exceptionalism ought to be called American narcissism. We look perfect only to ourselves.[12]

As Barbara Ehrenreich noted, "Major religious leaders, especially on the Christian right, buttress this conceit [American exceptionalism] with the notion that Americans are God's chosen people and that America is the designated leader of the world."[13]

Republican leader Mike Huckabee (who came in second for the GOP nomination for president in 2008 and was widely expected to run for president in 2012—but who chose not to run) praised Christian-nation mythologist David Barton (of WallBuilders) lavishly in spring 2011, saying Barton was one all Americans should learn from, and even joking that it would be helpful to have everyone required to hear Barton "at gunpoint."[14] Despite the obviously over-the-top rhetorical flourish (video of Huckabee alluding to the need to educate "at gunpoint" showed he was joking but was nevertheless edited out for later publication), it is clear that conservative candidates see no political risk from ringingly endorsing the false idea that the United States is constitutionally a Christian nation.

GOP 2012 presidential candidate Rick Santorum (US senator from Pennsylvania, 1995–2007, and runner-up to Mitt Romney for the 2012 nomination), famous for his very conservative social views, told a meeting of the Southern Republican Leadership Conference in New Orleans in April 2010,

> The founding documents upon which our founding documents were based and that's the Judeo-Christian ethics, that is the base. . . . We are a people of western civilization founded upon the Bible. We believe in the dignity of every human person. Why? Because we are created in the image of God. We believe in the ability, the collective ability of free and virtuous people to do more for our society than a benevolent authoritarian government in bestowing rights upon us.[15]

Santorum's claim that "we" are "a civilization founded upon the Bible" could be construed as an indirect or distant connection to Christianity (mostly incorrect even if that was all he meant), but he has consistently defended his political positions as being correct *because* they are biblical. And in that same talk in New Orleans he accused Barack Obama of trying to turn America into Europe, which Santorum identified as "a completely secular country."

Santorum later in the campaign was "nominated" by Frank Bruni for having "perhaps the most ridiculous hyperbole in a political season thick with it." That Santorum hyperbole was aimed at Barack Obama but through him at secularism itself; it was a by-product of lack of understanding and respect for secularism, the great American ideal. Bruni noted,

> He [Santorum] said that "the path of President Obama and his overt hostility to faith" would lead the country to "the guillotine," an apparent assertion that for Obama, hope and change are the smoke-screen, deficits and decapitation are the real agenda.[16]

Santorum was part of the bizarre attacks on Obama over the administration's rulings requiring Catholic (and other) institutions to make health insurance that includes contraception available to employees. Santorum drew an inference that the guillotine (apparently a metaphor for the excesses of the godless French Revolution) was a little farther along on the road Obama was leading us down. Santorum's remarks drew a variety of comments on their ahistorical and even un-American nature.[17] Not long after this, Santorum explicitly attacked Barack Obama for not being theologically correct, for failing to lead an administration based correctly on proper Christian principles and the Bible.[18] And Santorum, in an apparent attempt to make every new declaration more bizarre than the previous one, attacked his fellow Catholic, President John F. Kennedy, for his famous 1960 defense of separation of church and state. According to Santorum, Kennedy's commitment to separation "makes me [Santorum] throw up."[19] It seemed clear that Santorum could not grasp the possibility that secularism could be anything other than governmental promotion of atheism—or at least that he was convinced that conservative voters in Republican presidential primaries would be that ignorant.

Even Rick Santorum's wife, Karen, jumped into the fray regarding God, her husband, and the need for political leadership on behalf of religiosity. As Maureen Dowd noted, Mrs. Santorum attributed, in February 2012, her husband's successes to "God's will" and declared that a key purpose of her husband's campaign was "to make the culture a better culture, more pleasing to God."[20]

According to Andrew Sullivan, the attacks on Obama over contraception being included under required health insurance seemed to be entirely politically—not religiously—motivated, and not to be working politically. In Sullivan's words,

So with this new compromise, Obama has actually increased religious freedom, not restricted it. All of which makes one wonder exactly how genuine the current outrage is—whether it is part and parcel of a political campaign against Obama rather than a defense of religious freedom.[21]

As chapter 16, "God's Law," demonstrates, a biblically based government would be thoroughly unconstitutional, inimical to religious liberty, and profoundly un-American. Joe Nocera credited John M. Barry (*Roger Williams and the Creation of the American Soul*) with the idea that Rick Santorum's ideas on the right way to govern have roots in the John Winthrop versus Roger Williams disputes of over 350 years ago—and that the Santorum/Winthrop side lost that battle long ago.[22]

An especially telling irony developed in the 2012 campaign, as the candidates and public supporters apparently most fearful of Islam and Sharia law demonstrated that threats to a free and secular nation can come from Christians just as surely. As Charles M. Blow wrote just as Santorum gave up on his candidacy,

> Santorum surged by dragging the debate so far to the right he couldn't see the middle with a telescope. The base dropped all pretense of moderation or even modernity and followed Santorum down a slippery path that led to a political abyss of social regression. The rest of America watched in stunned disbelief and was left to wonder: Was this the rise of some sort of "Judeo-Christian Shariah" movement, as the political comedian Dean Obeidallah pointed out on CNN.com?
>
> Instead of small government and fiscal conservatism, Santorum overwhelmingly promoted—and the public overwhelmingly focused on—his apparent obsession with sex and religion.[23]

Blow's comments highlighted the fact that Santorum-style attacks on secularism make good fodder for political comics—but are also real dangers.

In 2008, Hillary Clinton drew fire[24] for being associated with the arch-conservative if unorthodox religious group known as "The Family" (led by Douglas Coe; see books by Jeff Sharlet for more on this) and even 2008 Republican vice-presidential nominee Sarah Palin was attacked over a video showing her being exorcised by Thomas Muthee to protect her against witchcraft.[25] The 2010 midterm elections had somewhat less drama and uproar regarding religion, though the US Senate Republican candidate in Delaware, Christine O'Donnell, lost quite probably in part because she felt compelled to air a television ad defending herself as not being a witch.[26] And many conservative candidates, especially those associated with the Tea Party movement, advanced themselves as Christian, religious, and therefore allegedly more moral and honest than their more progressive opponents. Insinuations of irreligiosity or unorthodoxy on the part of President Obama, who after all represented everything the Tea Party opposed, were used to undercut politicians at all levels. Pamela Geller declared, with only innuendo for support, that Obama's mother "was a communist."[27] For her snide claim that Obama is a Muslim, Geller offered as "proof" nothing more than that, "Apostasy is punishable by death in Islam. Yet there have been no calls for Obama's death from the Islamic world. Why is this? Islam gives no free passes."[28] Geller even devoted an entire chapter[29] to allegedly demonstrating that Obama is determined to convert America into "An Islamo-Christian Nation."

Nonsense similar to Geller's is this, from 2012 GOP presidential candidate Newt Gingrich in a 2006 screed: "There is no attack on American culture more destructive and more historically dishonest that the secular Left's relentless effort to drive God out of America's public square."[30] Gingrich neglected to tell anyone who the alleged "secular Left" really is or what he meant by "driving God out" beyond an intelligent application of separation of church and state. But that is not meant to suggest that absurd declarations of that type are not politically effective. With at least a substantial swath of the American electorate, they ring "true" even with no reasonable metaphorical bell to create the sound. For much more on Speaker Gingrich's history of distortion and bombast regarding secularism, both before and during the 2012 election, please see the next chapter of this book.

A particularly clear set of examples of simply assuming the accuracy of the false Christian-nation claim have been offered by 2008 Republican VP candidate Sarah Palin. Her declaration in 2010 that it is "mind-boggling" to claim, as prominent Democrats have, that America is "not a Christian nation," was accompanied by her evident confusion of the Declaration of Independence with the US Constitution.[31] She was hardly alone in that confusion—Republican Herman Cain of Georgia, in his 2012 presidential candidacy declaration, insisted that "We don't need to rewrite the Constitution of the United States. We need to reread the Constitution and enforce the Constitution." Cain then went on to attribute to the US Constitution a number of phrases and ideas that are found only in the Declaration of Independence.[32] At least he proved the wisdom thereby of his recommendation to actually read the US Constitution.

Washington Post columnist Eugene Robinson demonstrated that Herman Cain dramatically misunderstands the meaning and appropriate application of First Amendment protections for religious liberty—or at least that he is willing to subvert constitutional principles for political gain in attacking Muslims. Robinson denounced Cain's "unapologetic bigotry" against Muslims as similar to racial bigotry, anti-Catholic bigotry, and other prejudices Americans have used in the past to deny freedom, especially religious freedom, to those they perceive as un-American.[33] Cain later (in late 2011) declared that God had directly told him to run for president.[34] When Cain suspended his presidential run, near the end of 2011, he apparently made no public declaration as to whether God had changed his mind.

Slightly less recently, Palin declared in her book released in late 2010, *America by Heart: Reflections on Family, Faith, and Flag*, that "morality itself cannot be sustained without the support of religious beliefs."[35] (See chapter 15, "The Big Lie" for more on that.) Palin painted with a broad brush, for example attacking President John F. Kennedy because, among other things, he "repeatedly objected to any government assistance to religious schools."[36] Palin quite plainly neither understands nor supports church-state separation and secularism.

Michele Bachmann (Republican congresswoman from Minnesota and erstwhile 2012 presidential candidate) is a clear advocate of politics that include extreme examples of claiming God is on her side. She has even asserted that in effect God has acted as her political adviser on political questions. In April 2011, when asked in an Iowa forum about her long-standing activism opposing gay marriage, Bachmann said of her actions in the Minnesota Senate in 2003,

> I heard the news [about a Massachusetts court decision supporting gay marriage] on my local Christian radio station in Minneapolis-St. Paul, and I was devastated. And I took a walk and I just went to prayer and I said, "Lord, what would you have me do in the Minnesota State

Senate?" And just through prayer I knew that I was to introduce the Marriage Amendment in Minnesota.[37]

She also said in 2006 during a congressional campaign,

They're teaching children that there is separation of church and state, and I'm here to tell you it's a myth—that's not true. . . . The only reason we've been a great nation—guess why? Because at our founding we established everything we did on the lordship of Christ.[38]

In Bachmann's defense, she proved consistent even in defeat, describing her withdrawal from the 2012 presidential race (after she finished last among active candidates in the Iowa caucuses) as also part of "God's plan."[39] Comments like these certainly suggest that a President Michele Bachmann would have vigorously resisted maintaining church-state separation or seeing any need for a secular government and that any government she led would therefore be a serious threat to religious liberty.

While normally associated more with the libertarian wing of the Republican Party, Congressman Ron Paul had at least one embarrassing brush with Christian theocratic extremism in his campaign for the 2012 Republican nomination for the presidency. His campaign quickly pulled a webpage touting the endorsement of Nebraska pastor Phillip Kayser after it turned out Kayser's views include a belief in the modern enforcement of Old Testament laws, including not just the execution of murderers but in some cases the death penalty for unrepentant adulterers, apostates, blasphemers, homosexuals, and idolaters.[40] (As will be discussed in chapter 16: "God's Law: Sharia and the Ten Commandments versus the Constitution," "theonomy"—the radically un-American idea that we should implement biblical law in the United States—has been in circulation on the fringes of the American religious Right for decades now.) One might suppose the laissez-faire beliefs of the libertarian wing of the American Right would be at odds with the state-enforced piety of the religious Right. However, the extreme anti-federal-government views of some libertarians—including a willingness to effectively gut the Fourteenth Amendment in the name of "states' rights" and thereby abandon American citizens to the tender mercies of local majorities (or local activist minorities)—opens up the possibility of theocrats making common cause with those who might seem to be among their natural enemies in the hopes of carrying out an incrementalist strategy of imposing their views in, to begin with at least, the most susceptible parts of the country. (Again, see our "God's Law" chapter for more discussion of Christian theocrats advocating political activism by disciplined minorities to gain power, in the name of an explicitly theocratic agenda of Christian "world conquest.")

As already noted, possible Republican presidential nominees Mike Huckabee (former Arkansas governor and former preacher who later withdrew from 2012 consideration) and former Speaker of the House Newt Gingrich (who did become a 2012 candidate, with many ups and downs in the campaign—though he finally failed to get the GOP nomination) have both sought support based in part on identification with fundamentalist Christian voters—and both have been criticized by secularists over religious questions. Republican 2012 nominee (and former Massachusetts governor) Mitt Romney has struggled against conservative critics who often insinuate that his Mormonism is heretical[41] and simultaneously from more liberal critics. An example of the latter was Kathleen Kennedy Townsend, who criticized Sarah Palin for approvingly quoting Romney as condemning secularism.[42]

Romney has been criticized and attacked by anti-Mormon Christians who are apparently acceptable to Republican "Values Voters." One of these, Bryan Fischer of the American Family Association—who spoke after Romney at an event in October 2011—has gone so far as to declare that the First Amendment "was written by the Founders to protect the free exercise of Christianity" (this may be a good place to admit that some people are quite likely to be wholly immune to the arguments and facts presented in this book) and that Islam is not protected by the First Amendment. (Fischer went on to generously concede that "non-Christian religious traditions" ought to be given religious freedom as a "courtesy." Unless we—er, that is, the real Christians—decide that some non-Christian religion such as Mormonism or Islam is dangerous.) The fact that this would mean that the US government would then have the power, the right, and the duty to define "Christianity" as well as "dangerous religion" seems not to have occurred to Fischer.[43] Fischer wants, according to Jane Mayer, to "control the Republican Party"—and Mayer has made an excellent case that Fischer is both powerful and bizarre.[44]

Even now, evangelicals who reach out to Mormons must, according to Mormon history professor J. Spencer Fluhman, "fend off charges of getting too cozy with Satan's minions."[45] Interestingly enough, not all members of Romney's church consider Mormonism a Christian denomination, with at least one Mormon college professor, David Mason, denouncing "the Christian nation that persecuted, banished or killed them [Mormons] in the 19th century" and arguing that Mormonism is instead "a fourth Abrahamic religion, along with Judaism, Christianity and Islam."[46]

Romney has suffered, according to Frank Rich, because he hides his core because of the proportion of voters—somewhere between a fifth and a fourth of the electorate—who find Mormonism unacceptable. Rich wrote in early 2012 that

> in the current campaign, Romney makes frequent reference to faith, God, and his fierce loyalty to "the same church." But whether in debates, or in the acres of material on his campaign website, or in a flyer pitched at religious voters in South Carolina, he never names what that faith or church is. In Romneyland, Mormonism is the religion that dare not speak its name.[47]

And according to Rich, this means that we are prevented from getting to know the real Romney, the Romney who has devoted so much of his wealth and life to his church. Rich cited with approval Christopher Hitchens's statement a few weeks before he died that "we are fully entitled" to ask Romney about "the role of his religion in influencing his political formation." Rich insisted that "that faith is the key to the Romney mystery." A follow-up on the same subject, on whether for good or ill Romney hid his religion during the presidential campaign, was published shortly after Rich's article. Frank Bruni, in a column titled "Mitt's Muffled Soul," suggested that Romney is "editing out the core of his identity. He's muffling his soul."[48] Bruni also described some of the reasons Romney might be avoiding discussing Mormonism, since his own great-grandfather (Miles Park Romney) was a practicing polygamist who moved to Mexico to avoid the changes in the law and Mormon church rules prohibiting multiple wives.

The Romney campaign did try, at the Republican National Convention in Florida, to use Romney's religion to help present him as warmer or more human—though without allusion to any of the theologically controversial aspects of Mormonism. Romney himself, in his acceptance speech there, cited his religion, but only as a vague, generic faith, not as a distinctive path to religious truth.[49]

Mitt Romney even tried to use God-talk during the campaign in deflecting his problems, real or imagined, with being quite wealthy. In a televised interview, Romney said:

> You know, I think it's about envy. I think it's about class warfare. When you have a president encouraging the idea of dividing America based on 99 percent versus one percent, and those people who have been most successful will be in the one percent, you have opened up a wave of approach in this country which is entirely inconsistent with the concept of one nation under God. The American people, I believe in the final analysis, will reject it.[50]

The syntax and logic are hard (impossible?) to follow in this, but it is clear that Romney expected Americans to avoid envying wealth (his or anyone else's) because America is "one nation under God."

Republican presidential candidate Rick Perry, governor of Texas (he withdrew his candidacy for president just before the South Carolina primary in January 2012), is not merely a Christian politician eager to show off his religious bona fides to the right wing of his party. Perry is closely, openly, and voluntarily aligned with "a little-known movement of radical Christians and self-proclaimed prophets [who want] to infiltrate government," and, according to Forrest Wilder, "Rick Perry might be their man." Wilder went on to describe Perry's success, just before he officially announced that he would be a presidential candidate, with religious Right Christian supporters:

> Moreover, various media outlets have documented a possible coalescing of religious-right leaders around Perry's candidacy. *Time* magazine reported on a June [2011] conference call among major evangelical leaders, including religious historian David Barton and San Antonio pastor John Hagee, in which they "agreed that Rick Perry would be their preferred candidate if he entered the race," according to the magazine.[51]

The John Hagee referred to here is the same pastor that John McCain had to distance himself from in 2008. A further example of Perry's determination to win fundamentalist Christians to his campaign, even if it required displaying either ignorance or dishonest pandering, occurred not long after he announced his presidential candidacy. Perry declared as he campaigned in New Hampshire that "we teach both creationism and evolution" in Texas public schools. Kurt Anderson, who reported this, noted that Perry's claim was "an assertion that's a fiction itself; last month the Texas Board of Education unanimously rejected creationist biology textbooks."[52] Dana Milbank has made the case that Perry is best labeled a theocrat.[53] Theocrat or not, Perry was quite willing to declare that Christianity is the only way. At a "Thanksgiving Family Forum"—a Republican *political* debate—in Iowa in 2011, Perry said, "In every person's heart and soul there is a hole that can only be filled by the Lord Jesus Christ."[54]

Michael Gerson summed up neatly in 2011 the problems attendant on mixing religion and politics:

[The] use of religion in politics is a source of cynicism. It should raise alarms when the views of the Almighty conveniently match our most urgent political needs. A faith that conforms exactly to the contours of a political ideology has lost its independence. Churches become clubs of the politically like-minded. Political dialogue suffers, since opponents are viewed as heretics.[55]

Gerson followed up his comments with similar ones a few months later, though he declared then,

So maybe the message of Americans on religion and politics isn't that confusing after all. They don't like sectarianism. But they also reject secularism. There is, fortunately, a distinctly American alternative: religious pluralism, humanized by tolerance.[56]

This shows that Gerson, like most politicians, understands neither the correct meaning of secularism nor its exceptionally American place in the world. He seems not to understand the real ramifications of "tolerance," either—a common misunderstanding, as chapter 10, "Tolerance, Toleration, and Liberty" shows. The political climate in the United

States is such that there remains real doubt as to whether any candidate will effectively support the quintessentially American point of view: secularism and liberty, *not* pluralism and tolerance.

An example of the prevailing fearfulness of political leaders on all sides occurred during the lead-up to the 2012 election. Republicans led a successful effort to "reaffirm" the "In God We Trust" motto in November 2011; the *New York Times* reported that Rep. J. Randy Forbes (R-VA), the measure's sponsor, claimed, "Some public officials have stated incorrectly that there are different national mottoes. We heard the president make that mistake."[57]

The "mistake" Congressman Forbes referred to was in a speech in November 2010 in Indonesia, in which President Obama did indeed say, "In the United States, our motto is *E pluribus unum*—out of many, one"—but he was explicitly tying our motto to Indonesia's own national motto, *Bhinneka Tunggal Ika*, Old Javanese for "unity in diversity,"[58] which Obama also quoted. In that talk, Obama also said, "America is not, and never will be, at war with Islam. Instead, all of us must work together to defeat al Qaeda and its affiliates, who have no claim to be leaders of any religion—certainly not a great, world religion like Islam." So this was not, alas, evidence of any desire on Obama's part to get rid of the insulting McCarthyite "In God We Trust" as our national motto, but instead just good public diplomacy—playing up a way in which the United States and a foreign country are alike when giving a speech in that country. And *E pluribus unum* remains, as it has been since the earliest days of the republic, a de facto motto of the United States, is still depicted as a part of the US national seal, is still engraved on US coins, and appears as well in many other places. That some right-wing ideologues seem to prefer always insulting any other nation or any religion other than Christianity (and sometimes Judaism) to being diplomatic— as a part, presumably, of defending "American exceptionalism"—is perhaps a subject for another time.

The nonbinding resolution to "reaffirm" the religious motto passed the House 396–9 and did lead Obama to declare the whole process, correctly, as "political posturing." But no leader of either party exhibited the political courage to suggest changing the anti-American motto.[59] Later that same month, Obama was roundly criticized for failing to mention God in his oral Thanksgiving Day message, despite the fact that he did declare that we must be grateful to God in a written proclamation, and despite the fact that three of the prominent Republican presidential candidates had issued their own Thanksgiving messages without mentioning God.[60]

President Obama undertook his own effort to wrap political and policy decisions in religious armor when he addressed the 2012 National Prayer Breakfast and declared that his calls for higher taxes on the rich comported well with his Christianity. He even quoted the Bible, allegedly, on the subject, noting that "For me as a Christian, it also coincides with Jesus's teaching that 'for unto whom much is given, much shall be required.'" Obama also said that the reforms he champions "makes the economy stronger for everyone" and abides by God's command to "love thy neighbor as thyself." At least one Republican, US Representative Phil Gingrey, walked out in protest, declaring that he was angry that the president had used a prayer service for political purposes.[61] And conservative political columnist and blogger Erick Erickson immediately and sharply criticized Obama for his religious/political entanglement and for allegedly choosing to "pervert the words of the Living God."[62] Conservative columnist Cal Thomas excoriated Obama over the event, even going so far as to claim that Obama conveyed an attitude that suggested he wanted government "to replace God."[63] There is of course considerable hypocrisy in some of the same advocates of using religion to defend right-wing politics becoming so righteously upset at someone using religion to defend left-wing politics—one cannot help but be reminded of the biblical injunction about getting rid of the big wooden beam in one's own eye before helping someone else get rid of the little mote of dust in his. Defensive Democratic partisans would likely point out, not without some justification, that Obama was probably doing no more than trying to inoculate himself against the palpably unfair attacks by Republicans that claimed Obama had "declared war" on the Catholic Church or had committed "antireligious" acts (as Newt Gingrich declared a few days earlier).[64]

Secular purists (including us) would respond that doing the sort of thing the president did violates the spirit if not the letter of the First Amendment and that it only encourages the dishonest anti-secularists. A proud American leader, aware of our history and of the purpose of separation of government and religion, would not even attend a National Prayer Breakfast in any official capacity, much less use such an event as a vehicle for pandering to adherents of any religion.

Aside from the brouhaha over the president's Prayer Breakfast remarks, an Obama administration's ruling about the same time stirred up many attacks from religious and conservative political leaders. Newt Gingrich was especially over the top in his fiery rhetoric on the subject (see next chapter). That ruling, later amended and partially reversed by the Obama administration, required institutions and organizations, including Catholic hospitals and universities, to provide health insurance that included contraception coverage for all staff. While it was defended by many columnists, including, for example, a stirring defense by Gail Collins in two columns,[65] it was roundly attacked by others, including, for example, Kathleen Parker, who described it as meaning that "Catholic institutions are under siege by the federal government."[66] *Mother Jones* political blogger Kevin Drum provided a careful analysis of the contraception controversy[67] that applies as well to other church/state controversies. We apply and quote from that analysis in chapter 11, "Secular Schooling." Another *Mother Jones* writer, Stephanie Mencimer, wrote

> When it comes to religious organizations and their treatment by the federal government, the Obama administration has been extremely generous. Religious groups have benefited handsomely from Obama's stimulus package, budgets, and other policies. Under Obama, Catholic religious charities alone have received more than $650 million, according to a spokeswoman from the US Department of Health and Human Services, where much of the funding comes from.[68]

Mencimer went on to quote Amanda Knief, of the Secular Coalition for America, as reporting that "Religious organizations have greatly benefited from the Obama administration."

Libertarians and even some other secularists may be uneasy at government "intrusions" into the internal workings of religiously based organizations on issues like this, or on such issues as potentially forcing religiously based organizations to consider same-sex couples as foster or adoptive parents or to do other things which they say violate the teachings of the religions of which they are a part.[69] We believe, as James Madison said, in keeping religion and government separate. But if we look more closely at some of these disputes over "government intrusion" into the affairs of "religious charities," an interesting complication arises. Government money is funding some of their activities, in some cases a very substantial part—Catholic Charities reports that well over half its income (62 percent) derives from "Government Revenue" (by contrast "Community Support" accounted for 9 percent and "Diocesan Church Support" for 3 percent).[70] In exchange for this money they no doubt provide useful services, with secular purposes, helping people who genuinely need help. But it is also taxpayer money, from taxes paid by Catholics and non-Catholics alike—including citizens of no religion at all—and it raises the question of how an organization can call itself a "Catholic" charity, and insist that it be allowed to maintain its identity as a Catholic Christian religiously based institution, when well over half of its budget comes from tax dollars paid by everyone, not just Catholic Christians.

American Catholic bishops repeatedly insisted during the 2012 campaign that the Obama administration was undercutting "religious freedom" by mandating insurance coverage for birth control[71]—but neglected to explain why determinations of policy regarding coverage should be tailored to religious ideas (often enough, ideas that contradicted *other* religious ideas) in cases where taxpayers may be providing a substantial portion of the organization's budget. There are many social and political issues that involve tensions between sincere religious convictions and public policies for the common good, but especially in cases where taxpayer dollars are involved, organizational principles will not in every case prevail. While individuals must remain free to follow their religious convictions (when those do not impinge on the rights of others), public policy must be based on a more broadly defined common good.

Nicholas D. Kristof analyzed the controversy with an emphasis on economics and political interests and wondered about parallels between the politics that the Catholic hierarchy raised with other religious groups. Kristof noted, for example, that *The Christian Science Monitor*, a newspaper associated with a religion that traditionally opposes medical care, offers its employees "a standard health insurance package."[72]

There was, as there always is, considerable political posturing, some of it perilously close to being downright silly, in the 2012 election. Examples: Republican vice-presidential candidate Paul Ryan's obvious pandering to conservative religious voters, especially Utah voters, regarding giving states the right to defy the First Amendment and support school-sponsored prayer in public schools, despite the settled opinion of the courts.[73] On the other side, the Democrats managed to look craven and even dishonest as they scrambled to force delegates to add the word *God* to their platform at their convention in Charlotte, North Carolina, after it was discovered that the word (*not* the idea—*faith* was already repeatedly inculcated) was omitted. The Democrats at the same time revised their official platform to reaffirm that "Jerusalem is and will remain the capital of Israel."[74] Then Governor Romney tried to capitalize on the "error" the Democrats had made by piously declaring that he would fight to keep "under God" in the Pledge of Allegiance and "In God We Trust" on American money. Romney also asserted that our American rights come from God, not government.[75] If any other candidate had proposed that the pledge and motto be changed, we would have taken that effort quite seriously and as a positive sign. If any candidate had averred that Americans' rights come from government, we would have opposed that (see chapter 1, "Why Secularism?" for more on this false choice). Since, however, there had been no hint of such efforts by anyone else, we confidently considered Governor Romney's reassurances as more pandering silliness. For much more on the pledge and motto, see chapter 18, "What in the Name of God?" Obama's 2012 reelection outcome probably did not turn directly on religious issues (or religion-based silliness) or on the attacks against him as not being the "right" kind of religious. But as the 2012 election showed and as the ones thereafter unfold, religious orthodoxy and attacks on secularism are almost certain to be sustained subtexts throughout American elections and to bubble often to the surface more openly.

Chapter 4.

Why Newt Gingrich's Abuse of Language Matters to the Defense of Secularism

What if a political opponent of Newt Gingrich (former Speaker of the US House and 2012 Republican candidate for president) said of him that Gingrich was an "abuser of power, anti-American, bizarre, a cheater, corrupt, cynical, destructive, disgraceful, endangering, an excuse-mongerer, a failure, greedy, a hypocrite, ideological, incompetent, insecure, insensitive, intolerant, a liar, obsolete, pathetic, pessimistic, radical, self-serving, selfish, sensationalist, shallow, shameless, sick, and a threatening traitor who is willing to destroy freedom to win power"—with or without any specific grounds for the insults? We leave it to others to decide how much of that would accurately apply to Speaker Gingrich. But however accurate the name-calling would be, it would be fitting in one sense: it was Gingrich, more than any other modern politician, who established the practice of false or exaggerated name-calling and invective. We are certainly not fans or great respecters of the former Speaker of the House or of his substantial contributions to the loss of civility in American public and political life. Those unfortunate contributions include a 1990 memo, tellingly titled "Language: A Key Mechanism of Control,"[1] that recommended using all the invective included above (and more) against one's political opponents, that counseled using and abusing language for political gain. This is relevant to the appraisal set forth in this book because Gingrich demonstrably applied his abusive use of language not only to opponents (like Barack Obama) but as well to secularism as an idea. To cite but one egregious example, Gingrich wrote in his 2010 book that "the secular-socialist machine represents as great a threat to America as Nazi Germany or the Soviet Union once did."[2] Atlanta reporter James Salzer claimed that "the words of Newtspeak transformed US politics" and led directly to much of the nasty rhetoric to be found in recent American politics.[3] But Newt Gingrich's irresponsible verbal nastiness is nevertheless not the primary focus of this analysis of Gingrich. We accord him the "honor" of a chapter all his own because he is arguably the single most dangerous, prominent, and misleading opponent of maintaining the United States as an honorable secular society.

Breathtaking examples of Gingrich's dishonesty in service of his own power and in attacking secularism are to be found in this short excerpt from his 2005 book, *Winning the Future*:

> During the Constitutional Convention of 1787, Benjamin Franklin (often considered one of the least religious of the Founding Fathers) proposed that the Convention begin each day with a prayer. As the oldest delegate, at age eighty-one, Franklin insisted that "the longer I live, the more convincing proofs I see of this truth—that God governs in the Affairs of Men."
>
> Because of their belief that power had come from God to the individual, they began the Constitution "we the people." Note that the Founding Fathers did not write "we the states." Nor did they write "we the government." Nor did they write "we the lawyers and judges."[4]

If Gingrich were merely defending the framers' confidence in individual rights, some of this would be reasonable and correct, for the Founding Fathers assuredly did not trust governments, states, lawyers, or judges to automatically protect individual freedom. But his attempt to persuade his readers that the Founding Fathers wanted the government of the United States to rely on God is demonstrably sleight of hand and a slight as well on the intelligence of those framers and of his readers.

It is true that Franklin called for prayer at the convention, perhaps because of newfound religious conviction in his old age—but also quite possibly just because he thought invoking a deity might get the delegates past their fractious differences. Either way, his move completely failed to persuade his fellow delegates and *no prayers were offered*. Franklin wrote in his own notes on all this that "the Convention, except three or four persons, thought Prayers unnecessary."[5] And for Gingrich to declare, without any evidence whatever, that the Founding Fathers were alluding to God by saying "We the People" is illogical and insulting to those framers. If they wanted to invoke divine authority for their work and charter, as virtually all governmental charters in human history had done up until that moment, why did they neglect to do so? Does Gingrich think the framers just forgot to call on God? Gingrich went on, in the same chapter of that 2005 book, to give examples of cultural and literary allusions to God and the Bible in American history, with no hint of understanding how such allusions could—and were—made for political and dramatic purposes with no necessary theological ones.

Newt Gingrich went, in early spring 2011, to a megachurch in Texas led by the same preacher who had caused John McCain problems in the 2008 election: Pastor John Hagee. There Gingrich

> called for a return to historic, Christian roots he said were critical to protecting the nation's freedoms. . . . The audience gave him a standing ovation as he spoke of the nation's biggest threat: the growth of secular thought and an indifference to standing against militant Islam. [Gingrich] warned that America is headed toward becoming a godless society unless voters take a stand against President Barack Obama and liberal-minded college professors and likeminded media pushing his agenda.[6]

At that same event, Gingrich came up with the most irrational, most bizarre comment of any from the current aspiring national politicians on secularism, a comment that demonstrates an utter lack of understanding—and probably of honesty—about the matter. (A rival contender for most bizarre comment comes from another candidate for the GOP presidential nomination, Rick Santorum. See Santorum's comments on the "guillotine" in the previous chapter for more.) Gingrich's ability to be even weirder than Michele Bachmann, Sarah Palin, or Mike Huckabee may have proven to be a strength or a weakness with large swaths of the American electorate. The winner of the most outlandish comment on secularism in the 2012 campaign? Surely it was this comment from Gingrich: "I have two grandchildren—Maggie is 11, Robert is 9. I am convinced that if we do not decisively win the struggle over the nature of America, by the time they're my age they will be in a secular atheist country, potentially one dominated by radical Islamists and with no understanding of what it once meant to be an American."[7] According to Gingrich's spokesperson, Gingrich had intended, when he said this, to put in an "or"[8]—but even if he had done so, to perceive the two radically polar outcomes as alternatively likely results of our national "slipping" demonstrates no understanding at all of secularism. Whether one is considering Christianity or Islam, of whatever variety, a government in the name of either is fundamentally opposed to a secular one, and working to protect secularism is directly opposite to working to establish any religion.

Newt Gingrich followed up his comment that we would give the prize for "most bizarre" to with another, almost seven months later, that we would award another prize to: most outrageously inaccurate historical comment of the campaign. During one of the late 2011 Republican debates, Gingrich declared,

> A country that has been now since 1963 relentlessly in the courts driving God out of public life shouldn't be surprised at all the problems we have. Because we've in fact attempted to create a secular country, which I think is frankly a nightmare.[9]

Incorrect and thoroughly misleading comments like that one are the reasons this book is needed and that the Speaker deserves his own chapter. It is clear that a basic campaign strategy in Gingrich's run for president was to dare any opponent in either party to defend secularism. That dare was, unfortunately, not accepted by any candidate.

When Gingrich spoke after the Florida Republican primary at the end of January 2012 (it was the time and place for a concession speech, since he had just been soundly defeated by Romney—but Gingrich conceded nothing), he continued his attack on both Barack Obama and American secularism. The Obama administration had just issued some rules related to healthcare that did not sit well with conservative critics or, especially, with the Catholic Church. Reasonable conservatives, such as Ross Douthat, and less reasonable ones, such as Michelle Malkin, had raised possible concerns about the effect of the administration's policies on religious actors' scruples regarding including contraception in health-insurance policies.[10] Gingrich, according to Martin Schram, tried to turn legitimate concerns into incendiary politics:

By then, Gingrich was ecumenically pouring gasoline on all glowing embers. He went on to utter the sort of hateful overstatement that made him the fallen speaker that he is today. He said the Obama administration has "declared war" on the Catholic Church and other religious institutions. And he vowed to repeal "every anti-religious" Obama act.

It was classic Gingrichian deceit by distortion, a model for Romney of what not to do. Desperate to reclaim his shattered fame, Gingrich has become a man without shame. He is a self-deluded crusader in a holy war he cannot and will not win.[11]

Lest anyone conclude that perhaps Gingrich threw antisecular verbal firebombs only in hopes of attracting religious zealots to his own candidacy, he persisted with his nonsense even after that candidacy ended. After his tepid endorsement of Romney, Gingrich bizarrely declared, "We're up against a president who's trying to destroy faith by imposing a secular government and arguing that secular bureaucrats have greater moral authority than religious leaders."[12]

The former Speaker of the House, the author or inspirer of much of the dishonest and uncivil behavior and talk in recent American politics, the historian who ignores much of America's history and vigorously and unfairly fights to destroy the most exceptional legacy of America for human civilization—secularism—seemed to be on the cusp of flaming out in 2012. His own deceit by distortion about church and state seems destined, however, to survive—and to continue to need Americans willing to combat the lies of Speaker Gingrich and many others like—or even close to being like—him.

Chapter 5.

History Is Not on the Side of the Angels

The General History That Supports Secularism and Separation of Church and State

Y ou might think that a country can be a "Christian nation," that it can do without "separation of church and state," and still be free, even for non-Christians. After all, some European states have vestigial establishments of religion, but no one is persecuted in England for not supporting the Church of England. But the actual history of the entanglement of religion and the state should disabuse anyone of that view. It was only eighty years from the Emperor Constantine's proclamation that Christians were to have freedom of worship in the Roman Empire to Emperor Theodosius's proclamation that no one else did.[1] Thereafter for thirteen hundred years Christian rulers engaged in crusades against "heathens," heretics, and most notoriously Muslims; carried out forced conversions of entire populations; sought to control the church or were controlled by it; tortured and burned "witches"; and set up special courts to hunt down religious dissenters (the notorious "inquisitions"). When major theological divisions among Christians appeared, persecution turned into war and massacre, from the bloody thirteenth-century Albigensian Crusade against the Cathars of southern France,[2] to the French Wars of Religion in the sixteenth century and the infamous St. Bartholomew's Day Massacre of the French Protestants by French Catholics, to the Thirty Years' War between Catholic and Protestant princes that practically depopulated large areas of Germany in the seventeenth century.[3]

The Catholic Inquisition is well known for its persecutions, but the Protestants were no better: an example of infamous Protestant evil, an example cited by Thomas Jefferson, was that of Michael Servetus.[4] Servetus, a Spanish physician, wrote that the doctrine of the Trinity makes no sense, that it contradicts the idea that there is only one God. Servetus was condemned to die by the Catholic Inquisition, but he wasn't present, so they couldn't kill him. He went to Protestant Switzerland, expecting to be protected there. Instead, the city leaders in Geneva, with the approval of John Calvin (one of the great fathers of Protestant thought) and other Protestant leaders across Europe, had Servetus burned alive (with green wood to give him longer to repent) in 1553.[5]

When not persecuting their fellow Christians for practicing the wrong kind of Christianity, Christians would often turn against the adherents of Christianity's parent religion, Judaism. In 1290 Edward I of England decreed that every single Jew in England be expelled from the kingdom[6]—they were not officially allowed to return for over 360 years—and in 1306 King Philip "the Fair" followed suit in France.[7] In 1492 Ferdinand and Isabella did the same for Spain.[8] Sometimes, European Christians did worse than merely force their Jewish brethren from their homes; during the Crusades, Christians massacred Jews by the thousands, incited by the "blood libel," false stories that the Jews were carrying out infant sacrifices of Christian babies—and that the Jews had secret rites in which they ritually desecrated the sacred objects of the Christian religion.[9]

The American colonies did not escape this terrible history of religious persecution. The Puritans came to America to have freedom to practice their religion, then persecuted Quakers,[10] hanged nineteen "witches" (in Salem),[11] and bored holes into the tongues of other people for "blasphemy."[12] Vicious penalties for blasphemy were on the books, and occasionally carried out, in many different American colonies, not just in Puritan/Congregationalist Massachusetts.[13] One man, Charles Arabella, had his tongue bored with a hot poker in 1710 in Maryland, astonishingly (to modern sensibilities) because of a provision of a law that derived from Maryland's famous Act of Toleration of 1649.[14]

It embarrassed John Adams, as he noted in a letter to Jefferson in 1825, that his own state of Massachusetts had been among the places where blasphemy had been punished in horrible ways and that it remained illegal in his own day.[15] Blasphemy is *still* technically illegal (and can subject one to "jail for not more than one year or by a fine of not more than three hundred dollars") in Massachusetts,[16] as it is in many other states, though any attempt to enforce the law would probably—and certainly should—get it declared unconstitutional.

In Virginia just before the revolution, leaders of the Church of England (now known as Episcopalians), who were then in charge of church *and* state, threw Baptist preachers in jail for things like the "crime" of telling people to read the Bible for themselves.[17] Nor was this limited to Virginia. At least two different historical markers near Baptist churches in Georgia refer to Baptist preachers being jailed or hauled into court for daring to ignore the authority of the Church of England.[18] There were bright spots; the Baptist preacher Roger Williams led the colony of Rhode Island to champion religious freedom for all—and called for separation of church and state.[19] Quaker Pennsylvania was also an early champion of religious tolerance.[20] Intended as a haven for Catholics (persecuted in Protestant England), Maryland allowed for at least a limited form of religious toleration.[21] (For much more on toleration, see chapter 10, "Tolerance, Toleration, and Liberty.") By the eve of the American Revolution, many in the thirteen colonies were ready to reject not only European views on government but also views on the relationship of Christianity to the state, which had existed for centuries in Christian Europe. Angered and horrified at legal persecution of Baptist preachers in his native Virginia, James Madison, the "Father of the Constitution," wrote in a letter in 1774 (quoted in the previous chapter) that a lack of religious liberty strikes at the very heart of human freedom and human ability to think clearly.

As for those vestigial establishments, that's what they are: the last vestiges of a dying past of religious persecution. After the Reformation, Catholics and Protestants in England alternated in martyring each other for practicing their respective forms of Christianity; even as late as the nineteenth century, Britain discriminated against both Catholics and Protestant "dissenters" from the Established Church, who could not be elected to Parliament and were not permitted to attend the great universities in Oxford and Cambridge. Although the nineteenth century saw an end to such practices, centuries of English and British religious policy in Ireland helped lay the foundation for the sectarian violence that plagued that country for much of the twentieth century. The last remnants of religious establishmentarianism no longer lead to violence or injustice in Britain only because Britain's Jews, Catholics, and dissenting Protestants have struggled for generations to render establishment a quaint and toothless relic.[22] Britain's example hardly recommends religious establishment as a path to civic peace.

Because the Declaration of Independence does refer to God, the religious Right loves to quote from it, but we shouldn't be blind to the fact that the Declaration was a radical document. In fact, its theory of government, though not atheistic or *secular* humanist, was literally revolutionary:

> We hold these truths to be self-evident, that all men are created equal, that they are endowed by their Creator with certain unalienable Rights, that among these are Life, Liberty and the pursuit of Happiness.
>
> That to secure these rights, Governments are instituted among Men, deriving their just powers from the consent of the governed, — That whenever any Form of Government becomes destructive of these ends, it is the Right of the People to alter or to abolish it, and to institute new Government, laying its foundation on such principles and organizing its powers in such form, as to them shall seem most likely to effect their Safety and Happiness.[23]

With these words, the founders of this country swept away nearly fifteen hundred years of European Christian political thought: ideas of aristocracy, that some tiny segment of the people should be specially privileged above the rest; of "Divine Right of Kings," that some men are anointed by God to rule; and that the sole duty of the people is to obey their betters. (For more detail on the declaration, please see chapter 6, "The Unchristian Roots of the Fourth of July.")

Unlike the Declaration of Independence, the Constitution of the United States *is* godless: the word *God* (like the words *Jesus*, *Christ*, *Christianity*, or *Bible*) simply does not appear anywhere in our country's fundamental legal document. The Constitution, invoking the authority of "We the People," doesn't even pay lip service to any divine authority. The only mention of religion in the original seven articles of the Constitution is to proclaim, in Article VI, that "no religious Test shall ever be required as a Qualification to any Office or public Trust under the United States."[24] And the failure to endorse divine authority for the

Constitution was no accidental oversight. As historian Pauline Maier noted, "we know that some delegates objected to the lack of any reference to God in the Constitution's Preamble."[25]

The date of the Constitution at its end includes a standard Christian dating convention used on all formal documents at the time; there is a reference to Sunday not counting as a workday for some purposes; and affirmations are declared to be acceptable substitutes for swearing. But nowhere in the body of the Constitution is there anything substantial based on any religious beliefs.

Benjamin Franklin suggested to the delegates at the Constitutional Convention that they bring in clergy to help get them past some hard disagreements, but the delegates tabled Franklin's motion and never voted on it.[26] A somewhat similar motion was then proposed but voted down. As Franklin himself wrote on his copy of his speech proposing clergy aid, "The convention, except three or four persons, thought prayers unnecessary!"[27] And this was the same Benjamin Franklin, by the way, who wrote in a letter to Richard Price, on October 9, 1780: "When a Religion is good, I conceive it will support itself; and when it does not support itself, and God does not take care to support it so that its Professors are obliged to call for help of the Civil Power, it is a sign, I apprehend, of its being a bad one."[28]

When the Bill of Rights was added to the Constitution, it went even further: Congress was forbidden to pass any laws prohibiting the free exercise of *any* religion. Earlier colonial charters, such as Maryland's 1649 Toleration Act, had provided that anyone (Catholic or Protestant of any sect) who was a "professed Christian" was to be permitted to freely exercise his religion—but anyone denying the Christian religion was to be put to death.[29] The founders realized that toleration is not good enough; what they rightly demanded was religious *liberty*. As George Washington said in a 1790 letter to the Jews of Newport, Rhode Island,

> It is now no more that toleration is spoken of as if it was by the indulgence of one class of the people that another enjoyed the exercise of their inherent natural rights. For happily the Government of the United States, which gives to bigotry no sanction, to persecution no assistance, requires only that those who live under its protection should demean themselves as good citizens in giving it, on all occasions, their effectual support.[30]

Although some American Christians now and in the past have unfortunately clung to Old World theocratic impulses, other Christians, today and in the earliest days of the American republic, have spoken out in favor of separation. The Baptists in colonial America, who were certainly deeply religious Christians—led by men like John Leland and Isaac Backus—were *strong* supporters of separation of church and state. The Baptists of today, including the Southern Baptists, who you might think oppose separation of church and state, are also *officially* very much on the side of religious liberty and the need for separation to support it. The "Baptist Faith and Message," the official statement of the Southern Baptist Convention, is primarily a declaration of Christian, biblical principles. But it includes, in a section called "Religious Liberty," these sentences (emphasis added):

> *Church and state should be separate.* The state owes to every church protection and full freedom in the pursuit of its spiritual ends. In providing for such freedom no ecclesiastical group or denomination should be favored by the state more than others. Civil government being ordained of God, it is the duty of Christians to render loyal obedience thereto in all things not contrary to the revealed will of God. *The church should not resort to the civil power to carry on its work.* The gospel of Christ contemplates spiritual means alone for the pursuit of its ends. *The state has no right to impose penalties for religious opinions of any kind. The state has no right to impose taxes for the support of any form of religion.*[31]

Although most Americans unquestioningly accept the First Amendment's protection for the *free exercise* of religion, the other half of the First Amendment's edict on religion and government, the establishment clause or "separation of church and state," is more controversial. It is often claimed that there is some great "tension" between the establishment and free-exercise clauses; that while the free-exercise clause is in favor of religious liberty, the establishment clause is a limit on religious liberty, and that there must therefore be a careful "balancing" of these two apparently contradictory provisions of the First Amendment. In fact, *both* of the First Amendment's religion clauses are protections of the religious liberty of individuals. This is self-evidently the intent and effect of the free-exercise clause, but the establishment clause is a protection of individual liberty as well. To force someone to contribute "threepence only" to support a religion he or she disagrees with is already a violation of that person's rights of conscience—and, as James Madison noted,[32] sets a dangerous and unacceptable precedent regarding the proper limits of government power over matters of religious belief. The establishment clause also removes religion from the majoritarian sphere of politics. In a democracy the majority must, ultimately, prevail in all matters *that are legitimately the subject of government action*, but each person's beliefs about God and the meaning of life are not subject to a majority vote.

But despite what some would have you believe, there is no question that the authors of the Constitution and the Bill of Rights were unhesitatingly in favor of keeping government and religion separate. As already noted, Thomas Jefferson famously declared in 1782 that government had no legitimate authority over matters of religion, since someone else having different religious opinions from yours in no way violates your rights.

Perhaps the most telling comments of all came from John Adams. Adams was a religious man and, like many of the other Founding Fathers, believed it desirable that religion, by which he meant having and following a conscience, should be and was widespread; he believed that religion was necessary for morality (for a refutation of that idea, see chapter 15, "The Big Lie"). But Adams was unequivocal in roundly condemning at great length the idea that governmental principles must come from any god or that American political principles had any religious origins. In his 1787–1788 work *Defence of the Constitutions of Government of the United States of America*, which was widely circulated in London, John Adams reviewed in detail the history of attributing government and law to divinity and firmly declared that (emphasis added):

> It was the general opinion of ancient nations, that the divinity alone was adequate to the important office of giving laws to men. The Greeks entertained this prejudice throughout all their dispersions; the Romans cultivated the same popular delusion; and modern nations, in the consecrations of kings, and in several superstitious chimeras of divine rights in princes and nobles, are nearly unanimous in preserving remnants of it: even the venerable magistrates of Amersfort devoutly believe themselves God's vicegerents; Is it that obedience to the laws can be obtained from mankind in no other manner? — Is the jealousy of power, and the envy of superiority, so strong in all men, that no considerations of public or private utility are sufficient to engage their submission to rules for

their own happiness? Or is the disposition to imposture so prevalent in men of experience, that their private views of ambition and avarice can be accomplished only by artifice? — It was a tradition in antiquity that the laws of Crete were dictated to Minos by the inspiration of Jupiter. This legislator, and his brother Rhadamanthus, were both his sons: once in nine years they went to converse with their father, to propose questions concerning the wants of the people; and his answers were recorded as laws for their government. The laws of Lacedæmon were communicated by Apollo to Lycurgus; and, lest the meaning of the deity should not have been perfectly comprehended, or correctly expressed, were afterwards confirmed by his oracle at Delphos. Among the Romans, Numa was indebted for those laws which procured the prosperity of his country to his conversations with Egeria. The Greeks imported these mysteries from Egypt and the East, whose despotisms, from the remotest antiquity to this day, have been founded in the same solemn empiricism; their emperors and nobles being all descended from their gods. Woden and Thor were divinities too; and their posterity ruled a thousand years in the north by the strength of a like credulity. Manco Capac was the child of the sun, the visible deity of the Peruvians; and transmitted his divinity, as well as his earthly dignity and authority, through a line of incas. And the rudest tribes of savages in North America have certain families under the immediate protection of the god war, from which their leaders are always chosen. There is nothing in which mankind have been more unanimous; *yet nothing can be inferred from it more than this, that the multitude have always been credulous, and the few artful.* The United States of America have exhibited, perhaps, the first example of governments erected on the simple principles of nature: and if men are now sufficiently enlightened to disabuse themselves of artifice, imposture, hypocrisy, and superstition, they will consider this event as an æra in their history. Although the detail of the formation of the American governments is at present little known or regarded either in Europe or America, it may hereafter become an object of curiosity. *It will never be pretended that any persons employed in that service had any interviews with the gods, or were in any degree under the inspiration of heaven,* any more than those at work upon ships or houses, or labouring in merchandize or agriculture: *it will for ever be acknowledged that these governments were contrived merely by the use of reason and the senses.*[33]

(Adams could also have accurately noted that the belief that kings and governments are divinely established is certainly the biblical view in both

Old and New Testaments.) A little farther along in his preface, Adams reiterated his point regarding all the American state governments: "Thirteen governments thus founded on the natural authority of the people alone, without a pretence of miracle or mystery, which are destined to spread over the northern part of that whole quarter of the globe, are a great point gained in favor of the rights of mankind."[34] Adams did not, it must be said, prove to be much of a prophet, since many, many pundits—and not just recent ones such as Glenn Beck and Michele Bachmann—have indeed "pretended" that persons employed in that service (writing the Constitution) were "under the inspiration of heaven." But we can safely take the testimony of Adams, one of the founders and key players of the day, over that of religious followers or of demagogues or of, as Adams called them, "credulous multitudes" led by "the few artful."

Those who insist that the United States was founded as a Christian nation simply ignore the facts about the key founders. As David Holmes noted,

> Since the founding fathers did not hold identical views on religion, they should not be lumped together. But if census takers trained in Christian theology had set up broad categories in 1790 labeled "Atheism," "Deism and Unitarianism," "Orthodox Protestantism," "Orthodox Roman Catholicism," and "Other," and if they had interviewed Franklin, Washington, Adams, Jefferson, Madison, and Monroe, they would undoubtedly have placed every one of these six founding fathers in some way under the category of "Deism and Unitarianism."[35]

And, as Holmes makes clear in his book, these would not be the only key men of the age so categorized—Thomas Paine, Ethan Allen, Elihu Root, and others in America and in Europe would also fall in that grouping.

James Madison, in an 1822 letter, plainly called not merely for refraining from establishing any particular denomination but for separating religion and government entirely: "And I have no doubt that every new example will succeed, as every past one has done, in shewing that religion & Gov't will both exist in greater purity, the less they are mixed together."[36]

To sum up the history on all this and add more telling bits of historical evidence, see our two chapters that follow this one on important historic specifics. And remember this sequence, ending in 1797: In 1776, the Declaration of Independence was issued and the Revolutionary War officially began. Eleven years later, after mounting frustration with the weak alliance of states under the Articles of Confederation, the delegates to the Constitutional Convention agreed on the US Constitution, which was then ratified in 1789.

By November 1796, the United States was near the end of George Washington's second term, and America was having problems with Muslim terrorists—seriously. George Washington sent over a diplomat, Joel Barlow, to see if he could appease the leaders and pirates of several Muslim countries. The Bey—the leader—of one of these nations, Tripoli—then a nation where Libya is now—signed a short treaty with Barlow on November 4, 1796.

But what does all that have to do with the point of this book? The eleventh article of that treaty, written (very likely) by Joel Barlow, a former chaplain, is interesting. It says (emphasis added), "As *the government of the United States is not in any sense founded on the Christian religion*, . . . it is declared by the parties that no pretext arising from religious opinion shall ever produce an interruption of harmony existing between the two countries."[37] See chapter 8, "From the Shores of Tripoli . . ." for much more detail on this treaty and on Joel Barlow, its chief architect.

As noted above, in the late nineteenth century the National Reform Association tried repeatedly to officially change the preamble to the US Constitution.[38] They were most unhappy that the basic governing charter of the United States failed to even mention Jesus Christ or God, and they strove repeatedly to get an amendment passed to change the preamble so that it would begin by invoking what they saw as the correct source, by prefacing "We the People" as the ultimate source with "In the Name of Our Lord and Savior Jesus Christ, we the people . . ." A bill to do this was introduced into the US Congress repeatedly, but it repeatedly failed. (For more detail on this and other historical details, see Rob Boston's excellent 1993 book, *Why the Religious Right Is Wrong about Separation of Church and State*.)

One of Thomas Jefferson's three proudest achievements (the three he directed be recorded on the obelisk over his grave), alongside being the principal author of the Declaration of Independence and founder of the University of Virginia, was that he was the author "of the Statute of Virginia for religious freedom" adopted in 1786.[39] That law, widely regarded as a crucial forerunner for the First Amendment, has been described as "a vigorous, precedent-setting statute that totally separated church and state in Virginia" by distinguished historian Pauline Maier.[40] James Madison was reportedly "horrified" at Patrick Henry's "nearly successful effort in the mid-1780s [in Virginia] to derail passage of Thomas Jefferson's Bill for Religious Freedom, a move that threatened to undermine . . . the separation of church and state."[41]

David Goldfield makes a good case that many original founding members of the modern Republican Party in the 1840s and 1850s believed that God was on their side, that abolishing slavery was a righteous religious crusade, and that their other aims—such as undermining the Mormons—were also religious. Goldfield ignores, however, the openly fervently Christian motivation of slaveholders and Southern clergy who used the Bible to support them. Goldfield's core argument is apparently that the Civil War "should teach us that self-righteousness and religious certitude are more likely to lead to violent rather than peaceful resolution, and that even a good cause—the abolition of slavery—may be better served by peace than by war."[42] Goldfield's case would be stronger rather than weaker if he had taken note of the religious rhetoric and motivation on *both* sides of the slavery question. Slavery was in fact almost certainly a bigger factor for Southerners leading to war, a basis seen by its proponents and the preachers who spoke for them as a moral issue, than it was for many in the North. (For more on slavery as a key cause of that war, including some details on the explicitly Christian support for slavery, see this website for an interesting exercise: http://bellsouthpwp.net/m/e/mebuckner/civwarquiz.htm.)

Revisionism about the cause of the Civil War and the relative moral worth of the opposing sides flourishes in certain sectors of the Christian right. As detailed in a *New Yorker* profile of Republican congresswoman and then presidential candidate Michele Bachmann, such Christian writers as J. Steven Wilkins have proclaimed the South to be a "Christian nation" attacked by an allegedly godless North. According to this view, slavery, far from a shameful stain on our national history, was a largely benevolent Christian institution.[43]

If we travel forward in time to the last half of the nineteenth century, one of the surprising facts, in light of more recent American politics, is that the Republican Party was in that era the party most firmly committed to secularism. Many modern, twenty-first-century Republicans would almost certainly be appalled at the attitudes of "original" Republicans—those from the middle of the nineteenth century to the end of it. Abraham Lincoln himself was a fan of Thomas Paine's *Age of Reason*, the scathingly anti-Bible, anti-Christian deist work written in the late eighteenth century and popular among Americans, especially deists (it sold "tens of thousands of copies" in America). Lincoln was, apparently because of his reading *Age of Reason*, something of a religious skeptic, according to one historian.[44] A Lincoln biographer, Jackie Hogan, has speculated that Lincoln would be unlikely to be nominated by a "Tea Party"–influenced modern Republican party, for several reasons, among them,

> He didn't advertise his faith. The debate over Lincoln's religious beliefs is a heated one. But there is good evidence that he questioned Christian orthodoxy, perhaps not so surprising at a time when biblical verses were routinely used in defense of slavery, an institution he found morally repugnant. While it is true that Lincoln frequently evoked the divine in his speeches, he never took up membership in a church, and certainly never spoke publicly about his personal relationship with Christ.[45]

President Ulysses S. Grant called, in 1875 in an official message to Congress, for taxing churches.[46] Robert G. Ingersoll (1833–1899), probably the most famous American ever who was openly irreligious, toured the nation repeatedly, speaking to huge crowds.[47] And Ingersoll gave a key nominating speech, for James G. Blaine, at a Republican National Convention.[48] Blaine, though he never succeeded in being nominated for president, was a prominent Republican and ardent supporter of separation of church and state—famous for having introduced what later became known as "The Blaine Amendment" to the US Constitution, intended to prevent public monies being spent on private schools. The amendment never passed, but many states adopted it. Blaine served in the cabinet of several Republican presidents. Some critics, then and since, have insisted that the Blaine Amendment was based on nothing more than anti-Catholic bigotry, and controversy still swirls around how the history of these amendments should be interpreted. But the wording and effects of that amendment, in the proposed national version and in the versions adopted in various states, were not anti-Catholic and applied equally to any sectarian schools.[49]

It is also worth remembering, with regards to anti-Catholicism in nineteenth-century America, that the official position of the Catholic Church of the day was openly hostile to many basic American values, especially secularism but even to a basic right to rebel against a king. In his 1864 *Syllabus of Errors*, Pope Pius IX not only sternly condemned the idea that the "Church ought to be separated from the State, and the State from the Church" and attacked nonsectarian public schools; he also demanded that Catholicism must be "the only religion of the State, to the exclusion of all other forms of worship" and attacked the very idea of free exercise of religion, ending with a sweeping repudiation of (in the Holy Father's own words) "progress, liberalism and modern civilization."[50]

There is perhaps a parallel between nineteenth-century American anti-Catholicism and the anti-Muslim attitudes now on display in twenty-first-century America—an example of bigotry that nonetheless does in part spring from genuine conflicts between American ideals and those of a major world religion.

As a Republican congressman in 1874, James Garfield declared that

> The divorce between church and state ought to be absolute. It ought to be so absolute that no church property anywhere, in any State or in the nation, should be exempt from equal taxation; for if you exempt the property of any church organization, to that extent you impose a tax upon the whole community.[51]

While Garfield's argument is straightforward and eminently reasonable, it is hard to imagine a Republican congressman today making such a statement on the record. Yet Garfield was elected president of the United States just six years later, in 1880.

President Grant not only sent his Official Message urging taxing churches to Congress in 1875; he also said, in a speech in Des Moines, Iowa, as president:

> Encourage free schools, and resolve that not one dollar of money shall be appropriated to the support of any sectarian school. Resolve that neither the state nor nation, or both combined, shall support institutions of learning other than those sufficient to afford every child growing up in the land the opportunity of a good education, unmixed with sectarian, pagan, or atheistical tenets. Leave the matter of religion to the

family altar, the church, and the private schools, supported entirely by private contributions. Keep the church and state forever separated.[52]

The Republicans of the late 1800s were more firmly in the mainstream of American political theory—and far more representative of the ideas of the founders regarding secularism—than the fearful politicians of any major American political party today.

The US Supreme Court has, of course, been quite important in the history of establishing and maintaining secularism in this country. The overall take from the court can perhaps best be summed up by what Justice Robert H. Jackson wrote in a 1943 pledge case (before the "under God" phrase was added; this was a case about whether Jehovah's Witnesses could be compelled to pledge allegiance to the flag or the nation). Jackson wrote, in *West Virginia v. Barnette*:

> If there is any fixed star in our constitutional constellation, it is that no official, high or petty, can prescribe what shall be orthodox in politics, nationalism, religion, or other matters of opinion or force citizens to confess by word or act their faith therein. If there are any circumstances which permit an exception, they do not now occur to us.[53]

Justice Jackson thus summarized precisely the logical and historical rationale for the United States being a secular nation—*so that* her citizens could be free.

Chapter 6.

The Unchristian Roots
of the Fourth of July

The United States Constitution is, of course, literally a "godless" document: the word *God* (like the words *Jesus*, *Christ*, *Christianity*, or *Bible*) simply does not appear anywhere in our country's fundamental legal document.[1] If the founders of the United States meant to establish this as a "Christian nation" in any constitutional, legal, or political sense, they neglected to mention it in the document from which our federal government derives its authority. See the next chapter for more on the Constitution.

Often, though, supporters of the "Christian nation" ideology claim that the Declaration of Independence is the document that establishes this country as distinctively Christian. Leaving aside the fact that the Declaration, however important it may be in our history, technically has no legal standing in our government, this is at least superficially a more convincing claim. After all, the Declaration does at least use the word *God* and uses synonyms thereof three more times later in the Declaration.[2] To be sure, none of these words or phrases ("Nature's God," "Creator," "Supreme Judge of the World," "Divine Providence") is specifically Christian—there are no references to Jesus Christ or the Holy Trinity—but none of them is necessarily incompatible with Christianity either.

It should be pointed out that Thomas Jefferson, the principal drafter of the Declaration, declared "I am a Christian"[3] but did not accept the doctrines of the virgin birth, the resurrection of Jesus, the divinity of Jesus, or any miraculous powers ascribed to Jesus, nor did he believe in original sin or justification by faith. Although Jefferson often referred to himself as a "Christian," he viewed Jesus of Nazareth as a great man and a moral and religious reformer, and not as the Christ or Messiah. In a letter to William Short, October 31, 1819, Jefferson listed doctrines that he explicitly rejected: "the immaculate conception of Jesus, his deification, the creation of the world by him, his miraculous powers, his resurrection and visible ascension, his corporeal presence in the Eucharist, the Trinity; original sin, atonement, regeneration, election, orders of the Hierarchy, etc."[4] In a later letter to Short, in April 1820, Jefferson clarified further: "It is not to be understood that I am with him [Jesus Christ] in all his doctrines. I am a Materialist; he takes the side of Spiritualism; he preaches the efficacy of repentance toward forgiveness of sin; I require a counterpoise of good works to redeem it."[5]

Given Jefferson's religious beliefs and the lack of any distinctively Christian language in the Declaration, many have argued that the theism of the Declaration is the religion of deism and not the religion of Christianity. (Deism was a rationalist, monotheistic faith associated with the eighteenth-century Enlightenment in Europe; deism had no creeds or dogmas, but in general deists, while believing in God as Creator of the Universe and even as author of moral laws, rejected belief in miracles and considered reason and experience rather than revelation and faith to be the proper sources of religious truth. The modern Unitarians are probably the closest heirs to the deists of Jefferson's day.) It is also true that the Declaration contains no scriptural citations or even any obvious allusions to the Christian Bible, which is certainly peculiar for an ostensibly Christian document. However, what is most important to look at in the Declaration of Independence are the basic ideas it embodies, rather than the rhetoric with which they are presented.

In addition to numerous condemnations of the policies of King George III (explicitly identified as "the CHRISTIAN king of Great Britain" and attacked for supporting the slave trade in Jefferson's draft[6]), which need not further concern us here, the Declaration of Independence is most famous for setting forth a basic philosophy of government: people have certain natural rights deriving from their Creator; in order to preserve those rights, people establish governments; since governments derive their power from the establishment of the people, the people therefore retain an inherent right to change or even overthrow any government that no longer carries out its original purpose of protecting the rights of the people. This is far from an entirely atheistic or materialist philosophy—the Declaration does derive those natural rights from an endowment by a Creator—but it is far from being a Christian or Judeo-Christian view of government either. In the Old Testament, the ideal form of government is literally a theocracy. The laws of the ancient Israelites are handed down directly by God, not written by human legislators answerable to the people at large. The purpose of the laws is not to protect the inalienable rights of the people but to ensure that the Israelites would remain "a people holy to the LORD your God" (Deuteronomy 14:2). The leaders of the people—Moses, Aaron, Joshua—are selected by the deity, not elected (Exodus 2:14, 3:11–12, 4:14; Numbers 27:15–21; Joshua 1:1–2). When Israel first became a kingdom, the Bible teaches that Samuel—a prophet chosen by God and not responsible to any human constitution or institution—selected a king on divine instruction (I Samuel, chapter 8; this chapter also reveals the ambivalence of the biblical writers toward the whole institution of human kingship, which in the Old Testament is at times portrayed as tyrannical and even an affront to God; clearly, though, what is being preferred over monarchy is not a democratic republic but a continued theocracy in which divinely chosen priests, prophets, or "judges" rule by God's power). Later, when the first king (Saul) is abandoned by God, a new king (David) is again chosen by direct, divine intervention (1 Samuel 16:1–2). When kings of Europe claimed that the proper form of Christian government was a monarch who ruled by "divine right" as the "Lord's anointed," they were putting forth a view of government that is genuinely in accord with biblical, Judeo-Christian values.

The New Testament also upholds the view that government is an institution of God, not of the people. Romans 13:1–2, already cited in an earlier chapter but worth quoting again here, clearly forbids rebellion against the established authorities and was, moreover, written about the pagan government of the Roman Empire, which actively persecuted Christians:

> Let everyone be subject to the governing authorities, for there is no authority except that which God has established. The authorities that exist have been established by God. Consequently, whoever rebels against the authority is rebelling against what God has instituted, and those who do so will bring judgement on themselves.

George III, it should be noted, was a Christian monarch; if Paul commanded obedience by Christians to the pagan and tyrannical Roman emperors, surely he would have demanded equal obedience by Christians to the avowedly Christian (and far less cruel or oppressive) British king and parliament. The New Testament does, of course, present a major shift in viewpoint from the Old; now, obedience to secular authorities is commanded not so much because they rule over a divinely ordained theocracy as it is because secular authorities, along with everything else in the world, will soon be swept away by the Second Coming. Christians should act morally—which to Paul included obedience to a corrupt and tyrannical state—in preparation for Judgement Day, which he preached was quite near at hand in the first century CE (Romans 13:7–14).

The theory of government presented in the Declaration of Independence, then, represents a radical break with Judeo-Christian traditions that went back thousands of years. Government, it asserts, derives its powers not from the will of God but from the consent of the governed. From being an instrument of God's wrath, government is demoted to an invention of human beings, to be altered at the will of its creators. As Pauline Maier noted, "indeed, separation of church and state was one of the most radical innovations of the American Revolution."[7]

Our Constitution goes even further than the Declaration in its godlessness, not even bothering with a ceremonial invocation of God or "Divine Providence" in vesting ultimate authority in "We, the People."[8] What James Madison and John Adams, both quoted in the previous chapter, wrote is directly relevant here. As Madison, principal drafter of the Constitution, said, "religion and government will both exist in greater purity, the less they are mixed together."[9] And to reiterate what John Adams, second president of the United States, wrote (quoted at much greater length in our earlier chapter),

> Although the detail of the formation of the American governments is at present little known or regarded either in Europe or in America . . . [i]t will never be pretended that any persons employed in that service had interviews with the gods, or were in any degree under the influence of Heaven . . . ; it will forever be acknowledged that these governments were contrived merely by the use of reason and the senses.[10]

The leaders of this country went on not only to found what is likely the first entirely secular government in human history but also to guarantee religious liberty for all in the Constitution and the Bill of Rights. Article VI of the Constitution, in barring any religious test or oath for federal office, and the First Amendment, in protecting freedom of religion and the separation of church and state that guarantees that freedom, ended the long "Judeo-Christian" tradition of persecution, torture, and death for differences of opinion in matters of religion—a tradition that began with the Bible itself, which calls on the faithful worshippers of God to denounce even their own parents and children and to cast the first stone in putting them to death if they deviate from the "true" religion (Deuteronomy 13:6–11). That we do not have a government based on the Bible—or "God's law"—or "Judeo-Christian values"—is something that all Americans can be grateful for every Fourth of July: grateful not to any god but to the human beings who established this country as a free country, and *not* a Christian nation.

Chapter 7.

The Unchristian Nature of the US Constitution

The Declaration of Independence proclaimed the revolutionary doctrine that governments, rather than having been established by God as the Bible teaches, derive their powers from the consent of the governed—that is, from the people—who retain the right to change or even overthrow those governments if they cease to protect the people's rights. Within a few years of the Declaration, the colonies—now self-proclaimed states—moved to establish the first national constitution, the Articles of Confederation. It, too, was a largely secular document, although it did speak of "the Great Governor of the World" (in rather deistic language), and also bound the states to assist each other against any attack made upon any or all of them, including any attack that might be made "on account of religion."[1] For a variety of reasons, the Articles of Confederation proved to be inadequate as a framework for governing the new nation and—since American constitutions are not sacred scripture—it was decided to amend it, which led in fact to its being completely replaced by the Constitution of the United States (and its later amendments).

The current Constitution starts off by identifying in its preamble the source of its authority and the purposes for which it is written:

> We the People of the United States, in Order to form a more perfect Union, establish Justice, insure domestic Tranquility, provide for the common defence, promote the general Welfare, and secure the Blessings of Liberty to ourselves and our Posterity, do ordain and establish this Constitution for the United States of America.[2]

Again, the authority to form the new Constitution is said to derive from the people. Now there is no longer even a rhetorical flourish of invoking God, not even in the most vague and nonsectarian of terms. The purposes of the new Constitution are all secular. Though "the establishment of justice"—the making and execution of law in Christian Europe—had historically long been intimately intertwined with religion, the Constitution banned "religious tests" for office holders, and would soon be amended to ban laws regarding the exercise of or establishment of religion at all, along with guaranteeing freedom of speech. Though the new Constitution only constrained the federal government, there would be no national laws regarding "heresy" in the new country, and those remaining state laws against blasphemy were clearly against the ideals of the Revolution. Where earlier generations had sought domestic tranquility through enforced religious uniformity, the framers of the Constitution sought it through religious liberty and government neutrality with respect to different religions—as we have seen, men like George Washington defined good citizenship without reference to sect or dogma.[3]

Distinguished historian Richard Beeman noted that

> The United States Constitution was meant to be—and is, resolutely—a legal document, drafted in an age when the substance of the law was becoming more secular and when its leading practitioners were consciously purging their profession from legal imperatives derived from anything hinting of divine sanction. Although it remained the case that a few New England states persisted in attempting to maintain the connection between government, public order, morality, and religion, on the whole the independent American states were deliberately moving in the opposite direction.[4]

Beeman also commented on the religious beliefs of the framers and on the separation between their personal beliefs and the Constitution they created:

> some of the framers, whatever their denominational preferences, were men of great piety—men for whom the practice of the Christian religion was an active and important part of their daily lives. But whatever their private beliefs, the vast majority of the Founding Fathers operated on the assumption that temporal and spiritual aspects of public life should be kept separate.[5]

The secular language and purposes of the Constitution contrast sharply with the language and ideals commonly found in pre-Revolutionary American charters. The Mayflower Compact was "in the name of God" and "for the Glory of God," and specifically for the "advancements of the Christian faith and honour of our king and country." (Although the compact did arguably prefigure representative government and the idea of governments deriving their powers from the consent of the governed, being a contract between the settlers to set up a new government, the colonists nonetheless also continued to use the good biblical language of monarchy, proclaiming themselves to be "Loyal Subjects of our dread Sovereign Lord King James, by the Grace of God... King, Defender of the Faith."[6]) The "Fundamental Orders of 1639" of Connecticut, considered by some scholars to be the first true constitution in the Americas,[7] not only cited Almighty God and "the wise disposition of his divine providence" in the settlement of the colony but also proclaimed the purposes of the charter to include maintaining and preserving "the liberty and purity of the Gospel of our Lord Jesus" and "the discipline of the Churches."[8] The First Charter of Virginia proclaimed the desire of the colonizers to bring "Christian Religion to such People, as yet live in Darkness and miserable Ignorance of the true Knowledge and Worship of God";[9] the Second Charter reiterated the goal of "the Conversion and Reduction of the People in those Parts unto the true Worship of God and Christian Religion" (while also making it clear that "the true Worship of God and Christian Religion" did not mean the Catholic Church, or as the charter put it, the "Superstitions of the Church of Rome," adherents of which were to be kept strictly out of the new colony).[10] The Charter of Maryland begins by commending the king's "well beloved and right trusty Subject Caecilius Calvert, Baron of Baltimore" for his "laudable, and pious Zeal for extending the Christian Religion."[11]

There is absolutely no such language in the Constitution; its authority is of the people and its purposes are concerned with the here and now, not the saving of souls, which was no longer considered by the Revolutionary generation to be the proper duty of government. Its ban on religious tests and (after the adoption of the First Amendment) ban on restrictions on free exercise of religion is absolute—no more is there the sort of "religious toleration" seen in Maryland's 1649 Toleration Act, which, although guaranteeing the free exercise of religion for any person "professing to believe in Jesus Christ" nonetheless also proclaimed that any person denying the doctrine of the Trinity should be put to death.[12] Even the much more progressive 1663 charter of Rhode Island, which guaranteed

> that noe person within the sayd colonye, at any tyme hereafter, shall bee any wise molested, punished, disquieted, or called in question, for any differences in opinione in matters of religion, and doe not actually disturb the civill peace of our sayd colony; but that all and everye person and persons may, from tyme to tyme, and at all tymes hereafter, freelye and fullye have and enjoye his and theire owne judgments and consciences, in matters of religious concernments

without any such Trinitarian restrictions, nonetheless couched its guarantee of freedom of conscience as a matter of "true pietye rightly grounded upon gospell principles" and of preserving "the true Christian ffaith and worshipp of God."[13] As the Thirteen Colonies moved toward becoming the United States, and toward full freedom of religion, language speaking of "the inestimable privilege of worshipping Almighty God in a manner, agreeable to the dictates of [one's] own conscience" remained common (and, alas, such language about "the natural and inalienable right to worship God" is still to be found in many state constitutions to this day).[14] By contrast, the religious tests clause in Article VI of the US Constitution not only contrasts favorably with Maryland's "Toleration Act" in prohibiting any religious test (not just tests that discriminate against some Christians over others), but this complete ban on religious discrimination in government is (like the rest of the Constitution) not justified with any reference to a need to preserve the "true Christian faith" or "gospel principles" or any other such sectarian ideals. The First Amendment simply proclaims that there shall be no law "respecting an establishment of religion or prohibiting the free exercise thereof" without any reference to any "inestimable privileges" of worshipping God (not even "according to the dictates of one's conscience"). The Constitution (including the Bill of Rights) is resolutely, breathtakingly secular.

Some believers have sought respite from this relentlessly secular language at the very end of the Constitution, where the document is dated "the Seventeenth Day of September in the Year of our Lord one thousand seven hundred and Eighty seven and of the Independence of the United States of America the Twelfth."

Though sometimes triumphantly held up as unanswerable evidence of our allegedly Christian heritage, this is awfully weak tea compared to the colonial charters' bold proclamations about the "advancement of the Christian faith" and "the liberty and purity of the Gospel of our Lord Jesus" or even the quite progressive Rhode Island charter's grounding of freedom of conscience in "true pietye" and "gospell principles" and "the true Christian ffaith and worshipp of God." Now collective proclamations of Christianity are reduced to the conventions of calendars. And anyone seeking to discern an official religion of the United States by its calendar will likely come away awfully confused: we are apparently a country whose Lord is Jesus Christ (the familiar *Anno Domini* or "In the Year of Our Lord" of the Gregorian Calendar triumphantly cited by some disappointed Christians perusing the Constitution), but we *also* (based on the names of the days of our weeks and our months) worship the gods of the Sun and the Moon, the old Germanic gods Tiu and Woden and Thor and the goddess Frigg, and the Roman gods Saturn and Janus and Mars, not to mention the deified Caesars, Julius and Augustus.[15] These conventional forms of dating have little to do with religious commitment or belief; all formal documents in 1787 were dated "in the Year of Our Lord." Note that the framers also included a then much more recent conventional dating form, one that has not persisted as perhaps they hoped, additionally dating the Constitution by the year "of the Independence of the United States of America." The somewhat archaic formalities of dating of documents certainly cannot override the absence of any religious reference in the body of the Constitution, the straightforward and unadorned ban on religious tests in Article VI, and the First Amendment's unsentimental language in favor of free exercise of religion and against religious establishment.

As previously noted, in the generations closer to the Constitution's adoption, rather than simply denying its secular nature, the would-be establishers of Christianity of the day repeatedly, openly—and unsuccessfully—sought to change it, by amending the preamble to include an allusion to the source of authority as Our Lord and Savior Jesus Christ.[16]

It is also sometimes claimed that one of the most distinctive and familiar features of the American Constitution—its division of the government into three branches, judicial, legislative, and executive—is actually rooted in the Bible, specifically in Isaiah 33:32—"For the LORD is our judge, the LORD is our lawgiver, the LORD is our king; it is he who will save us."[17] This is more evidence of desperate grasping at straws. Though the idea has even been attributed to James Madison, "Father of the Constitution," no one seems to have found any real basis for that in Madison's known writings. In fact, though the Isaiah verse can be made to sound like evidence that basic American constitutional principles are rooted in the Bible by a glib propagandist, the notion quickly falls apart under further examination. The most obvious implication of this verse is that all three functions come from "on high," not—as in this nation—from "We the People." And it ignores the crucial idea of *separating* the powers—"the LORD" is judge, lawgiver, and king. It is, in other words, easier to see this verse as completely missing the mark when it comes to American governance. Only those who want to deny the importance of democratic elections, freedom of religion, separation of powers, and much else about American government would be willing to accept this as evidence of any congruence of the Bible and the Constitution.

In reality, the idea of separation of powers as a necessary protection of liberty dates (like so much else in American political thought) to eighteenth-century Enlightenment thinkers like the French Baron de Montesquieu, who argued, in his 1748 treatise *The Spirit of the Laws*, for the need for the separation of government power into the executive, legislative, and judicial branches familiar from countless high-school civics classes. These Enlightenment notions of checks and balances in government are in turn much more influenced by classical (Greco-Roman) thinkers than they are by Judeo-Christian ones.[18]

It is often claimed by some on the political Right—not necessarily the religious Right—that this is a *republic*, not a *democracy*. It is true that the Constitution itself never uses the words *democracy* or *democratic*. However, both the Declaration of Independence and the Constitution root the basis of political power in the consent of the governed, which is a principle which it is hard to see as anything but "democratic" (albeit one as compatible with "indirect democracy" or a "democratic republic," as it is with some imaginary implementation of direct town hall–style democracy on a continent-wide scale). Even this indirect democracy is hard to square with the top-down, literally theocratic teachings of the First Book of Samuel or the thirteenth chapter of Paul's Letter to the Romans, in which rulers are chosen by God, not by the people.

One important way in which the Constitution differs from any sort of sacred scripture is that it contains a provision for amending itself—indeed, some of the most cherished parts of the Constitution are to be found in its amendments. Those amendments also show a clear pattern of moving toward more democracy in the United States, never less—sometimes in ways that conflict with biblical teachings, even beyond the basic conflict between the theocracy of the Bible and the democracy of the Declaration of Independence. The basic democratic principle of participation in government by voting for those who make and execute the laws has repeatedly been strengthened: eliminating racial discrimination in voting, directly electing US senators, guaranteeing the vote in presidential elections for residents of the District of Columbia, forbidding the use of nonpayment of poll taxes as a basis for denying voting rights, guaranteeing voting rights for eighteen-year-olds—there is a very clear pattern in which changes to the Constitution have consistently expanded the basic democratic right to vote and never limited it. (The only *possible* exception to this pattern would be term limits for the president of the United States, which could be construed as limiting the democratic rights of the people to reelect a president more than once.)

One such expansion of democracy, the Nineteenth Amendment—women's suffrage (made a part of the Constitution as of August 1920[19])—stands out in particular as being directly in conflict with biblical teaching about the relationship between men and women. The fifth chapter of Paul's Letter to the Ephesians teaches that women should "submit" to their husbands; in fact, they should submit to their husbands "as you do to the Lord" (Ephesians 5:22). Husbands are called "the head of the wife as Christ is the head of the church" (Ephesians 5:23). Christians will undoubtedly say that Paul's depiction of marriage is a loving one, not a cruel or tyrannical institution—Paul does exhort husbands to love their wives as Christ supposedly loves the church (Ephesians 5:25–33)—but it is not an egalitarian or democratic institution. In 1 Timothy 2:11–12, Paul writes that a woman must not "assume authority over a man"—hard to square with women voting on which man will be senator or governor or president (let alone becoming senators and governors and presidents themselves). In fact, religious arguments were often used in opposition to women's suffrage, and the clergy were prominent opponents of the notion.

The original Constitution, under the cultural influences of the times, did not really explicitly exclude women—it just did not say one way or another anything about women. The no doubt very Christian *laws* and society before the Constitution mandated that women not vote, that husbands control property, and so forth. The Constitution continued this more by default than otherwise. Ironically, it was the great Fourteenth Amendment that first explicitly discriminated against women in the Constitution, by specifying "male citizens" in Section 2, dealing with voting rights. Even under the Fourteenth Amendment, women are considered *citizens*—in addition to the "all *persons*" language, the phrase "male citizens" logically implies non-male citizens. But not all citizens were equal—*male* citizens are guaranteed certain rights with regards to voting. Going a step further to make the US Constitution—and the United States itself—less biblical required a struggle of well over half a century (from about 1848 to the passage of the Nineteenth Amendment in 1920).

Annie Laurie Gaylor has written about and collected the writings of other women on these subjects in well-written and carefully documented books like *Woe to the Women: The Bible Tells Me So* and *Women without Superstition: "No Gods—No Masters": The Collected Writings of Women Freethinkers of the Nineteenth & Twentieth Centuries*. The most effective woman who led the efforts of the suffrage movement (Gaylor has documented that there were large numbers of courageous women freethinkers who led the efforts over many years) was almost certainly Elizabeth Cady Stanton. Like many of the other leaders, she was adamant about the causal connections between Christianity and oppression of women.

Elizabeth Cady Stanton wrote and spoke on the subject often, fearlessly, and—though she did not live to see it—finally successfully, at least as far as winning the vote for women (she was the first to call for women's suffrage). She wrote the text of the Nineteenth Amendment[20] and issued, in 1848 at the Seneca Falls, New York, convention, a stirring declaration demanding rights for women and denouncing the clergy (the "black-coated gentry").[21] Gaylor quoted Stanton as writing, in "The Degraded Status of Women in the Bible" (1896),

> For fifty years the women of this nation have tried to dam up this deadly stream that poisons all their lives, but thus far have lacked the insight or courage to follow it back to its source and there strike the blow at the fountain of all tyranny, religious superstition, priestly power, and the canon law.[22]

The Nineteenth Amendment, probably more than any other major change to the Constitution (even the Thirteenth Amendment abolishing slavery—though that, too, qualifies—see below), was not merely unbiblical but starkly anti-biblical.

Even in the twenty-first century, there are still occasional sputters of religiously based opposition to equal civil rights for women (for example, one "Christian Reconstructionist" pastor's claim that women's suffrage is unbiblical,[23] or the statement back in 2001 that the Nineteenth Amendment is a "symptom" of a "society that does tear families apart" because "the man should be the head of the family"—astonishingly enough uttered by a woman who herself was a state senator in Kansas at the time.[24]

Another way (besides its original, default omission of women as citizens with rights) in which the Constitution was more biblical than revolutionary was in its original acceptance—though refusing to ever name the institution—of slavery. Approval of slavery is readily apparent in the Bible, from the Old Testament injunction to the Israelites to buy slaves from the nations around them, to become property that could be bequeathed to their children (Leviticus 25:44–46) to the law in Exodus 21:20–21 that says since slaves are their masters' property, they can be beaten, so long as they are not beaten to death. Biblical principles were also clearly reflected in the antebellum laws of the slave states; see for example the 1819 constitution of Alabama:

> Any person who shall maliciously dismember or deprive a slave of life, shall suffer such punishment as would be inflicted in case the like offence had been committed on a free white person, and on the like proof; except in case of insurrection of such slave.[25]

Nor is acceptance of slavery in the Bible limited to the Old Testament. It is clear in the New Testament command that slaves submit to their masters, not only to the "good and considerate, but also to those who are harsh" (1 Peter 2:18). And the Bible never condemns slavery. Supporters of slavery often justified the institution in explicitly biblical terms—the *Confederate States of America—Declaration of the Causes Which Impel the State of Texas to Secede from the Federal Union* proclaimed

> That in this free government all white men are and of right ought to be entitled to equal civil and political rights; that the servitude of the

African race, as existing in these States, is mutually beneficial to both bond and free, and is abundantly authorized and justified by the experience of mankind, and the revealed will of the Almighty Creator, as recognized by all Christian nations.[26]

Following the bloody Civil War, this "biblically correct" institution was finally officially done away with by the Thirteenth Amendment. (As is made abundantly clear in *Slavery by Another Name* by Douglas Blackmon, slavery in many respects continued in the Deep South until the beginning of World War II—with frequent support of the racism that undergirded it from religious leaders and ideas.) The Thirteenth Amendment was followed by the crucial Fourteenth Amendment, which established that

All persons born or naturalized in the United States, and subject to the jurisdiction thereof, are citizens of the United States and of the State wherein they reside. No State shall make or enforce any law which shall abridge the privileges or immunities of citizens of the United States; nor shall any State deprive any person of life, liberty, or property, without due process of law; nor deny to any person within its jurisdiction the equal protection of the laws.[27]

This reinforced that American citizenship, as Washington proclaimed, has nothing to do with religious belief.

In the 2012 presidential campaign, as noted in chapter 3, "Religion and Politics Now," much hot air was expelled and much ink was spilled over the notion of "American exceptionalism" and whether certain candidates truly accepted this principle. The most strident expounders of this theme were also the most determined attackers of the principle of secularism in government. This is deeply ironic, because secularism—the separation of church and state—is truly one of the most important ideals that Americans have given to the world. Nor are we the only ones to point this out. For a recent example, according to reviewer Damon Linker, see *The New Religious Intolerance* by Martha C. Nussbaum.[28] For thousands of years, it had been assumed across the world that the duties of kings and magistrates naturally included leading the community in the worship of its gods. The rise of Christendom merely exchanged paganism for Christianity. The idea of freeing the conscience of the individual from the control of the state—albeit often with limitations, such as John Locke's refusal, in "A Letter concerning Toleration," to extend liberty of conscience to atheists, even as he was arguing for the protection of such rights for "Jews" who rejected the New Testament and even "heathens" who rejected the Bible entirely[29]—had been tentatively proposed before the American Revolution. But it was in the United States of America that the ideal of individual religious liberty for everyone, protected by a secular state in which all citizens—of whatever religion or lack thereof—are nonetheless equal, was perfected and first put into practice.

Chapter 8.

From the Shores of Tripoli . . .
Why a 1796–1797 US Treaty Matters

As noted in the introduction and in chapter 5, relations between the United States and the nation now called Libya have been troubled since before the official beginning of US national history. And religious conflict, or often more accurately, imagined religious conflict, has also been a part of that turmoil or an excuse for it since the earliest days. Americans witnessed, for example, turmoil there in late 2012 that took the life of the American ambassador to Libya, J. Christopher Stevens, and of other diplomatic staff. That attack was most likely al Qaeda–related terrorism—and not merely a part of the broader violent uproar over an allegedly blasphemous video[1] (see chapter 17 for more on that). A US treaty of the late eighteenth century, commonly called the Treaty with Tripoli, was officially titled "Treaty of Peace and Friendship between the United States of America and the Bey and Subjects of Tripoli, of Barbary" (Tripoli is part of what later became known as Libya). It is of little importance as a treaty or legal document (it was superseded nine years later by another treaty). It has, however, been frequently cited, sometimes carelessly, as evidence against the claim that the United States was founded as "a Christian nation." The relevant language in the treaty, written in 1796, probably by diplomat Joel Barlow (more about him, below), is to be found in the eleventh article of the treaty, which reads in its entirety:

> **Article 11.** As the government of the United States of America is not in any sense founded on the Christian Religion.—as it has in itself no character of enmity against the laws, religion, or tranquility of Musselmen,—and as the said States never have entered into any war or act of hostility against any Mehomitan nation, it is declared by the parties

that no pretext arising from religious opinions shall ever produce an interruption of the harmony existing between the two countries.[2]

"Musselmen" was a term of the times for *Muslims*; "Mehomitan" was similarly a term then for *Mohammedan* or *Islamic*. The treaty was brokered between Tripoli and the United States in late 1796 (initially signed and agreed to by both sides on November 4) at the very end of the second term of George Washington. Richard O'Brien, sent to Tripoli by Joel Barlow, negotiated the agreement. There is no evidence that Washington was personally involved with or aware of the famous article, and it is therefore not wise, as some have done, to attribute the key words to Washington, though they are indeed a product of Washington's second presidential administration. There is no reason to believe that he would not have agreed with the idea. One Washington biographer, Paul F. Boller, has written that "Very likely Washington shared Barlow's view, though there is no record of his opinion about the treaty."[3]

PURPOSE

The treaty that grew out of negotiations between the Bey and O'Brien/Barlow, and that Barlow wrote or at least translated into English, was intended by the Americans to protect American shipping interests and American seamen, then and for some years before that under serious attacks and threats of more from "Barbary pirates." The threats included selling seamen into slavery and was partly grounded in religion.

An ambassador from Tripoli told John Adams in 1786, according to Adams, that "a war between Christian and Christian was mild, with prisoners, on either side, treated with humanity; but a war between Turk [Muslim] and Christian was horrible, and prisoners were sold into slavery."[4] That ambassador met with both Adams and Jefferson later that winter in London and, according to historian Frederick Leiner,

> The Tripolitan ambassador in London had explained to Thomas Jefferson . . . that the Barbary states' policy toward the Christian world "was founded on the Laws of their Prophet, that it was written in their Koran, that all nations who should not have acknowledged their

authority were sinners, that it was their right and duty to make war upon them whenever they could be found, and to make slaves of all they could take as Prisoners, and that every [Muslim] who should be slain in battle was sure to go to Paradise."[5]

The slavery feared was not precisely the same as that in the United States at the time—slaves on the Barbary Coast could escape slavery by converting to Islam (Muslims were forbidden to hold other Muslims as slaves) or by being ransomed by their families or governments. The two different sorts of slavery were historically intertwined and each affected the other. But conditions were quite harsh under either version of slavery—and none of this was merely academic. Leiner quotes historian Robert C. Davis (who wrote *Christian Slaves, Muslim Masters*) as estimating "that in the 250 years of peak slave-trading by the Barbary corsairs, from 1530 to 1780, at least one million, and perhaps as many as one and one-quarter million, white Christians were enslaved in Islamic North Africa."[6]

It is worth noting that religious differences—Islam versus Christianity—were only a part of the motivation for captures by Barbary pirates. However much Islam was used as a rationale, economics (whether seen as greed or merely as a way of surviving) played a part. And the long history of the corsairs involves great variety and complexity.

The young American republic, lacking at that day a meaningful navy, spent significant amounts of its treasure on the problems. According to Leiner, in 1796, with no navy, "the United States paid the astronomical sum of $642,000—about one-fifteenth of all federal outlays that year—to ransom 107 American seaman from the bagnio [slave prison] of Algiers, some of whom had been held more than ten years."[7]

The treaty agreed to with Tripoli in November 1796 specified that the United States would pay the Bey "twelve thousand Spanish dollars" and provide a variety of other items, including, for example, "twenty-five barrels tar," to secure the peace.[8] The treaty was somewhat successful in the short term, but in the end US Naval and Marine forces had instead to win the peace through force. The reference to Tripoli in the famous first line of the US Marine Hymn, "From the Halls of Montezuma to the shores of Tripoli," refers to Marine participation in the war against the pirates of the Barbary States (1801–1805) in Thomas Jefferson's administration.

CONTROVERSY

There has been great controversy about the treaty, probably because of its explicit rejection of Christianity as the basis for the government of the United States. There have been some grounds for the controversy but no serious basis for rejecting the treaty as solid though secondary evidence of the framers' intent to establish a secular, non-Christian government. The US Constitution, lacking as it does any affirmative reference to religion, is both necessary and sufficient evidence of that secular intent, but the treaty provides weighty additional evidence of it less than a decade after ratification of the Constitution.

There are explicit connections between senators who voted for this treaty and those men who earlier approved the Declaration of Independence and then the Constitution itself. Senator Richard Stockton of Princeton, New Jersey, was the son of Richard Stockton (of the same city) who signed the Declaration.[9] Two of these senators signed the US Constitution—William Blount, then from Tennessee, represented North Carolina at the Constitutional Convention in 1787 and signed the Constitution then. (Tennessee was later carved out of North Carolina). And US senator John Langdon of New Hampshire was the same John Langdon who signed the Constitution almost ten years earlier (in September 1787).[10]

Among the objections to the treaty as evidence of the non-Christian nature of the American government is the possible fact that the Arabic version of the treaty, the one the Bey and his representatives agreed to, did not include Article 11. The surviving Arabic version has in place of Article 11 a page of what can be best described as a diplomatic cover letter with some flamboyant Arabic gibberish, and no one seems to know why.[11] Someone other than Barlow could well have substituted an Arabic page, perhaps even by accident at the time, or at some later time between the date it was written and the date the non-treaty page was discovered (in 1930). Barlow was very likely by 1796 a deist, though he had served earlier as a military chaplain, so one other possible (but unlikely) explanation is that Barlow wrote Article 11 and included it only in the English version—and therefore only for domestic consumption. If so, his motives may be suspect, but the Barlow translation, with the famous language, is the one sent to the US Senate for ratification by then president John Adams—the process of getting the treaty language approved and the documents back to the States took several months. And it is the Barlow translation that is and always has been recorded as the official version of the treaty in American diplomatic archives and publications.[12]

Another occasional objection is that the treaty was later superseded after Jefferson's war with the Barbary pirates without any such language in the new treaty. Indeed, some later treaties with nations such as Russia or Great Britain had flowery ceremonial language about the Christian Trinity. But it must be noted that the later treaties with such language were with nations that were at the time officially Christian nations—and none of those treaties reversed the earlier one and declared or even implied that the US government was after all founded on the Christian religion. The current importance of the treaty with the famous Article 11 language is, it must be remembered, not formal or legal, but historical. The "not in any sense founded on the Christian Religion" wording merely reinforces what the US Constitution had recently established—a secular basis for government.

Adams, inaugurated in March, sent the 1796–1797 Tripoli treaty to the Senate in late May 1797.[13] Copies were printed for the Senate and the committee considering it. The committee reported favorably to the Senate a week later, and on June 7, 1797, the Senate voted to ratify, with all twenty-three senators present recorded in favor: "Bingham, Bloodworth, Blount, Bradford, Brown, Cocke, Foster, Goodhue, Hillhouse, Howard, Langdon, Latimer, Laurance, Livermore, Martin, Paine [no, not Thomas Paine], Read, Rutherfurd, Sedgwick, Stockton, Tattnall, Tichenor, and Tracy."[14] The Senate, like the United States, was smaller then and a few senators were not present. For only the third time in the history of the Senate, a recorded vote was requested and approved despite unanimity, which is why we know the names of every senator voting in favor. There were up to that point (by our own personal tally as we combed through the official record[15]) 339 recorded Senate votes (out of thousands of votes in Senate history by then), but 336 were on matters where the Senate was divided and where, presumably, those in the minority wanted their own or their opponents' votes shown on the historical record. There is no record of any debate or dissension in the Senate on the treaty.

President Adams signed the treaty and proclaimed it to the nation on June 10, 1797. His statement on it was a bit unusual:

Now be it known, That I John Adams, President of the United States of America, having seen and considered the said Treaty do, by and with the advice and consent of the Senate, accept, ratify, and confirm the same, and every clause and article thereof. And to the End that the said Treaty may be observed and performed with good Faith on the part of the United States, I have ordered the premises to be made public; And I do hereby enjoin and require all persons bearing office civil or military within the United States, and all other citizens or inhabitants thereof, faithfully to observe and fulfil the said Treaty and every clause and article thereof.[16]

The wording of the treaty, including its now-famous Article 11, as well as Adams's proclamation, were printed in the newspapers of the day. Originals of some of those newspapers (for example, the Philadelphia *Gazette and Universal Daily Advertiser* for June 17, 1797) and microform copies of others (such as the very similarly named *Gazette of the United States, and Philadelphia Daily Advertiser* for June 16, 1797) can be read at the US Library of Congress. Philadelphia was of course the capital city of the United States then. The treaty was short—only three or four pages long in most texts, even including the ceremonial signature section—so the famous Article 11 was not likely to have been overlooked. Searches of the newspapers in the days and weeks after the treaty language was published revealed no record of any public dispute or protest over Article 11.

JOEL BARLOW
(AND THE OTHER MAJOR PLAYERS)

Joel Barlow, American poet, diplomat, translator into English (and probable author) of the treaty, was born on March 24, 1754, in Redding, Connecticut—where there is today a high school named after him.[17] Barlow likely wanted most to be remembered as a poet, especially as the author of *The Columbiad*, a long epic he worked on for years and envisioned as the great American poem. *The Columbiad* got mixed reviews then and has not since become the basis for literary fame. An earlier version, "Vision of Columbus," did produce more fame and acclaim when published in

1787. He served as an American chaplain at the end of the Revolutionary War. Barlow, a member of a group who called themselves "The Connecticut Wits," graduated from Yale in 1778 and is best known now for "The Hasty Pudding," a short satirical mock epic poem that probably inspired Harvard University's famous club of the same name.[18]

Barlow also wrote radical political philosophy, publishing "Advice to the Privileged Orders" (1792) in London, which the British government proscribed, and he later published political essays in France. Thomas Paine entrusted his draft of the first part of *Age of Reason* to his friend Barlow just as the guards of the French Revolution hauled Paine off to prison in 1793, and Barlow assisted later with getting *Age of Reason* published. Barlow also corresponded with Thomas Jefferson.

Barlow died in Poland in 1812 while on a diplomatic mission from the United States to Napoleon. As he drew near Napoleon, the French Army was in retreat from the Russians, and Barlow died of pneumonia in the exodus. His tombstone inscription in Poland roughly translates as "Joel Barlow, diplomat from the United States of America to the Emperor of France and the Queen of Italy; died here while traveling." He was fifty-eight.[19]

Also of interest is the fate of the senators who voted that day in May 1797 that the United States "government is not in any sense founded on the Christian Religion." A search through biographical information available[20] on the twenty-three revealed that none seems to have paid a political price for his vote; among the twenty-three were many who were reelected as senators. One senator, Theodore Sedgwick of Massachusetts, went on to become the Speaker of the House[21] (Henry Clay is the only other American in history to be first a senator, then Speaker). Imagine, if you can, former Speaker Newt Gingrich running for president or wielding influence with the conservative wing of the Republican Party if he had publicly voted for Article 11. An aside of interest to many Americans: Senator Sedgwick's direct descendant (great-great-great-great granddaughter) is the popular American actress Kyra Sedgwick.[22]

Another senator, Isaac Tichenor,[23] became governor of Vermont and then returned to the Senate for many years. A Georgia senator, Josiah Tattnall,[24] did not return to the Senate, but he did serve thereafter as one of the youngest governors in Georgia's history and has a county in Georgia and a number of streets, squares, and so forth, named after him.

(His father was a Tory; his son by the same name was a famous officer in the Confederate Navy.)

Any who might be tempted to recommend the senators or President Adams or Joel Barlow or even George Washington as atheist or freethought heroes for their actions should instead reflect, with satisfaction, that this secular declaration was apparently considered ordinary and was broadly known and accepted at the time. There was no confusion then about whether the American government is and should be secular.

Chapter 9.

Ten Commandments
Religious Manifesto or Political Gimmick?

The Ten Commandments, or rather various of the many versions of them, have been the source of confusion and controversy since the beginning of the United States in 1789, if not before. Thomas Jefferson engaged in disputes about these. And fights over posting some version or another in courtrooms or public schools still seem to erupt somewhere in the United States every week.[1] As the Reverend Barry W. Lynn has written,

> I'm tired of lawmakers using a religious code that's important to hundreds of millions of Christians and Jews all over the world as a cannon to fire off salvos in a "cultural war." It's offensive. It's time for it to stop. . . . The purpose of such displays is not to educate. It's to make a political statement that religion and government should be joined at the hip. Such displays do a disservice to our residents.[2]

Widespread claims that "our laws are all based, originally at least, on the Ten Commandments of God" quite often accompany claims that American government is Judeo-Christian in nature even if not in so many words in the Constitution. Adherents often seem baffled that anyone should oppose public posting of such basic moral guidelines; and the Decalogue (another term for the Ten Commandments) is sometimes even declared (ludicrously) not to be religious at all—only legal and moral.

Those who believe that the Judeo-Christian Commandments (that all good Christians and Jews "know" came directly from the one true God) seem at times immune to facts, history, logic, and the actual words of the commandments they champion. The false claims go well beyond the nature of the Decalogue, extending even to details as to where they are allegedly posted. Many a preacher or political demagogue will assure you, as proof of the hypocrisy of the US Supreme Court, that the commandments are prominently displayed over the heads of the US Supreme Court Justices in their courtroom *and* posted on the main doors opening into the courtroom. And these advocates imply or say things like "Given this fact, would anyone but a fool claim that this is not a Christian nation?" Also intoned often enough are questions like "Where's the harm, as long as the government doesn't favor Methodists over Presbyterians?" A related, frequent, baseless question relies on a fabricated quotation from Madison and is usually cast something like "Since Madison, who wrote the Constitution, said good government is dependent on the Ten Commandments, isn't it obvious that the Constitution is profoundly Judeo-Christian?"

The answer to questions like these is based on a simple notion that, at times, we can all have trouble remembering. As already noted and as Jefferson wrote, anyone who cares about freedom of conscience should work to protect it for others if he wants his own protected.[3] Only two concepts are relevant in these cases: (1) US citizens are not unanimous in their views on religion, including the precepts summed up in the commandments (and the differences are important ones), and (2) neither the majority nor any government acting on behalf of the majority has any right to make any religious decisions for any citizens. If a fundamentalist questioner can be persuaded of the truth of these two ideas, then it follows as a matter of straightforward logic that governmental neutrality regarding religion is necessary and desirable, as much for any Christian as for any non-Christian.

Many claim that the words of the Ten Commandments are posted in the US Supreme Court Building and that it is therefore hypocritical for the Court not to allow them to be posted in other schools or courtrooms. (On a related issue, the depiction of Mohammed in the courtroom, see chapter 17, "Blasphemy and Heresy.") Though often repeated, that is a false claim. We have been in the US Supreme Court chambers ourselves[4] and walked carefully all around the outside of the building, too. There are sculptural allusions, several of them, to Moses, just as there are to Confucius and Hammurabi and Napoleon and Mohammed and many others—but in every case these figures are presented as *lawgivers*—some religious, some not. In no case are the words of the Ten Commandments presented in English (there are a few Hebrew-looking fragments and there are some roman numerals that could be interpreted as referring to the Ten Commandments or, more likely, to the Bill of Rights). If government buildings—courtrooms or classrooms—did post and endorse the Ten Commandments, the very first commandment would directly oppose the First Amendment. "Thou shalt have no other gods before me" may be a clear religious rule for Christians and Jews to follow, but if *government* is allowed to endorse *or* oppose it, *government* becomes the authority on religious truth, instead of each American citizen. As we note in chapter 16, "God's Law," not only are the Ten Commandments not the basis of American law, but it is a very good thing they are not. Those who *genuinely* argue for a government based on the Decalogue—fortunately they remain on the fringes even of American Christianity—want a government that would more resemble a Christian version of Iran than the United States we know. For more on the policy implications of taking the Commandments seriously, see that chapter.

Posting a religious or antireligious document is and assuredly should be every citizen's right, and it is a right that is nowhere in the United States under any serious threat from government or the courts. But asking or even allowing the government to post similar documents in a way that suggests that the government endorses the religious ideas included in the document is a direct threat to the same individual religious liberty. And it is nonsense to argue, as some have, that if the government does not directly pay for printing or engraving or framing a document like the Ten Commandments (whichever version is used), then it is acceptable.

Any public-school teacher (or other public official) who gets involved directly in the struggle over using the Ten Commandments in any way in a public school or other state-controlled institution, should consider referring to *The Decalogue: Bible Scholarship for Use Today*, by Brant Abrahamson and Frederick C. Smith. It includes thoughtful, scholarly discussions of the different versions of the Ten Commandments, the development of "The Golden Rule," comparisons of ancient and modern history writing, suggested activities, and more information for teachers as background. Probably few fundamentalists would accept using this in the schools, but that is part of the point. The book is scrupulously respectful of diverse views and, if it were actually used by a classroom teacher, should satisfy believers and nontheists alike.

To any American in any state who asserts that posting the Ten Commandments in all the schools is acceptable, ask if posting one of the Humanist Manifestos (at the expense of, say, the Council for Secular Humanism) would be acceptable. If the reply is that such a slogan or manifesto would offend most Americans instead of just a few atheists, ask if a majority of voters *did* convert to atheism, would that make one of these acceptable? It is crucial that, as atheists or secular humanists, we understand that not all Christians are our opponents on church/state separation. It should be stressed, we argue, that offending a few thin-skinned atheists is *not* the problem with an official religious slogan; the problem is that if the majority has the right to endorse any religious (or antireligious) idea, then a later majority will have the right to endorse some other different or even opposite view. All of us (atheists, secular humanists, Christians, Jews, Muslims, Buddhists, etc.) are either in some way now in the minority about religion or could easily be in the future. The important thing is not who is offended or who has the votes—the important thing is to protect religious liberty.

Alabama judge Roy Moore tried—and for a while succeeded—to build his whole political career on the political gimmick of treating the Ten Commandments as a tool for winning political support. Most famously, Moore arranged, as Alabama chief justice, for a two-ton-plus graven image (literally) of the Decalogue to be installed—sneaked in under cover of darkness—in the Alabama Judicial Building. Moore insisted that, despite the plain language of the First and Fourteenth Amendments declaring that Alabamans are US citizens with full rights to religious liberty, Alabama officials (or at least one official named Roy Moore) could establish Christianity in Alabama, could decide for Alabamans what counted as sacred commandments.

Earlier in his career, Moore had successfully used his willingness to use the Ten Commandments as a political tool (posting them in his Gadsden, Alabama, courtroom and daring anyone to order him to take them down) to create controversy, stir publicity, and make himself famous. He was elected, in 2000 in a statewide election, to be the chief justice of the Alabama Supreme Court. And it was as a judge on that court that he pulled his infamous two-ton trick. But it ultimately back-fired. A federal court ruled that his rock was unconstitutional and ordered it removed. Chief Justice Moore refused. But his colleagues on that court and others on the Alabama Court of the Judiciary drew a line in the sand (they apparently knew about the First Amendment) and unanimously voted to remove Moore from office. Not long before, Roy's rock was also removed from public display.[5]

Moore summarized the events leading up to November 12, 2003, when he appeared as a witness before an ethics panel—the one that voted unanimously to remove him from office:

> The Ten Commandments monument that I had placed in the rotunda of the building to acknowledge God had already been declared unconstitutional by a federal district judge, ordered removed from the rotunda, and locked in a storage room by my colleagues on the court. But on this day, I was being questioned before an ethics panel because I had refused to move the monument.
>
> "And your understanding," Attorney general [Bill] Pryor asked me, "is that the federal court ordered that you could not acknowledge God. Isn't that right?"
>
> "Yes," I responded.[6]

Moore spent the rest of his 2005 book *So Help Me God* explaining and insisting that his interpretation of the law and the Constitution and his understanding of his duty to God superseded every possible authority available, regardless of what documents or officials were brought to bear. As the Rev. Barry W. Lynn has noted, "41 law professors and legal historians" in the Alabama dispute wrote to debunk "the idea that U.S. law springs from the Ten Commandments."[7] Moore's attention seeking, using the Ten Commandments, did not end with his book. He flirted with the possibility of running for the Republican nomination for president in 2012,[8] and he sought election, again, as chief justice of Alabama in 2012.[9] Moore will certainly keep using his favorite prop whether or not he is holding any public office.

As to the alleged Madison quotation on the Ten Commandments, that, too, is readily rebutted as a serious claim. But that doesn't mean it is all that simple. It is related to another false claim the Christian-nation mythologists love to make: the idea that even if the framers did not *label* the US government as Christian, they did base all our laws and procedures on the Bible and especially on the Ten Commandments. Despite frequent, confident repetition, this is demonstrably false. But the main issue here is an apparently fabricated quotation attributed to Madison. Robert S. Alley explored this almost certainly false history at length and in sufficiently well-documented detail to persuade any reasonable person in a 1995 essay.[10] According to Alley, David Barton quotes James Madison as saying:

> We have staked the whole future of American civilization not upon the power of government, far from it. We have staked the future of all our political institutions upon the capacity of mankind for self-government, upon the capacity of each and all of us to govern ourselves, to control ourselves, to sustain ourselves according to the Ten Commandments.

Alley noted that Barton gave as his only sources two twentieth-century writers: "Harold K. Lane, *Liberty! Cry Liberty!* and Fredrick Nyneyer, *First Principles in Morality and Economics: Neighborly Love and Ricardo's Law of Association.*" Based on our own knowledge of Madison and on Alley's essay, we deny that Madison is likely to have ever written or said what Barton claimed, regardless of how many sources are cited. But how can we know, and how can we prove to any doubting Thomases that we are right? The answer, of course, is that we cannot *know*, and we cannot *prove* it. The only way anyone could "prove" a quote is inaccurate is by having a complete, verified transcript of everything a person ever said or wrote—practically speaking, an impossibility. But that does not mean we should accept every quote anyone attributes to someone famous. As thoughtful, skeptical atheists and secular humanists, our only reasonable course, when provided with a quote (no matter whose side it supports) is to ask critical questions. Is it consistent with other things we know the man or woman wrote or said? Is there any specific written evidence from a primary source for the quote? If so, is the context in which it is found consistent with the apparent meaning of the quote? To return to the alleged Madison quote, no such quote has ever been found among any of James Madison's writings. None of the biographers of Madison, past or present, have ever run across such a quote, and most if not all would love to know where this false quote originated. Apparently, David

Barton did not check the work of the secondary sources he quotes. (He has since admitted that the quote, like a number of others he has cited and that others have repeated, cannot be confirmed.) For more, please read Alley's excellent essay.

As Thom Hartmann has noted, Thomas Jefferson's entanglement with those who claimed US law or government is based on the Decalogue was long-standing and his rejection of their claims—of Moses as the author of our Constitution—was complete.[11] Jefferson himself addressed, clearly, the whole idea that American law or the US Constitution is somehow based on the Ten Commandments. Jefferson wrote a long, detailed, and heavily documented account explaining in 1814 to John Adams why he had concluded that neither American law or before it English common law rested on the Ten Commandments or Christianity. Jefferson first expressed skepticism that anyone could even have a record of the alleged Ten Commandments, as they were supposedly

> written by the finger of god on tables of stone, which were destroyed by Moses: it specifies those on the 2d. set of tables in different form and substance, but still without saying how the others were recovered.[12]

Jefferson then went on, at great length, to show how errors and mistranslations were the only basis for anyone concluding that English law was based not on Anglo-Saxon development of law but on Christianity and the Ten Commandments:

> Thus we find this string of authorities all hanging by one another on a single hook, a mistranslation by Finch of the words of Prisot, or on nothing.[13]

Aside from the detailed refutation by Jefferson of the idea that our laws and Constitution are based on the Ten Commandments, an even more straightforward reason for understanding that the connection is tenuous (at best) exists. If one reads the Ten Commandments, in whatever version one prefers, and examines our laws and Constitution even briefly, it is apparent that they have little connection. Not only are none of the religious commandments to be found enshrined in our legal system, but even the more secular ones—save false testimony, stealing, and murder—are also absent. We may have similar values inculcated in us by our culture—that we should honor our parents, for example—but not written into law. And arguably if following the last commandment became widespread even in the culture, our economic system might collapse. "Madison Avenue," not James Madison, bombards us hourly with messages urging us to covet pretty much anything and everything.

Every religious American—Catholic or Protestant, Jew or Muslim, or any other sort—has the unrestricted right to believe that the Ten Commandments (whatever version) constitute direct commands from an all-knowing and all-powerful god. Each such American is fully within his rights to carefully obey those commands insofar as doing so does not impinge on the rights of others. But it is openly un-American to demand that your fellow Americans agree with you on any such understanding or to play political games regarding the posting of whatever you consider to be sacred words in governmental places.

Chapter 10.

Tolerance, Toleration, and Liberty
The Historical Context

Possibly the most famous preacher around when the United States was officially born, Baptist John Leland (1754–1841), vigorously *opposed* "toleration." His fame was mostly based on his preaching but also rested on at least one extraordinary event unrelated to religion—he led a highly publicized effort by the people of his hometown, Cheshire, Massachusetts, to deliver a "Mammoth Cheese" to President Jefferson on the very day in 1802 that Jefferson wrote his famous letter to the Danbury Baptists.[1] Leland is also credited by some as inspiring James Madison to write and support guaranteeing religious liberty in the First Amendment to the US Constitution. Modern Americans are likely to be startled, at first, on learning that a man so important in our history disparaged anything like tolerance. Surely toleration should be encouraged in everyone, liberal or conservative, religious or atheist!

Here's some of what Leland wrote in 1790 in the *Virginia Chronicle*:

> Here let it be observed, that religion is a matter entirely between God and individuals. No man has the right to force another to join a church: Nor do the legitimate powers of civil government extend so far as to disable, incapacitate, proscribe, or any ways distress in person, property, liberty or life, any man who cannot believe and practice in the common road. . . .
>
> The principle, that civil rulers have nothing to do with religion, in their official capacities, is as much interwoven in the Baptist plan, as Phydia's name was in his shield. The legitimate powers of government, extend only to punish men for working ill to their neighbors, and no ways effect the rights of conscience. . . .

Government should protect every man in thinking and speaking freely, and see that one does not abuse another. The liberty I contend for is more than toleration. The very idea of toleration is despicable; it supposes that some have a pre-eminence above the rest to grant indulgence; whereas *all* should be equally free, Jews, Turks [Muslims], Pagans and Christians. Test oaths and established creeds should be avoided as the worst of evils. A general assessment (forcing all to pay some preacher) amounts to an establishment; if government says I must pay somebody, it must next describe that somebody, his doctrine and place of abode. . . . This doctrine turns the gospel into merchandise, and sinks religion upon a level with other things.[2]

Nor was Leland alone in such views. Rev. John Witherspoon, the only clergyman to sign the Declaration of Independence, president of Princeton, teacher to James Madison, declared, "Tolerance is not enough, since it implies superiority or condescension. The only religious principle worthy of adoption in a republic is the liberty to worship as one wishes, or not at all."[3]

The sequence of history is needed to explain how toleration (sometimes called "tolerance," as by Witherspoon) could be so despised by a religious leader. While toleration legislation, such as the 1649 Maryland Act of Toleration or the British Toleration Act of 1689, was seen by those in power as great progress and as generous and magnanimous treatment of minorities, it was rightly perceived as condescending by the minorities. As David L. Holmes wrote,

Religious freedom means that citizens are free to worship in any way or not at all—and that the state protects that freedom. *Religious toleration* means that the state allows a group to exist and to worship, but retains the right to withdraw or limit that permission at any time.[4]

The whole question does not resolve into simple matters, however. The most famous writings related to this are the *Bloody Tenent of Persecution* (1644) by Roger Williams (b. 1603?–d. 1683) and the 1689–1693 letters by John Locke (b. 1632–d. 1704) concerning toleration,[5] and these in turn had great influence on the American Founding Fathers and American ideas regarding freedom of religion. Official "toleration" of dissident religious ideas was of course much better than its predecessors:

beheadings or imprisonment or torture for not accepting the approved religion. Sort of like "separate but equal" Jim Crow laws being easily superior to slavery, even as it left some feeling understandably "uppity." (*Uppity* was a racist term of derision in and before the mid-twentieth century in the American South for African Americans who dared to exhibit the sort of pride one takes for granted in truly free and equal citizens.) Such toleration was ultimately well short of what was wanted by dissidents like Leland. To oversimplify a little, such acts and the rationales behind them were seen as saying, "Well, you people are obviously wrong, but we will graciously allow you to make these grave mistakes without governmental interference." The nonconformist reply was something like "Who are you to decide for me what is a mistake in these matters? I take my orders from God via my conscience, not from some worldly government via a magistrate."

Nor were religious leaders such as John Leland and John Witherspoon in revolutionary America the only ones to reject toleration emphatically in favor of liberty. Thomas Paine, crucial philosophical leader during the American Revolution, declared in the *Rights of Man* (1791), which he addressed to George Washington, that "Toleration is not the *opposite* of intolerance, but is the counterfeit of it. Both are despotisms. The one assumes to itself the right of withholding Liberty of Conscience, and the other of granting it."[6]

George Washington addressed this as well, eloquently, as president, in his famous letter to the "Hebrew Congregation" (of Touro Synagogue) in Newport, Rhode Island, in August 1790:

> It is now no more that toleration is spoken of as it was by the indulgence of one class of the people that another enjoyed the exercise of their natural rights. For happily the Government of the United States, which gives to bigotry no sanction, to persecution no assistance, requires only that those who live under its protection should demean themselves as good citizens in giving it, on all occasions, their effectual support.[7]

Washington's famous declaration, important enough that it has already been quoted (in chapter 5, "History Is Not on the Side of the Angels") is unambiguously in favor of liberty over the old ideas of toleration, even as he clearly opposes intolerance.

John Adams, key revolutionary leader and second president, wrote on October 2, 1818, "I will not condescend to employ the word Toleration. I assert that unlimited freedom of religion, consistent with morals and property, is essential to the progress of society and the amelioration of the condition of mankind."[8]

Jefferson and Madison, the key architects of religious liberty in the United States (though assuredly assisted in this by Adams and many others), were the key Founding Fathers who thought John Locke had not gone far enough in developing his ideas on toleration. As Jefferson noted,

> Locke denies toleration to those who entertain opinions contrary to those moral rules necessary for the preservation of society, as for instance, . . . [those] who deny the existence of a god (it was a great thing to go so far—as he himself says of the parliament which framed the act of toleration—but where he stopped short we may go on).[9]

As John Noonan has argued, the historical evidence is that, "Overshadowed by Jefferson, Madison was the better workman [in developing religious freedom]."[10] Noonan declared,

> To follow Madison is to catch the quintessence of the drive, at once deeply religious and deeply political, for more than religious tolerance—for free exercise itself. It is Madison whom American experience has vindicated.[11]

We disagree with Noonan in finding religious liberty or ideas of freedom of conscience necessarily religious, but we share his respect for Madison and his conviction that the "American Experience of Religious Liberty" (as his subtitle calls it) is a matter worthy of great American pride. The very essence of the modern American idea of secularism, the idea developed and founded in the Constitution and First Amendment, is an idea that is neither religious nor antireligious, neither Christian nor opposed to Christianity, and that idea is to proclaim, unmistakably and even fiercely, not toleration but freedom.

Modern Americans are pretty uniformly committed, at least in common parlance, to "tolerance," meaning accepting another's right to see things—especially religious ideas—in ways that disagree, even sharply, with our own conclusions. In the main, this idea of tolerance is quite positive, quite desirable, as an individual virtue. But it does not follow that toleration—meaning official *permission* for those who dissent from the accepted religion to exist—is therefore a national virtue. That would imply that some have the choice to allow others to disagree—and if it is a mere choice, it can be taken away.

All of us are right to prefer and work for individual tolerance but not for governmental toleration—in short, we should trust in freedom, with liberty for all. This is at the heart of the importance of secularism.

Chapter 11.

Secular Schooling
Public-School Policies and Curriculum Questions Affecting Religious Liberty

To educate a child perfectly requires profounder thought, greater wisdom, than to govern a state.

—William Ellery Channing, Boston, September 1838[1]

- Why should secular parents support public schools (or oppose "vouchers")?
- Is moral education possible in the public schools (where it would have to be taught without a religious basis of some kind)? Isn't it in fact impossible to separate religious belief or ideas from education, unless education is taken to mean nothing more than rote learning?
- Why should parents support the separation of church and state within public schools?

These are questions that any parent should take seriously, consider with care, and answer. This chapter includes some suggested answers.

SUPPORTING PUBLIC SCHOOLS

All thoughtful citizens, even people who aren't parents and never expect to become parents, should support public schools. The same goes for parents who want to homeschool their children or who pay to have them attend private schools, whether religious or secular.

Our society is more interdependent than ever, and we all gain by a better-educated population; we are all threatened by a less well-educated one. Our whole economy—not just our own jobs or businesses—depends directly on workers having and maintaining complex skills. Our democratic governance will cease to be self-governance if most of us don't understand our own society and its political philosophy. And our culture will be cheapened instead of enriched if we do not have a broadly educated citizenry, a populace able to appreciate all that life and art have to offer.

Only a public-school system has any chance of educating nearly everyone, and only such a system can hope to instill a common education, language, historical knowledge, and basic moral values across the population. Public schools deserve universal support for all these reasons. That's why "vouchers"—grants of tax dollars to individual parents to spend at the private schools of their choice—supposedly a way to encourage freedom and improve education—are a bad idea. Vouchers encourage, and may even guarantee, socially debilitating segregation. They certainly endanger religious liberty. Our children need to learn firsthand that different isn't worse. All our children can gain greatly by seeing other children cope and succeed, the more so if those other children have a wide range of different abilities, ethnicities, interests, geographical origins, and cultures.

A major argument advanced by private-school and voucher supporters is that we have, under another very successful program, done exactly what proposed school vouchers would do, without harm to public universities or to church/state separation or liberty. Veterans since World War II have had various public funding, usually known as "GI Bill" educational benefits, for going to whatever institution of higher learning they wish. And Notre Dame or Bob Jones University can be chosen as easily as State University. But the comparison of vouchers with the veterans' benefits misses a crucial set of differences: veterans are adults making choices that are optional, including the choice to attend at all. As adults, they are full citizens, entitled to make choices that may not be deemed wise or in the best interests of the society at large. But children are generally unable to decide with any effective power of their own how much to let the beliefs of their parents affect their educational decisions—and parents deciding for their children is not the equivalent of adult veterans deciding for themselves.

An occasional argument advanced by voucher supporters against church/state objections is that education is a local matter, not a matter to be addressed by the federal government or the federal courts. That argument ignores the Fourteenth Amendment (and the bloody civil war that led to it) that proclaimed in 1868 that the rights of a citizen of the United States cannot be abridged by state or local governments.[2] And many state constitutions explicitly protect religious liberty.

The other major basis for supporting public schools and opposing vouchers is, as already noted, that vouchers would encourage destructive segregation in our society. Taking tax dollars out of public schools and sending those dollars to private schools, even nonreligious institutions, would greatly increase the chances that a student would spend most of his time with others much like himself. Racial segregation has proven in the past to be extremely effective in undercutting justice, and voluntary segregation along racial, ethnic, class, sexual-orientation, political, or religious lines would be harmful as well. Our society is strengthened by having most of our citizens educated in settings where they rub shoulders with people quite unlike themselves and where a common curriculum, with more or less consistent standards and with guaranteed access for all, prevails. Tax incentives for people to abandon this common education would unmistakably weaken it, making it most likely that public education would soon be reserved only for those with expensive problems and for those whose parents are too lazy or ignorant to move them. To those who say a common, standard curriculum, with free access to all, could be required as a condition of vouchers, the question must be, how will that be any better or any freer than what we have now? Public schools need more resources and more public support, not less. A much more fractured society, with much less practical understanding of what other people are like, would be the result of vouchers.

And, as much as many secular parents might believe it would benefit our own children in some ways to be educated apart from others with irrational religious beliefs, it seems likely that even our own children would lose more than they would gain by being segregated.

MORAL EDUCATION

All parents must of course have primary responsibility for the moral education of their children, including encouraging and supporting social institutions and organizations that have moral education as part of their purpose. While other parts of this book, especially chapter 15, "The Big Lie," address moral education more generally, this chapter will offer advice for secular parents on the role public schools should play in moral education. One frequent false belief is that public schools are prevented from engaging in moral education by separation of church and state. If moral education were dependent on religious beliefs, that might be true—but it isn't.

Religious believers often think morals come ultimately from God, but that ultimate basis need not be part of the education, and of course those of us without any religious beliefs don't agree about the source of morals anyway. No God is needed for—and it can even be reasonably argued that religion interferes with—moral development. How we treat each other, whether we lie or have integrity, whether we care about what is right and follow our code of right and wrong—all of this can and should be taught in public schools. Good teachers have always helped their students develop self-respect, an understanding of justice and fair play, respect for differences, and moral understanding. Good parents should encourage and appreciate this.

The philosophical questions related to whether morality needs an absolute basis, a source beyond humankind, have engaged theologians and philosophers for centuries. Atheists and many other secularists come down, usually, on the situational side of the question, in agreement with the idea that no absolute basis—no god—is needed. But whatever the philosophical conclusions, the practical matter is that agreed-upon moral standards can be inculcated without referring to any nonhuman source even if there is one.

Education certainly means more than making students acquire facts or information. The main goal of education should always be to learn how to learn, to become an independent thinker. While teaching students to think, any good teacher will always also teach them to treat themselves and others wisely and well. No secular parent can hope to do this alone, but every parent should consciously plan to do it.

RELIGION OR SCIENCE IN THE SCHOOLS: "INTELLIGENT DESIGN" AND "SCIENTIFIC CREATIONISM"

A common complaint from conservative Christians is that the courts will not allow rival scientific theories, primarily those thought to contradict Darwinian evolution, to be taught in the public schools. These critics usually insist that a bias against Christianity (or at least against theism) is the real motivation for depriving schoolchildren of learning about "intelligent design" or "scientific creationism." Such opponents of evolutionary theory, most of them quite sincere, argue that teaching only evolutionary theory is somehow a violation of separation of church and state, that evolutionary theory is itself a religious idea. Extreme variations on this theme even occasionally enter the legislative arena, as with New Hampshire state representative Jerry Bergevin. He was reported in December 2011 as having introduced antievolutionary theory legislation, calling evolutionary ideas "criminal ideas" and equating evolution with "godless" atheism. Among other bizarre statements, Bergevin declared that teaching evolution caused terrible things like the Columbine High School shootings and that this amounted to "evidence right there" against teaching evolution.[3]

We have neither the expertise nor the space in this book to analyze the arguments regarding evolutionary theory. Excellent works like *The Greatest Show on Earth* by Richard Dawkins; *God, the Devil, and Darwin* by Niall Shanks; and *Why Darwin Matters* by Michael Shermer should be consulted for much more on Darwinian evolution.

But the key point to understand is that decisions about what is taught in secular public-school science classrooms need to be made based on the current state of understanding in the scientific establishment, not on religious or antireligious ideas. No serious analyst, for example, thinks that a rival to the germ theory of disease should be taught in health or science classes, even though some religions do teach that prayer is superior to antibiotics or that blood transfusions are unbiblical. Similarly, creationism (including intelligent design, which is by most accounts nothing more than creationism labeled anew) must be seen as a serious rival explanatory theory *by scientists* before it can be presented in science classes. In 2005, in *Kitzmiller v. Dover Area School District* the judge ruled[4] (the whole decision is well worth reading) that intelligent design is plainly a religious, not a scientific, theory.

Some scientific theories have, in the views of atheists, clear implications about the truth or falsity of traditional religions, and public-school teachers must draw the line between teaching students the scientific facts about the world they live in and going on to say, "So you see, children, that the Book of Genesis is therefore false." In the context of battles over school curricula, some believers have insisted that almost *any* concept—especially "Darwinism," "evolutionism," or "secularism"—is a "religion." But if everything is a religion, then a concept like the separation of church and state—or, in James Madison's words, the separation of religion and government—becomes meaningless. Even "free exercise of religion" becomes problematic—perhaps "tax evasion" is simply "my religion."

A useful way to analyze controversies over public policy versus religious objections was provided in a quite-different context by Kevin Drum, a political blogger for *Mother Jones*. As he wrote,

> You have to look at two separate issues: (1) How important is the secular purpose of the policy? (2) How deeply held is the religious objection to it? . . .
>
> Some matters of conscience are worth respecting and some aren't. If, say, Catholic doctrine forbade white doctors from treating black patients, nobody would be defending them. The principle of racial nondiscrimination is simply too important to American culture and we'd insist that the church respect this.[5]

For the most extreme fringe of the religious Right—the Christian Reconstructionists (see chapter 16, "God's Law" for much more) who proclaim that "There is no neutrality"—this is the whole point of the argument; if neutrality is impossible, then we have no choice but to establish some religion or another (and of course, they go on to say we might as well establish the One True Religion, i.e., *their* religion). Never mind the establishment clause; anyone who believes in individual free exercise of religion must reject such "Darwinism /Copernicanism/geometry is just another religion" arguments as fundamentally corrosive of the notion of religious liberty. This is not to say that there are not nontheistic belief systems that, though they may not be "religious" in a philosophical sense, must nonetheless be treated as religions in a constitutional sense, both positively and negatively. Congress (and American governments more generally) surely can make no law outlawing atheism or secular humanism; conversely, a public school could not do something that *genuinely* constituted an official endorsement of a nontheistic belief system (such as leading all the students in a daily recitation of the Affirmations of Humanism—even if it was "student-initiated," "voluntary," and "non-proselytizing").

SUPPORTING SEPARATION OF CHURCH AND STATE IN PUBLIC SCHOOLS

Every citizen benefits from separation of church and state or, in the case of public schools, from the separation of religious education from common public education. Despite myths to the contrary, separation is not a matter of being careful not to offend either people without religion or people who follow a minority religion. Nor is separation of church and state an antireligious principle. "Secular" means "not based on religion"—it doesn't mean "hostile to religion." As every public-school teacher and every parent should know, the purpose of separation is to protect religious liberty. Only by consistently denying government agents, including public-school teachers, the right to make decisions about religion is this liberty secure.

Four basic ideas together form the basic logical underpinnings of separation of church and state and should be applied to public schools (these four are discussed in more detail in chapter 1, "Why Secularism?"):

1. Not all American citizens hold the same opinions on religion and on important matters related to religion (like whether or not there is a god and, if so, what his nature is; or, how or when or whether to worship God; or what God says to us about how to live).
2. *Human* judgement is imperfect. The question is not whether any *God's* judgement is perfect—only whether man's is.
3. Religious truth cannot be determined by votes or by force. In

America, neither a majority of citizens nor the government acting on the majority's behalf can make religious decisions for individuals.

4. Freedom, especially religious liberty, is worth having and protecting.

Any citizen who understands American political philosophy should not disagree with any of these four ideas, and it is equally hard to understand how anyone who agrees with all four would oppose separation of church and state. Since the fight waged in Virginia in 1784–1785 by James Madison and others—a struggle that almost certainly produced the archetype for the religious liberty established by the First Amendment—it has been clear that letting majorities or governments decide religious matters risks destroying religious liberty.

As noted in chapter 1, "Why Secularism?" Madison, a leader in that Virginia battle, wrote "A Memorial and Remonstrance"—a petition signed by enough people all over Virginia to defeat "A Bill Establishing a Provision for Teachers of the Christian Religion." That bill, supported by a group led by Patrick Henry, was one designed to do what some claim the First Amendment does: support Christianity without choosing among denominations and specifically to do so regarding education. The logic and facts that caused those wanting a "multiple establishment" to lose in Virginia are the best reasons for rejecting those interpretations of the First Amendment.

What does this have to do with separation in public schools? Keep in mind that the Virginia bill was intended to *support Christian teachers*, and remember what Madison wrote.[6]

Madison understood and persuaded most Virginians in his day that governments must stay out of matters related to religion, or liberty is at peril, and this is especially true regarding public schools in our day. For the good of the whole society, students not yet adults are required to attend these schools. Secularism requires that students not be forced to undergo religious or antireligious indoctrination while gaining their common education.

Many do oppose separation of religion and public education, of course, but most who oppose it do so because they lack good understanding of the principle and its purpose. The most common misunderstanding is that separation is designed to protect religious minorities, especially atheists, from being offended. Offending people without good reason isn't ever a good idea, but that *isn't* the point of separation. Separation is necessary to protect everyone's religious liberty.

Another set of misunderstandings relates to which behaviors are actually prohibited by separation of church and state, especially in public schools. A related pernicious set of myths about separation being used to attack religion or to deny schoolchildren their religious rights has been around for years. In 1995 John Young, an editorial-page writer for the *Waco* (TX) *Tribune-Herald*, noted that "urban myths" or "unholy hoaxes" about school prayer and related matters have persisted even when shown to be completely baseless.[7] As he pointed out, "the hoaxers go merrily on their way. They make public schools the bad guys, anti-God and anti-good, for making the tough calls that come with accommodating a nation of many faiths."

Students can pray, including saying grace before lunch or praying that they'll pass the algebra test (studying longer would be more effective). Students can bring a Bible or other religious book to school and can read it in free time at school. Teachers can also pray if they wish. Rules that do apply, reasonably enough, include the following:

- Students may not disrupt classes to pray or witness about their religious or antireligious beliefs.
- Students may not proselytize others who don't want the attention.
- Teachers may not lead students in prayer or direct students to pray or not to pray.
- Teachers and administrators may not use government property or school time to promote or oppose religion.

Restrictions on teachers and administrators are the most important ones, and they are in every case intended to ensure that no one is using the power of government to impose religious decisions on students. Much more detailed information on the exact rules is available from Americans United for Separation of Church and State.[8]

American parents, especially nonreligious parents, owe it to their children and to their society to support public schools, to plan thoughtfully for and support the moral education of their children, and to support separation of church and state (especially the separation of religion and education in public schools).

Chapter 12.

Holy Days and Holidays in a Secular Society
Who Could Be against a Day off, Anyway?

There are acres of nonsense, in the media and in common understandings in American society, regarding a secular society and holidays (a term that originally was a variation of "holy days" but no longer has any necessary religious connection). The "War on Christmas" declared to be under way by the more sensationalistic media every year is the silliest and most ill-founded example, but it is not the only one. There are some real issues, some real decisions and need for sensitivity on these matters, but most of the "controversy" surrounding these issues is phony. The principle that governments in a secular society must follow is that everyone's ideas about religious special days should be respected, but that no one should get government endorsement of one's religion in the process. Government employees should be given some leeway about what days to take off to worship or to engage in other religious activities, with those not following a given religion trading off (directly or indirectly) with others to keep essential services in place.

Government offices should *not* generally be closed to honor or encourage a religious holiday, since that is a plain endorsement of the religion in question. But closing for a holiday that is widely celebrated in secular, nonreligious ways by people of various faiths or of none—particularly December 25—can readily be justified without endorsing religion. As Tom Flynn has demonstrated beyond doubt in *The Trouble with Christmas*, the celebrations of that holiday have little to do with religious Christianity. Most if not all of the usual trappings of the date—gift

133

exchanges, trees, decorations, traditions, and even the date itself—trace back to pagan or seasonal ideas. Christians adopted the date as the alleged date of birth for Jesus Christ to co-opt pagans and Mithraists, and much about it is associated with the winter solstice.

The Christian celebration of Easter has much in common with Christmas, except that not even the name "Easter" is Christian. Easter bunnies and Easter eggs point in an uncomplicated way to the real roots of the holiday: it is a celebration of the renewal and fertility that comes around every year in the spring (in the Northern Hemisphere). "Easter" is named after the fertility goddess Eostre or Eastre, a "Great Mother Goddess of the Saxon people," and the word literally refers to spring.[1] It is plain that the Christians chose this season for celebrating a "resurrection," or life after dying, because the season fits perfectly with their message. That the exact date of Easter is determined based on a combination of phases of the moon and the spring equinox is another indication that the date is not a simple anniversary of a historical event. Many Americans celebrate non-Christian aspects of this holiday—and it rarely causes controversy or problems or "War on Easter" nonsense because it always falls on a Sunday, already a day off for many people. In parts of the United States with substantial Catholic populations, the Friday before Easter, known to Christians as "Good Friday" and considered the anniversary of the crucifixion of Jesus, does cause conflicts. An argument sometimes advanced in such areas in favor of closing government offices on this Friday is that so many workers will want the day off as to make it hard to maintain services. Many times, such a rationale is more an excuse than a real explanation for wanting to close the office. Ultimately, government decisions have to be made based on the needs of the citizens and not made in a way that endorses or appears to endorse a religious belief.

The adoption of Sunday as a day of rest, no longer associated with worshipping the Sun, was related to some Christian beliefs or interpretations but not universally agreed upon even by Christians. "Blue Laws" instituted to help keep Sunday as a different sort of day are mostly ignored or have been declared unconstitutional now.[2] Seventh-Day Adventists,[3] Seventh Day Baptists,[4] and others—some Christians, Jews, Muslims, and others—do not consider Sunday to be a holy day. The treatment in the US Constitution of Sunday as different in some small ways from other days is almost certainly a matter of tradition and convenience, not a nod to encouraging religious belief. (See our section, below, on frequently addressed questions for more on Sunday in the Constitution, Richard Johnson, Sunday mail delivery, and related matters.) An accommodation to most—but not all—religious attitudes about days off in the United States is to generally honor Saturday and Sunday as weekend days of rest. (Muslim ideas to treat Friday as such a day are not usually honored in the United States because there are such small numbers of Muslim citizens in most areas.) The tradition of weekends allow for off days that many people, and many government offices, can close in honor of, without endorsing religious beliefs.

In a secular society, especially one as ethnically and religiously diverse as the United States, accommodation of holidays and days off can sometimes be tricky. But the principles that support religious liberty require religious neutrality to the extent practically possible by governments.

Chapter 13.

He Who Is Not with Me Is against Me

Contrary to the Reported Words of Jesus, Secularism Is Not Anti-Christian

Secularism (and the separation of church and state) is, despite repeated false and hysterical claims to the contrary, *not* anti-Christian, in intent or necessarily in effect. The idea of a "Christian nation" is an obvious threat to those of us who are not Christians, but it is also a trap for those who are. In a "Christian nation," even Christians will not be free; their faith will become a political question, and their consciences will be subject to the dictates of those who hold political power. Every Christian, like every other "person of faith," should contemplate whether he wants a school-board member or county commissioner—or legislator at any level—to vote on any religious issue, whether in someone's opinion a "minor" matter or one so momentous that not correctly understanding it or obeying it will cause one to "lose one's soul." If we cannot have neutrality on the part of government agents, when they act as agents, the only alternative is to empower religious or political leaders to make society-wide decisions about how best to interpret religious rules. A Muslim may well want an imam she trusts to advise her on how best to follow the Qur'an's teaching. But if she cannot accept neutrality on such matters from government agents, no peace is finally possible unless everyone with power agrees with her. This is no less true if it is a Christian citizen who seeks guidance from the Bible, a preacher, a bishop, or an archbishop.

Neutrality can sometimes be difficult to achieve in actual cases—is teaching evolution a matter of giving students sufficient understanding of the scientific process or is it, somehow, a religious indoctrination? (See chapter 11, "Secular Schooling.") But neutrality must be accepted by all as the ideal, and it must be actively sought. Irresolvable conflict is the only alternative.

A free country—where each citizen is free to follow his or her conscience on questions of religion, and the state must remain secular—allows both Christians and non-Christians to follow their consciences. In one of the great apparent paradoxes of American history, this freedom has demonstrably benefited rather than harmed the flourishing of religion even as it has afforded liberty to people who are not persuaded by any religion. Whether the freedom in question is viewed as a valuable end in itself, as an ultimate value, or only as a means to a greater end, it is impossible without government neutrality. This view, this support for secularism, is not pro-government; it is rather the result of profound distrust for governmental power. It not only treats individual liberty as worthwhile, but it opposes the arrogance of anyone—atheist, Christian, Muslim, or Wiccan—who is so sure he is right about ultimate questions as to demand government support for imposing them on all. One of the great values of avoiding pretensions of certainty, as Cullen Murphy has noted, is that "doubt can be a bulwark."[1]

A "Christian nation" is actually hostile to Christianity, if Christianity is understood to be a religion of individual conscience and free commitment, while the United States as a free country has demonstrably allowed Christianity to flourish as a faith freely chosen by millions of Americans. The apparent paradox—that a non-Christian nation can actually be good for the Christian religion—is partially resolved in terms of a religion's ability to do well, or at least survive, without government's help. Neutrality by the state in matters of religion is not Christian but does allow any religion to compete freely in the public sphere.

Only those who follow a religious or atheistic philosophy in which they hold no real confidence should oppose governmental neutrality. As the elderly Benjamin Franklin noted in a letter quoted in chapter 5, "History Is Not on the Side of the Angels," religions (or by implication, antireligious philosophies) that are so weak that their followers insist on government support for them are not well founded.[2]

HOUSES OF WORSHIP
IN A SECULAR NATION?

Beyond any reasonable doubt, the national organization best suited to present the facts on what the relationship between religious bodies—"houses of worship"—and the federal government is and should be in the United States is Americans United for Separation of Church and State. Its website, http://www.au.org, and literature available from the organization are comprehensive, specific, and accurate.

A summary of the relationship is that each must not unduly tread on the other's turf, though precise definitions of where the boundaries are can be tricky. The general "bargain" arrived at is that "churches" (and mosques, synagogues, temples, etc.—all such terms are equivalent in this discussion and "churches" should be read in this section as including them all) are not to engage in electoral politics in exchange for which they will avoid having to pay taxes on, or even having to account for, their income. When churches break the rules of this bargain, they can lose their tax exemption and suffer financial penalties. And that is, according to Americans United, not an empty threat, since some have had such penalties applied.[3]

Churches must, like every other sort of organization, nonprofit or otherwise, collect (by withholding) income taxes on clergy and other staff members, match portions of payroll taxes, and report on withheld taxes, and so on. Churches do have some tax benefits not available to nonreligious nonprofits. Some of these are subtle, related to how a religious leader's benefits (housing or travel allowances) are taxed or reported, but may nevertheless be quite valuable financially to clergy. One advantage that churches have over nonreligious nonprofit organizations is massive and by its very nature unknown in size: *only* churches do not even have to account for their income. Organizations as disparate as American Atheists and the American Red Cross can achieve 501(c)(3) status as nonprofits—and thus gain tax advantages for supporters who donate to them. But, *except* for churches, these 501(c)(3) nonprofits do have to file forms describing where the money came from and how it is spent. This total lack of accountability for churches, we argue, is dangerous, is unnecessary to protect religious liberty, and imposes a strong disadvantage on those of us without religion.

To the occasional religious leader of any sort who chafes under the restrictions that come with the "bargain" mentioned above—who wants, in other words, to freely endorse candidates or back political parties and to lobby in more than general ways—the bargain requires agreement from all. Any church that wants to be political in these ways can eschew the advantages of nonprofit status and have at it.

Property or real-estate taxes are the perquisites of state and local governments, and they are imposed quite differently in different areas. Churches get quite unreasonable and unnecessary advantages over non-religious nonprofits in many but not all jurisdictions. This means in effect that those who do not support the main religious organizations in many areas—atheists and followers of minority religions alike—are forced to subsidize the Catholics or Baptists or whoever predominates. After all, churches and their members rely on public streets, fire and police services, an educated citizenry, and much else that is financed with real-estate taxes. As one of the authors wrote more than a decade and a half ago,

> treating all nonprofit nonresidential property alike, with neither pref-
> erence nor penalty assessed in the name of religion . . . is the only way
> to ensure that all governments, county or federal or others, avoid
> making any religious decisions for citizens, which is the fundamental
> purpose of First Amendment protection of religious liberty.[4]

ARE CHRISTIANS PERSECUTED IN SECULAR AMERICA?

There are in the United States Christians who claim that this is a Christian nation, that the vast majority of Americans are Christian, *and* that Christians are "persecuted" in the United States. Aside from the bizarre image this brings to mind of hordes of people being picked on by elites and unable to defend themselves, it simply is not true. This is a free society, because it is secular, and one price of a free society is that everyone and every organization can be the object of satire or ridicule (justified or not). When writers like David Limbaugh (brother to right-wing radio talkmaster Rush Limbaugh) produce book-length compendiums of Christian grievances, they apparently count on selling books by discussing "persecution." Limbaugh's *PersecuTed: How Liberals Are Waging War against Christianity* (and yes, the special *t* in the title is similar to the one, in red, on the book's cover) is a heavily footnoted 350-plus pages of whining. Many of the examples Limbaugh cites are of comics and others failing to be sufficiently respectful to the faith. But many—perhaps most—are examples of American secularism at work in support of all faiths, including Christianity. Limbaugh distorts and exaggerates with abandon, and he accepts discredited "quotations" from Washington, Jefferson, and others without even acknowledging any possible problems with the quotations. Many of the examples Limbaugh cited are quite likely to be circumstances where Christians were denied the "right" to enlist government as an agent for promoting their religion. He does not present even one case that is a convincing example of a government agency depriving a Christian of religious liberty. What Limbaugh fails utterly to understand is that if such cases did exist, secularists like those in Americans United (attacked at length in his book) and like the authors of this book would work to support the Christians, not the government. What Limbaugh did not do, despite insisting that he did, is explain how the US Constitution is based on Christian principles. He also failed to show that in fact Christians are in any meaningful sense persecuted in the United States.

If fundamentalist Christians want to abide literally by Jesus's reported words and biblical principles—"He who is not with me is against me" (Matthew 12:30)—or if Muslims want to live in a society governed throughout by qur'anic principles, secularism and neutrality will not be possible. But then, neither will a modern, progressive, or free society be possible.

Chapter 14.

The Naked Public Square?
Clearing Up Confusion,
Even among Secularists, about the
Differences between "Public" and "Civic"

In discussions of the proper relation between church and state, one will often encounter the claim that the separation of church and state has left behind (as the title of a 1984 book by Richard John Neuhaus dubbed it) a "naked public square." The late televangelist Jerry Falwell laid the responsibility for the terrorist attacks of September 11 a few days after it happened on those who he blamed for "throwing God out of the public square." A few hours after that, he sort of apologized even as he seemed to simultaneously reassert what he had earlier declared.[1] It is claimed that the insistence upon a strict separation of church and state is an attempt to, or will have the effect of, driving religion solely into the private lives of believers, and out of "public life." There is often a whiff of the catacombs in these claims, as if believers were forced to resort to secret meetings in the dead of night to avoid the dreaded secularist police.

Part of this revolves around the question of whether matters of religious belief, of conscience, are properly considered as exclusively private matters, or, as writers as diverse as Austin Dacey, Barack Obama, and Neuhaus have all argued, whether it is instead proper to ground political principles in conscience. (Neuhaus is alone among these—and profoundly mistaken—in claiming that religion or God is crucial for morality.) Dacey, Obama, and Neuhaus are correct that deeply held beliefs, including religious ones, are appropriate bases for political choices, while such beliefs are never sufficient grounds to carry the day. As Obama put it, "To say that men and women should not inject their 'personal morality' into public-policy debates is a practical absurdity. . . . [But] what our deliberative, pluralistic democracy does demand is that the religiously motivated translate their concerns into universal, rather than religion-specific, values. It requires that their proposals must be subject to argument and amenable to reason."[2] Dacey's entire book, *The Secular Conscience*, is aimed at elaborating on this same point from a secular perspective. For many, however, all this also betrays a smaller but still serious confusion about entirely different meanings of the word *public*. There is public in the sense of something controlled or owned by the state or the government, or an activity carried on by the state or the government, and financed with tax dollars; but this is far from the only sense in which something may be public.

Anyone who thinks public can mean only something like "controlled by or pertaining to the state or the government" is invited to try doing a variety of perfectly legal activities on his or her own front lawn to be quickly disabused of this notion. The laws of the state of Georgia, for example, define a "public place" to be "any place where the conduct involved may reasonably be expected to be viewed by people other than members of the actor's family or household."[3] There is thus public in the sense of "in public"—among strangers or even acquaintances, but not at home with one's family. Much of our life takes place in public; in the main, we work, shop, and meet new people in public. Sometimes we play in public, eat in public, or pray in public. Schools, stores, theaters, malls, parks, stadiums, auditoriums, and streets are all public places, but only some of them are owned by the state or financed by the taxpayer. Churches are also public places in this sense, even though under our Constitution they can never be public in the same sense that city hall or the local public high school are public.

Institutions may exist to serve the public even though they are private (nongovernmental) entities. In England, a "public school" is (confusingly enough to Americans) a private school—that is an institution that relies on private sources for funding rather than the taxpayers or the *public* treasury—but is "public" in the sense of being open to the public at large, as opposed to a private tutor. In our own country the Internal Revenue Service defines "public charities" as being those that (i) are churches, hospitals, qualified medical research organizations affiliated with hospitals, schools, colleges and universities, (ii) have an active program of fundraising and receive contributions from many sources, including the general public, governmental agencies, corporations, private foundations or other public charities, (iii) receive income from the conduct of activities in furtherance of the organization's exempt purposes, or (iv) actively function in a supporting relationship to one or more existing public charities. Private foundations, in contrast, typically have a single major source of funding (usually gifts from one family or corporation rather than funding from many sources) and most have as their primary activity the making of grants to other charitable organizations and to individuals, rather than the direct operation of charitable programs.[4]

Thus, a *public* charity may be a private institution—private in the sense of not being controlled by the state—it may even be a church; it is public in the sense that it solicits funds from the public at large (and in that it serves the public).

US federal law (42 U.S.§ 12181) for some purposes defines *public* accommodations to mean everything from bus terminals or hotels to laundromats or bakeries:

(7) Public accommodation

The following private entities are considered public accommodations for purposes of this subchapter, if the operations of such entities affect commerce—

(A) an inn, hotel, motel, or other place of lodging, except for an establishment located within a building that contains not more than five rooms for rent or hire and that is actually occupied by the proprietor of such establishment as the residence of such proprietor;

(B) a restaurant, bar, or other establishment serving food or drink;

(C) a motion picture house, theater, concert hall, stadium, or other place of exhibition or entertainment;

(D) an auditorium, convention center, lecture hall, or other place of public gathering;

(E) a bakery, grocery store, clothing store, hardware store, shopping center, or other sales or rental establishment;

(F) a laundromat, dry-cleaner, bank, barber shop, beauty shop, travel service, shoe repair service, funeral parlor, gas station, office of an accountant or lawyer, pharmacy, insurance office, professional office of a health care provider, hospital, or other service establishment;

(G) a terminal, depot, or other station used for specified public transportation;

(H) a museum, library, gallery, or other place of public display or collection;

(I) a park, zoo, amusement park, or other place of recreation;

(J) a nursery, elementary, secondary, undergraduate, or post-graduate private school, or other place of education;

(K) a day care center, senior citizen center, homeless shelter, food bank, adoption agency, or other social service center establishment; and

(L) a gymnasium, health spa, bowling alley, golf course, or other place of exercise or recreation.

Note that *public* accommodations here are explicitly *private* entities; that is, they are not owned and controlled or financed by the government and the taxpayers. Nonetheless, they serve the public at large, and what happens in them is part of public life.

Public companies (as opposed to sole proprietorships or privately held companies) are owned by the general public, with the owners—the stockholders—free to buy and sell their share of the company on an open market, a stock exchange. Many of these public companies are businesses that are "open to the public." These senses of *public* have nothing to do with being paid for with tax dollars or being owned and controlled by the government.

A "public square" taken literally—the open space at the center of a town, either paved or perhaps with a park—represents a mixture of these different meanings of the word *public*. Such a place would likely be publicly owned, in the sense that the land itself is owned by some state entity, usually a municipal government. It is open to the public and used by the public, but not everything that goes on there—from family picnics to musical concerts—is controlled, financed, or explicitly sanctioned by the state. Such phrases as "the naked public square" or "throwing God out of the public square" artfully—but disingenuously—mix these different meanings of public.

Most important in the context of religious freedom is that aspect of public life expressed by the phrase "the marketplace of ideas." It is here that the citizens of a free country come together—not just sitting at their own kitchen tables but also standing on soapboxes in parks, sitting in taverns, assembling in convention halls, writing in letters to the editor for the local newspaper, standing on street corners passing out pamphlets, declaring on billboards and signs, broadcasting on public-access cable TV, and blogging in cyberspace—to persuade, cajole, or argue with each other about the issues of the day or the meaning of life, about entertainment or the doings of the rich and famous, art and music, sports, politics, or philosophy and religion.

A strict separation of church and state does demand that the activities of the government be secular and that no one be compelled to support any religion by anything except for his or her own reason and conscience. But an insistence upon keeping government separate from religion has absolutely nothing to do with driving Christianity, or any other belief or philosophy, religious or irreligious, from the public square in this sense of the marketplace of ideas. Even with the most absolute and strict separation of church and state, Christians would still be free to publicly defend and promote their religion, as individuals or as members of churches and other voluntary associations.

Christians are free to promote their beliefs in this marketplace of ideas and, in the United States, do so with great vigor. In this sense, churches are very much in the public square. So are Christian bookstores, Christian television and radio broadcasts, Christian websites, and the bumper stickers Christians put on their cars. Churches openly advertise their services and almost universally all members of the public are invited to attend. Christians put up billboards that contain what purport to be messages from the Almighty Himself. Christians seek to carry out their "Great Commission" in every corner of the country and in the virtual corners of cyberspace. And discussions of religion are far from limited to "Christians only" ghettoes. Not only are Christian books openly sold in bookstores solely devoted to Christianity, but general-purpose bookstores and public libraries have shelves of books about Christian theology, Christian spirituality, and Christian life; even the local grocery store may have a display of Christian devotional books at the end of the aisle. It's not just the Christian-run radio and TV stations—of which there are many—that broadcast sermons and gospel music; religious programs on the airwaves and cable TV channels are common at any time but become almost ubiquitous on Sunday morning. Newspapers of no discernible sectarian bent publish columns by Christians about their Christian faith. General-interest newsmagazines run frequent cover stories about the Virgin Mary or the Resurrection of Christ.

The phrase "public life" may also be used to mean "politics." More broadly, this aspect of civil society is sometimes referred to as the "public sphere"; the arena in which citizens of a free country can discuss among themselves the problems their society faces and the possible solutions to those problems.[5] Here is an area where the different meanings of *public* do indeed intersect, an area where Obama, Dacey, and even Neuhaus have a legitimate point. As Phillip E. Hammond argues:

> Does the modern "public square" require that the church stay out? Most assuredly not. Many who might want the church to stay out base their position, ironically, on the same fallacy held by those who see the square as "naked." That fallacy revolves around the issue of so-called "privatized" religion.
>   . . . Can religion offer public reasons, falsifiable arguments, or secular purposes? If so, religion is as welcome as any other participant in the public square. . . .
>   Religion, then, is not merely tolerated in the public square but has the liberty to pursue its objective, provided only that it recognize that, in the interests of religious liberty for all, the ground rules are secular.[6]

In a free country, there can be no religious tests for holding office or doing any other right or duty of citizenship, and no law can restrain or promote any religious belief. However, there is nothing to prevent Americans from making political judgements that are grounded in their fundamental religious beliefs. Not only voters but also officeholders can and should be guided by their consciences, which for many Americans are deeply affected by their religious beliefs. Candidates are still free to profess religion and to use religious language, to use religious images and metaphors—and even the most cursory look at American politics quickly reveals that few American politicians, Democratic or Republican, left, right, or center, refrain from invoking God, however sincerely, along with Mom and apple pie in their stump speeches.

It may well be that, as the Revolutionary-era Baptist preacher John Leland advised, we ought to "Guard against those men who make a great noise about religion, in choosing representatives."[7] A prudent citizen, even a devoutly religious citizen, ought to consider whether expressions of religious faith and devotion from politicians are truly intended to honor God or are only, as the Rev. Leland put it, "electioneering" intended to distract voters from the consideration of their and the nation's true interests or the true worthiness for public office of the pious politician at hand. Nonetheless there is a difference between that healthy skepticism and a court striking down a law that is in violation of the constitution. Whatever we as citizens ought to do in the privacy of the voting booth, no law ought to prevent anyone from invoking God in a campaign speech. One thing we must insist on is that if religion is to be brought into this marketplace of ideas, and especially if it is to be used to justify positions in politics and public policy, then religious ideas must be as subject to thorough and unrestrained examination as are libertarianism or socialism, or healthcare reform or cutting the capital-gains tax, or any other ideology or proposal for public policy. Certainly there is no place in a free society for blasphemy laws or anything of that sort. But even beyond that, religion in the marketplace of ideas cannot be allowed to occupy a privileged position or to be placed above criticism, while simultaneously being used as a political weapon, or to impugn the virtuousness of nonbelievers (or adherents to different religions), or even in support of political ideals with which we may happen to agree.

Theists often complain of the "stridency" or "coarseness" of the so-called new atheists. But those who would bring religion into the political sphere would do well to remember that, as Finley Peter Dunne quipped, "politics ain't beanbag." In recent years, books about politics have been published with titles like *Treason: Liberal Treachery from the Cold War to the War on Terror* (Ann Coulter) and *Lies and the Lying Liars Who Tell Them: A Fair and Balanced Look at the Right* (Al Franken). There can be no expectation that their ideals of personal faith will be treated any more gently once they have been brought into the rough-and-tumble world of partisan politics.

Religion has flourished in the marketplace of ideas in the United States, in the "public square," but without public—governmental—support. Indeed, the experience of the Old World has shown that state support for religion can be soporific or even toxic to religion's health in the public square. Many European countries have practices such as church taxes levied on all members of a denomination on that church's behalf, or even full-fledged established churches. Many of these same countries also have far lower rates of church attendance and expressions of belief in the fundamentals of Christianity than does the United States, where religion has been left free to fight for itself in the public square in a Darwinian—or, if you prefer, free-market—fashion.

Chapter 15

The Big Lie
Morality and Conscience
in a Secular Society

Quite likely the most persistent idea used to defame atheists—and sometimes anyone who is not a follower of an approved sect of an approved religion—is the claim that religious belief and morality are causally interdependent. This "big lie" is often used, explicitly or implicitly, to attack the whole idea of a secular society. And if the lie is believed, support for secularism can crumble. After all, no one in his right mind wants a society where moral standards are not generally understood and taken quite seriously by all or nearly all citizens. Social order, individual freedom, economic functioning, and more depend on agreed-upon ideas of what constitutes proper behavior toward one's fellow citizens. Deeply religious people often sincerely believe that the moral standards they cherish come to them from God, but in a free society where individual liberty is protected, everyone, from the most deeply religious to the most militantly atheistic, must maintain the theoretical possibility that he does not have everything exactly right about ultimate values. The alternative is some kind of conflict, even war, or sustained repression of one set of ideas or another.

Theists, especially fundamentalists, repeatedly and successfully (in political terms, not in philosophical or realistic terms) claim morality requires theism. This approach has been used so often that it is unnecessary to offer many examples, but Billy Graham offered a typical version in his weekly newspaper column. Replying to an atheist who declared that knowing the difference between right and wrong and how to get along with people, not belief in God, are what matters, Graham wrote:

First, if God doesn't exist, then how do we know what is right and what is wrong? Some things may seem more "right" than others—but how do we know they really are? The answer is—we don't. The only reliable way to know what is right and wrong, and how we should treat others, is if God tells us—and He has done this in His Word, the Bible.

My second question is this: What about your children? Will they grow up with the same values you have—or will they do like so many atheists do, and simply make up their own moral standards?[1]

Though they are demonstrably incorrect, the *political* success of claims like Graham's is a threat to secularism and hence to liberty, not merely a threat to nontheists. It is for that reason that what we call "the big lie"—the often-unquestioned assertion that religiosity and morality go hand in hand—is refuted here. Many works by moral philosophers and others have shown the false correlation (see such works in our bibliography as *Living without Religion*, by Paul Kurtz; *The Moral Sense*, by James Q. Wilson; *Six Great Ideas*, by Mortimer Adler; *The Moral Landscape*, by Sam Harris; *Biblical v. Secular Ethics*, edited by R. Joseph Hoffmann and Gerald LaRue; and *Ethics*, edited by Peter Singer), but the main points of those arguments will be reiterated here. A recent succinct and effective summary of the biological, evolutionary basis for morality —and of the reasons we should understand that as positive, not dangerous—appeared in an essay by professor Jerry A. Coyne titled "As Atheists Know, You Can Be Good without God."[2]

The most common variation of this approach—or at least a closely related argument—by anti-secularists is to pretend that the only choice for the origin of human rights, like morality, is God and not government. They often cite the American Declaration of Independence as showing that the founders of the United States unequivocally chose God, not government, as the source. The language in the Declaration does indeed attribute the source to "Nature's God" (not, please note, to the Christian God), but in the US Constitution—our governing charter—there is no allusion even to this more deistic version of a god. (For much more on the Declaration, see chapter 6, "The Unchristian Roots of the Fourth of July." For more on the source of rights, see our chapter "Why Secularism?") If any source for rights can be inferred from the Constitution, that source would be from "We the People," the source implied in the preamble. But it is all a false dilemma in any case. Rights can indeed be considered "natural"—essentially derived from a major societal consensus—without being treated as coming from a government *or* from a god. Moral standards, in a somewhat similar way, can be derived from individual rights or societal needs or, in practice, from long cultural evolution and deep-seated consensus. Such standards, embodied most obviously but not comprehensively in criminal codes, do have to be very broadly socially accepted to be effective, but religious ideals are as likely to interfere with the needed consensus in a pluralistic society as to support them.

Most Islamic understanding of morality is quite different from the approach most modern Christians take, but Islamic opposition to secularism is frequently rooted in fears related to morality. As Melanie Phillips summed it up in *The World Turned Upside Down*,

> America is the principal target of the Islamists because it is the fount of modernity. It is therefore immoral, because modernity is identified with secularism, which has led away from God's laws. The Islamists use secularism to mean both atheism and separation of religion from state. To them, both are equally reprehensible. In the Western world, they are very different. America is a secular society in that it rigorously separates church and state, keeping religion out of public life. But in cultural terms, it is also still a deeply religious, Christian society. The idea that the political separation of religion and state can coexist with a religiously inclined popular culture is, however, not understood by the Islamists because in Islam that distinction does not exist. They assume that any society that is not a theocracy is by definition godless and thus immoral.[3]

One need not agree with Phillips on how deeply religious or Christian American society is (and we do not agree with her) to accept her point about Islamists and perceived immorality.

There is really no good reason to believe that any moral standard is absolute or that any ethical principle is not a product of biological and cultural evolution. The religious debaters who like to claim a God-given absolute moral foundation for morality cannot escape the fact that moral ideas change over time and from one group to another within the doctrines of any religion. Christians in the Southern United States 150 years ago, including leading preachers, believed—with plenty of biblical support for their ideas—that human slavery was not only acceptable but explicitly ordained by God. As Nicholas Kristof and Sheryl WuDunn note,

> For most of history, slavery had been accepted as sad but inevitable. The Athenians were brilliant philosophers and abounded in empathy that made them wonderful writers and philosophers, yet they did not even debate their reliance on slavery. Jesus did not address slavery at all in the Gospels; Saint Paul and Aristotle accepted it; and Jewish and Islamic theologians believed in mercy toward slaves but did not question slavery itself. In the 1700s, a few Quakers vigorously denounced slavery, but they were dismissed as crackpots and had no influence. In the early 1780s, slavery was an unquestioned part of the global landscape—and then, astonishingly, within a decade, slavery was at the top of the British national agenda. The tide turned, and Britain banned the slave trade in 1807 and in 1833 became one of the first nations to emancipate its own slaves.[4]

Other sources that make plain the failure of religions to recognize the grievous immorality of slavery or even to use religion to support slavery abound. For example, Douglas A. Blackmon described a wedding in 1868 in Alabama of two people who had until quite recently been slaves:

> Henry was suddenly a man. Mary was a woman, a slave girl no more. Here they stood, bride and groom, before John Wesley Starr, the coarse old preacher who a blink of an eye before had spent his Sundays teaching white people that slavery was the manifestation of a human order ordained by God, and preaching to black people that theirs was a glorified place among the chickens and pigs.[5]

It would be hard to imagine a more telling example of the disassociation of religion and morality.

In the period around and during the American Revolutionary War, Christian rhetoric was used, in Connecticut newspapers for example, both to defend and to attack the institution, in both cases invoking God as being on the side of the arguer.[6] And R. G. Grant noted, "The rise of Christianity and Islam changed attitudes to slavery, but certainly did not end it."[7] Few Christians or Muslims today in America or elsewhere would attempt to defend "the peculiar institution" of slavery, though God does not seem to have issued any corrected Scriptures in the meantime. It is hard to believe that an omniscient God would not have foreseen how ambiguous his commandments are; believing that it is all up to us human beings to determine what is right, and to do it, is much easier to accept. Conscience, the critical idea on which C. S. Lewis hangs his own belief (in *Mere Christianity*[8]), is much more readily understood as the product of education. The Aztec who could, in good conscience, sacrifice a virgin to the gods and the Christian Southerner who could, also in good conscience, justify owning his fellow human beings both demonstrate that consciences are not divine products.

Dan Barker wrote in *Losing Faith in Faith* that those of us who lack religion can say to believers,

> You are an intelligent human being. Your life is valuable for its own sake. You are not second-class in the universe, deriving meaning and purpose from some other mind. You are not inherently evil—you are inherently *human*, possessing the positive rational potential to help make this a world of morality, peace and joy. Trust yourself.[9]

And as philosopher Paul Kurtz has written,

> Critical ethical inquiry enables us to transcend unquestioned customs, blind faith, or doctrinaire authority and to discover ethical values and principles. Humanists maintain that a higher state of moral development is reached when we go beyond **unthinking** habits to ethical wisdom: This includes an appreciation of the standards of excellence and an awareness of ethical principles and one's moral responsibilities to others.[10]

Those who support the "big lie" that morality depends on religiosity ignore or forget the strong biblical support for such Christian but decidedly anti-American values as accepting human slavery, denying women and children any meaningful rights at all, punishing people's descendants for their sins, blind obedience to purportedly divine authority, unquestioning obedience even to governmental authority, giving religious ideas and leaders special rights in the name of avoiding blasphemy, and many others. Less directly biblical but nevertheless strongly associated with

Christian orthodoxy are opposition to questioning authority and opposition to the healthy skepticism that is required for good science and progress in understanding the universe.

Supporters of the alleged dependence of morality on absolute religious standards also ignore human history. Horrific destruction of individuals, societies, and moral standards has certainly come at the hands of absolutist, totalitarian regimes not trumpeting Christian values—Russia's Stalin and Cambodia's Pol Pot, for example. But such evils have quite often come directly from Christian authorities like popes or John Calvin of Geneva and from villains like Adolf Hitler, who declared in 1926 that he was doing God's work, that he was extending Christ's work: "Christ was the greatest early fighter in the battle against the world enemy—the Jews. The work that Christ started but did not finish, I, Adolf Hitler, will conclude." And Hitler counted himself a good Catholic until he died. There is considerable evidence of Christian and church support for and entanglement with the rise of Nazism.[11]

The number of people, especially women, who have died horrible deaths because of a single Bible verse—"Do not allow a sorceress to live" (Exodus 22:18)—is unknown but huge. Both Christians and Islamic warriors committed almost unimaginable atrocities in the name of God or Allah in the Crusades. The Catholic Church itself directly engaged in torture and murder in the Inquisition. Man's inhumanity to man has often been spurred by man trying to do God's will.

It is worth noting that "moral values" voters in American elections are, despite apparent popular misconceptions, as likely to be voters of the right or left, of religious or secular preferences. Support for or opposition to wars and welfare programs and any other government action is certainly sometimes publicly associated with religious ideas, but the connections are rarely, if ever, simple or required. As Louis Menand wrote in the *New Yorker*,[12] just after George W. Bush defeated John Kerry in the 2004 presidential election, "The phrase 'moral values' is open to interpretive license. Peace and social justice are moral values; they just don't happen to be values associated with the Bush Administration."

According to a review article by James Wood, Dutch primatologist Frans B. M. de Waal reports that there are sound biological reasons to conclude that religion is unnecessary for morality, that in fact morality developed first in human evolutionary history:

In an account of spontaneous altruism and empathy in chimpanzees—
acts of "genuine kindness" that he and his researchers have recorded—
de Waal speculates that human morality "must be quite a bit older than
religion and civilization," and "may in fact be older than humanity
itself."[13]

If in fact our moral standards developed *before* our religious ideas did,
it would seem difficult indeed to continue to support the claim that religion is needed for morality.

Those of us who lack religious beliefs should steadfastly rebut the
false claims of causal correlation between religion and morality for the
sake of our own reputations and social standing. But everyone, religious
or not, who values individual freedom and understands that secularism is
required to protect it should reject the persistent "big lie." Neither logic
nor historical evidence supports the idea that religiosity is even helpful,
much less necessary, for ethical behavior.

Freedom for individuals is of course no guarantee of ethical behavior.
But oppressing anyone on religious grounds is itself immoral and breeds
much other immorality as well. The unquestionably central need for
morality in any nation is served better, not less, by a secular government
in a secular society.

Chapter 16.

God's Law

Sharia and the Ten Commandments versus the Constitution

In 2010 voters in Oklahoma overwhelmingly passed a ballot measure banning courts in the state from considering or using Sharia (Islamic law) when deciding cases. (The measure also banned Oklahoma courts from considering "international law," the wisdom of which is outside the scope of this book.) Although the measure passed by over two to one, a judge later issued a permanent injunction against the measure going into effect.[1] As of this writing, measures have been introduced in at least twenty-two states to ban the use of foreign or international laws by state courts, with a number of them explicitly disallowing Sharia by name; thus far, apart from one bill in Arizona (which did not explicitly name Sharia or any other religious code), none have been enacted into law.[2]

The Oklahoma measure was officially dubbed the "Save Our State Amendment" by its drafters:

> B. Subsection C of this section shall be known as the "Save Our State Amendment."
> C. The Courts provided for in subsection A of this section, when exercising their judicial authority, shall uphold and adhere to the law as provided in the United States Constitution, the Oklahoma Constitution, the United States Code, federal regulations promulgated pursuant thereto, established common law, the Oklahoma Statutes and rules promulgated pursuant thereto, and if necessary the law of another state of the United States provided the law of the other state does not include Sharia Law, in making judicial decisions. The courts shall not look to the legal precepts of other nations or cultures. Specifically, the courts

shall not consider international or Sharia Law. The provisions of this subsection shall apply to all cases before the respective courts including, but not limited to, cases of first impression.[3]

Given that Muslims are pretty thin on the ground in Oklahoma, this seems perhaps a trifle overwrought. (The British newspaper the *Daily Mail* reported fifteen thousand Muslims in a total Oklahoma population of 3.7 million, or less than 0.5 percent. The official US government census does not ask questions about religious beliefs, so it is hard to get reliable statistics on the numbers of adherents of various religions in the United States.)[4]

Amy Sullivan has written an interesting essay on this subject, in which she concluded, "Political scoundrels have been using the fear of Islamic-imposed law to stir xenophobia in America—even though this 'threat' is actually nonsense."[5] She drew telling parallels with the McCarthyism of the 1950s and sarcastically noted that, "If you are not vitally concerned about the possibility of radical Muslims infiltrating the US government and establishing a Taliban-style theocracy, then you are not a candidate for the GOP presidential nomination." Eliyahu Stern has noted parallels between the recent hysterical reactions to *Sharia* law and declarations in Europe two hundred years ago that Jewish law was dangerous to society.[6]

Still, it is hard to disagree that implementing Sharia would be fundamentally un-American, not to mention a really bad idea. Laws explicitly based on the teachings of *any* particular religion would violate the establishment clause of the First Amendment. Beyond objections to sectarian law in general, there are serious concerns about Sharia in particular. There are legitimate concerns about the status of women and the protection of their equal rights under Sharia. Under Sharia, homosexual acts between consenting adults are illegal, even punishable by death, whereas the United States (in the wake of *Lawrence et al. v. Texas*, and a long line of state supreme court cases) has finally done away with such barbaric invasions of personal freedom[7] (even in the armed forces, lately), and has even, in a few states, begun to move toward true equality with same-sex marriage laws. In such countries as Pakistan, laws against "blasphemy"— including actual prosecutions, as well as the threat of lynch mobs if no official action is taken—have been used to marginalize and oppress religious minorities (including minority Islamic sects as well as Christians).

Such laws are affronts to the basic human rights of freedom of religion and freedom of speech, and these archaic and inhumane laws have rightly been condemned by advocates of human liberty, atheists and believers alike. Various authorities—both Shi'ite and Sunni—agree that "apostasy" (leaving Islam for another religion) should be illegal under Sharia, even punishable by death.[8] *That* would certainly be unacceptable in a country that treasures individual freedom, where religion is seen as a personal matter of conscience, and where whole new denominations can spring up overnight in some little church a few people have gotten together to establish in a storefront or even in someone's private home.

As recent turmoil from elections and democratic protests in places such as Egypt, Libya, and Bahrain has amply demonstrated,[9] attempting to implement Sharia law even in a Muslim-majority nation is a recipe for trouble and for undercutting democratic ideals. (The turmoil surrounding the 2012 election in Egypt also showed—as has been demonstrated many times throughout history—that merely formal commitment to such important ideals as secularism, individual rights, and democracy will be largely meaningless without a widespread, sustained social consensus in favor of such and the civil society and human capital to support them. A constitution that ostensibly guarantees democratic rule or even—on paper—an ideal secular democratic state will still be insufficient to prevent military takeover or theocracy or other forms of tyranny without such a consensus.)[10] But the same conservative Christians who so often lead the charge against Islamic law have a long history of enthusiastic support for religious law—if it is the *right* religion.

From Sarah Palin, we are told we need to "go back to what our founders and our founding documents meant. They're quite clear that we would create law based on the God of the Bible and the 10 Commandments."[11] And this was hardly the first time a conservative has spoken in such terms about the Ten Commandments and the Bible. The "social conservatives" in the United States have been saying for years that we need to get back to the Ten Commandments, that they're the foundation of our laws, and (of course) that they should be posted in schools, courthouses, and other public buildings. We are told that the Ten Commandments are "the foundation of American society."[12] Numerous organizations, from the American Legion to the ironically named "WallBuilders," file amicus briefs before the courts in defense of public displays of the commandments.[13] (Bizarrely, at least one such brief filed by WallBuilders—home to noted Christian Right historical propagandist David Barton—*proudly* details various colonial laws calling for the death penalty for "idolatry" and "blasphemy."[14]) Indeed, the colonial America they describe seems little different from an Islamic Republic or a Wahhabite monarchy—only that a different religion is on top and calling the shots. Thank ~~God~~ the Founding Fathers for the Fourth of July!—see chapter 6, "The Unchristian Roots of the Fourth of July." For more on blasphemy and heresy, see the next chapter of this book.

But the Ten Commandments are full of ideas that would warm the heart of any good Muslim theocrat, like bans on idolatry and blasphemy (not to mention decrees on such topics as honoring your parents and refraining from coveting your neighbor's goods, not generally subjects of American jurisprudence):

> I am the LORD your God, who brought you out of Egypt, out of the land of slavery. You shall have no other gods before me.
>
> You shall not make for yourself an image in the form of anything in heaven above or on the earth beneath or in the waters below. You shall not bow down to them or worship them; for I, the LORD your God, am a jealous God, punishing the children for the sin of the parents to the third and fourth generation of those who hate me, but showing love to a thousand generations of those who love me and keep my commandments.
>
> You shall not misuse the name of the LORD your God, for the LORD will not hold anyone guiltless who misuses his name.
>
> Remember the Sabbath day by keeping it holy. Six days you shall labor and do all your work, but the seventh day is a sabbath to the LORD your God. On it you shall not do any work, neither you, nor your son or daughter, nor your male or female servant, nor your animals, nor any foreigner residing in your towns. For in six days the LORD made the heavens and the earth, the sea, and all that is in them, but he rested on the seventh day. Therefore the LORD blessed the Sabbath day and made it holy.
>
> Honor your father and your mother, so that you may live long in the land the LORD your God is giving you.
>
> You shall not murder.
>
> You shall not commit adultery.
>
> You shall not steal.

You shall not give false testimony against your neighbor.

You shall not covet your neighbor's house. You shall not covet your neighbor's wife, or his male or female servant, his ox or donkey, or anything that belongs to your neighbor. (Exodus 20:2–17)

The broader code of biblical law of which the Ten Commandments are a part is as clear on the subjects of "apostasy" and the worship of "false gods" as any legal code ever written by any Islamic theocrat:

> If a man or woman living among you in one of the towns the LORD gives you is found doing evil in the eyes of the LORD your God in violation of his covenant, and contrary to my command has worshiped other gods, bowing down to them or to the sun or the moon or the stars in the sky, and this has been brought to your attention, then you must investigate it thoroughly. If it is true and it has been proved that this detestable thing has been done in Israel, take the man or woman who has done this evil deed to your city gate and stone that person to death. On the testimony of two or three witnesses a person is to be put to death, but no one is to be put to death on the testimony of only one witness. The hands of the witnesses must be the first in putting that person to death, and then the hands of all the people. You must purge the evil from among you. (Deuteronomy 17:2–7)

> If a prophet, or one who foretells by dreams, appears among you and announces to you a sign or wonder, and if the sign or wonder spoken of takes place, and the prophet says, "Let us follow other gods" (gods you have not known) "and let us worship them," you must not listen to the words of that prophet or dreamer. The LORD your God is testing you to find out whether you love him with all your heart and with all your soul. It is the LORD your God you must follow, and him you must revere. Keep his commands and obey him; serve him and hold fast to him. That prophet or dreamer must be put to death for inciting rebellion against the LORD your God, who brought you out of Egypt and redeemed you from the land of slavery. That prophet or dreamer tried to turn you from the way the LORD your God commanded you to follow. You must purge the evil from among you. (Deuteronomy 13:1–5)

That an enticement to "apostasy" happens in the privacy of one's own home is no excuse; rather like the totalitarian police states of modern times, biblical law, as already noted, expects family members to inform upon one another:

> If your very own brother, or your son or daughter, or the wife you love, or your closest friend secretly entices you, saying, "Let us go and worship other gods" (gods that neither you nor your ancestors have known, gods of the peoples around you, whether near or far, from one end of the land to the other), do not yield to them or listen to them. Show them no pity. Do not spare them or shield them. You must certainly put them to death. Your hand must be the first in putting them to death, and then the hands of all the people. Stone them to death, because they tried to turn you away from the LORD your God, who brought you out of Egypt, out of the land of slavery. Then all Israel will hear and be afraid, and no one among you will do such an evil thing again. (Deuteronomy 13:6–11)

Given the large overlap between the proponents of Bible-based law and the supporters of "states' rights," it is worth pointing out that biblical law has no truck with local authorities going their own way, at least in questions of religion:

> If you hear it said about one of the towns the LORD your God is giving you to live in that troublemakers have arisen among you and have led the people of their town astray, saying, "Let us go and worship other gods" (gods you have not known), then you must inquire, probe and investigate it thoroughly. And if it is true and it has been proved that this detestable thing has been done among you, you must certainly put to the sword all who live in that town. You must destroy it completely, both its people and its livestock. You are to gather all the plunder of the town into the middle of the public square and completely burn the town and all its plunder as a whole burnt offering to the LORD your God. That town is to remain a ruin forever, never to be rebuilt, and none of the condemned things are to be found in your hands. Then the LORD will turn from his fierce anger, will show you mercy, and will have compassion on you. He will increase your numbers, as he promised on oath to your ancestors—because you obey the LORD your God by keeping all his commands that I am giving you today and doing what is right in his eyes. (Deuteronomy 13:12–18)

Of course, it seems absurd to contemplate the prospect of twenty-first-century Americans being put to death for "worshipping false gods." When Christians talk loftily of "law based on the God of the Bible and the 10 Commandments," surely they simply mean that we have laws against murder and stealing, and that we should all be honest and forthright and respect our mothers and not bear false witness against our neighbors (whether or not all of that is actually written down in anyone's legal code).

But real-life, un-watered-down biblical law was exactly what the late American theologian and political theorist Rousas J. Rushdoony wanted, and it is what his followers, called "Christian Reconstructionists"—fortunately few in numbers, as far as anyone can tell—still want today. In his 1973 magnum opus, *The Institutes of Biblical Law*, Rushdoony wrote:

> Deuteronomy 13 cites three cases of instigation to idolatry, *first*, in vv. 1–5, by the false prophet; *second*, in vv. 6–11, by a private individual; and, *third*, by a city, vv. 12–18. The penalty in every case is death without mercy. To the modern mind, this seems drastic. Why death for idolatry? If idolatry is unimportant to a man, then a penalty for it is outrageous. But modern man thinks nothing of death penalties for crimes against the state, or against the 'people,' or against 'the revolution,' because these things are important to him. The death penalty is *not* required here for private belief: it is for attempts to subvert others and to subvert the social order by enticing others to idolatry. Because for biblical law the foundation is the one true God, the central offense is therefore treason to that God by idolatry. Every law-order has its concept of treason. No law-order can permit an attack on its foundations without committing suicide. Those states which claim to abolish the death penalty still retain it on the whole for crimes against the state. The foundations of a law-order must be protected. . . .
>
> Basic to the health of a society is the integrity of its foundation. To allow tampering with its foundation is to allow its total subversion. Biblical law can no more permit the propagation of idolatry than Marxism can permit counter-revolution, or monarchy a move to execute the king, or a republic an attempt to destroy the republic and create a dictatorship.
>
> It should be noted that Deuteronomy 13:5–18 does not call for the death penalty for unbelief or heresy. It condemns false prophets (vv. 1–5) who seek to lead the people, with signs and wonders, into idolatry. It

does condemn individuals who secretly try to start a movement into idolatry (vv. 6–11). It does condemn cities which establish another religion and subvert the law-order of the nation (vv. 13–18), and this condemnation must be enforced by man to turn away the judgment of God (v. 17).[15]

Rushdoony was at pains here to disclaim any desire to outlaw or execute mere "heretics," as opposed to idolaters. Later, he went on to write:

> Deuteronomy 13 is not a popular chapter of Scripture. Several ministers have expressed to me their hostility to biblical law by citing Deuteronomy 13; or 17:2–7 (or, Ex. 22:20); going back to biblical law, they declare, means going back to burning heretics. Do I want that? . . . It is important to face this issue squarely. Either the whole of Scripture is defensible, or it is not. . . . [I]t is important to note that it is not heresy which is condemned but idolatry. There is an important difference. Heresy is wrong thinking about the word of God, but it is not idolatry. . . . The Bible requires us to separate ourselves from a heretic (Titus 3:10; cf. Acts 24:14; I Cor. 11:19; Gal. 5:20; II Peter 2:1), but it does not go beyond that. . . . All who are content with a humanistic law system and do not strive to replace it with biblical law are guilty of idolatry. They have forsaken the covenant of their God, and they are asking us to serve other gods. They are thus idolaters, and are, in our generation, when our world is idolatrous and our states also, to be objects of missionary activity. . . . Only as God's law is made the practice of men can it become the practice of nations. . . . Scripture emphatically requires us to reject both the earlier and the present law systems in favor of a rigorously biblical, covenantal law structure.[16]

It is instructive to note that even when he is explicitly disavowing the idea of criminalizing "heresy"—mere disagreement within a religion, as opposed to following a false religion—he winds up calling every single Christian who opposes his doctrine of "theonomy" (literally "God's law"; the belief in the enforcement of biblical law by the state) an idolater, and thus subject to criminal punishment—once the Reconstructionists have taken over. Shades of the fear that allowing Islamic radicals to compete in elections will lead to "one man, one vote—once."

Elsewhere, Rushdoony says:

The god of the Arminians is the god of their imagination, not the God of Scripture. The fact that many of them are "good, moral people" no more alters the fact of their idolatry than does Jeroboam's obvious ability and character negate his sin.[17]

Arminianism is the set of theological doctrines opposed to Calvinism, and includes a denial of strict predestination in favor of human free will. Since most mainline Protestant and many modern Protestant evangelicals are probably at least de facto Arminians, all should qualify for Rushdoony as "idolaters." Those of us outside these religious groupings entirely are naturally unconcerned about whether one Christian thinks another is an "idolater"—but everyone should recognize that if a theocrat of Rushdoony's persuasion achieved real political power, it would not just be atheists and agnostics at risk, even at risk of execution. Seemingly depending on what day it was, Rushdoony apparently believed that just about all of his fellow Christians were "idolaters," with the implication that they should be put to death if they so much as tried to advocate peacefully for their religious views in the privacy of their own homes ("attempts to subvert others and to subvert the social order by enticing others to idolatry"; "individuals who secretly try to start a movement into idolatry").

The works of Rushdoony and his followers (notably the late Greg Bahnsen and Rushdoony's son-in-law, Gary North) call for the death penalty for a whole list of offenses—all scrupulously proof-texted from the Bible, of course. The ban on "idolatry" is arguably the most sweeping and dangerous in its suppression of all competing ideas: "The law thus enjoins us as individuals and as a community to be totally separated from idolatry in any form. Our lives, families, churches, schools, states, and vocations, as well as all things else, must be totally dedicated to God and free of idolatry, from man's self-worship in any form."[18] But that would also be matched with laws mandating the death penalty for adultery, blasphemy, cursing one's mother or father, sodomy, and witchcraft, along with more conventional capital crimes like murder, rape, and kidnapping.

According to Gary North, only Christians should be allowed to vote, assuming anyone else is even left, after the Reconstructionists are through.[19] Given the Apostle Paul's reported admonition to women that they "should learn in quietness and full submission. I do not permit a woman to teach or to assume authority over a man; she must be quiet"

(1 Timothy 2:11–12), the legal status of women would also be in grave danger in a Christian Reconstructionist republic. Indeed, Joseph Morecraft III, pastor of Chalcedon Presbyterian Church in Cumming, Georgia (and one-time Republican nominee for the US House of Representatives in Georgia's Seventh Congressional District), forthrightly declared that on biblical grounds not only should women not be permitted to hold elected office, but that "since voting is a key element of civil government" Christians should also be opposed to women's suffrage.[20] From time to time news stories from places like Iran, Afghanistan, or Somalia will report that an execution by stoning has been carried out, or has been ordered and may happen soon. The reaction in any civilized place to such stories is, rightfully, one of revulsion. Yet Gary North wrote a paean to stoning as a means of execution, in which he noted that rocks are cheap—"the implements of execution are available to everyone at virtually no cost"—and more important, that stoning is a public and collective act by the whole community.[21]

Among some opponents of Islamic radicalism, we find discussions of the alleged Islamic practice of *taqiyya*, which can mean anything from a predominantly Shi'ite doctrine that it is permissible to conceal one's faith in the face of religious persecution, to (according to the more vigorous—not to say paranoid—crusaders against Islamic extremism) a widespread doctrine of duplicity and double-dealing by Muslims in order to spread Islam and Islamic law across the world.[22] Here, too, the most extreme fringes of Christianity give as much cause for paranoia as do the Islamic radicals.

In his discussion of the Ninth Commandment (against bearing false witness) in his *The Institutes of Biblical Law*, Rushdoony is at pains to argue that this commandment does not mean Christians must always tell the truth to hostile nonbelievers.[23] Rushdoony cites such biblical stories as that of Rahab in the second chapter of the Book of Joshua and the Egyptian midwives in the first chapter of the Book of Exodus to argue (not unreasonably) that Christians are free to lie to those who are seeking to persecute or murder Christians. While a humanist would likely agree with such a principle (surely it was not unethical for those sheltering Jews against the Holocaust to lie to the Nazis who were seeking to commit genocide), Rushdoony's statements that we live in "a world at war" and that lying is a permissible tactic in times of war are just as legitimate causes for paranoia about deceitful Christian theocrats using stealth tactics to undermine our

Constitution as the notion of *taqiyya* is for paranoia about Muslim jihadists using stealth tactics to implement Islamic law in Oklahoma.

Gary North also wrote of using talk of "religious liberty" as a (deceptive) "tactic" to "buy time" for the Christian Reconstructionists in their goal of imposing their "world-and-life view" on the majority.[24] In one of his books, Reconstructionist author George Grant included a primer on how a committed minority can take political power all out of proportion to its size, complete with discussions of voter registration and precinct workers and the actual percentage of the population you need to win an election, given that most people don't bother to register to vote, and most registered voters don't bother to show up and vote—with the ultimate goal of (in his words) "world conquest" and "dominion," *not* "influence" or "equal time."[25]

Reconstructionist author David Chilton wrote that Christian Reconstructionists must literally try to take over the world: "The Christian goal for the world is the universal development of biblical theocratic republics, in which every area of life is redeemed and placed under the lordship of Jesus Christ and the rule of God's law."[26]

The Christian Reconstructionists and other, more idiosyncratic homegrown American theocrats are on the fringes of our culture. Although the Christian Reconstructionists are the most organized and—relatively speaking—largest avowedly theocratic group among Christians in the United States, other theocrats can be found on the far reaches of American Christianity, often in the form of self-published books or crackpot websites. For example, the web domain http://www.ten commandments.org has long belonged to the rabidly theocratic "Society for the Practical Establishment and Perpetuation of the TEN COM-MANDMENTS"—but the "Society" is almost certainly one person. The right-wing radio talk-show host Bob Enyart broadcast his own idiosyncratic but avowedly theocratic form of Christian Dominionism in the 1990s.[27] One occasionally runs across books calling for bans on "idolatry" in the United States, such as *Creating a Nation under God: Rebuilding America with Biblical Principles*, by one David James King, MD—evidently a lone autodidact on the subject of Christian theocracy.[28] That said, it is important to note that, biblically speaking, all of these people—both the Rushdoonyites and the lone wolves—have a pretty good point. There is nothing in the Bible about "freedom of religion"; to the contrary, worshipping any god but the *true* God, or worshipping the true God in the wrong way, are the subject of unequivocal and consistent condemnation in the Bible. There is also nothing in the Bible about freedom of speech generally, or free elections, or the desirability of abolishing slavery. If we are going to have "biblical law" or laws based on the Ten Commandments, religious liberty will have to go. Any attempt to establish "laws based on the Bible" will inevitably wind up with a nasty, repressive, Middle Eastern–style theocracy, with no respect whatsoever for individual religious rights. All attempts to create any system recognizing some kind of official Christianity will likely end up the same way—as noted in an earlier chapter, it took less than a century for Christians to go from the persecuted to the persecutors in the Roman Empire (the emperor Constantine issued the Edict of Milan in 313 CE, legalizing the practice of Christianity in the Roman Empire; Emperor Theodosius ended toleration of pagans in the 380s),[29] and for well over a thousand years thereafter the history of Christianity was one of official establishment and varying degrees of official persecution of "heretics," "blasphemers," and "infidels."

As far from the mainstream of American political thought as serious advocates of biblical law may seem to be, less explicit but still frighteningly all-encompassing forms of Christian Dominionism are as close to that mainstream as Michele Bachmann—who, despite her reputation among many as a flake or extremist, is a member of the United States Congress and (as of the summer of 2011) was a leading candidate for the Republican nomination for the presidency in 2012. (After losing badly in the Iowa caucuses in January 2012, she withdrew.) Profiles of Bachmann from the *New Yorker* and *Mother Jones* magazines in 2011 and a column by Frank Bruni in 2012 detailed her deep, dangerous, and long-standing ties to the Christian Right.[30] When she warns about the allegedly "toxic" influence on small children of the soundtrack to the movie *The Lion King*[31] or confuses John Wayne and John Wayne Gacy,[32] Bachmann may come off as more laughable than scary. But the *New Yorker* article quotes Bachmann's reaction to the 1977 film series "How Should We Then Live?" by Francis Schaeffer, an evangelical theologian often cited as one of the driving forces behind the rise of the modern Christian Right, and an advocate of a form of Christian Dominionism. In a speech in Iowa in the spring of 2011, Bachman discussed her reaction to Schaeffer's films:

That also was another profound influence on Marcus's life and my life, because we understood that the God of the Bible isn't just about Bible stories and about Bible knowledge, or about just church on Sunday. He is the Lord of all of life. Every bit of life, including sociology, theology, biology, politics. You name the area and walk of life. He is the Lord of life.[33]

While it may lack the lurid details of the hard-core Reconstructionists, with their paeans to stoning, this is as sweeping a call for total Christianization of American society as anything Rushdoony ever wrote.

Conversely, Islam is no more *fundamentally* incompatible with good citizenship than is Christianity. The "Five Pillars" of orthodox Islam, required of all Muslims, are the *shahada* (the statement of faith that one believes in the One God and that Mohammed is the Prophet of God), *salat* (daily prayers), *sawm* (fasting during the holy month of Ramadan), *zakat* (a kind of Islamic tithe or almsgiving), and the *hajj* or pilgrimage to Mecca.[34] As atheists, the authors of this book do not, of course, agree with any of these religious requirements (although the principle of *zakat* or almsgiving, if done properly, is admirable even from a secular humanist viewpoint). However, none of these things are incompatible with being a good, law-abiding, taxpaying, patriotic American citizen. The practice of daily prayers throughout the day might possibly cause some conflict with the neighbors over noise issues, but apart from that, none of these things (or the possibility that our neighbors may choose not to eat pork or drink alcohol) "picks our pockets or breaks our legs" (to paraphrase Thomas Jefferson). *Sharia*—Islamic law—would be a grave threat to American values, if implemented. *Jihad*—struggle or, in some contexts, "holy war"—as interpreted by the extremists, poses a threat to individual American lives and to the interests of the United States abroad. But these are no more *necessary* to the practice of Islam than biblical law or witch-burnings are to Christianity. In considering the possibility that Islam is a "threat" to the United States or to the American way of life, we must distinguish—as far too many Americans, including some atheists, fail to do—between what we might term "security threats" and "political threats." Security threats are the possibility of terrorism and violence. As we have seen all too often in recent decades, at home and abroad, small conspiracies of violent men, or even lone fanatics, can cause terrible death and destruction. This is so whether the perpetrators are Islamic extremists, Christian extremists, or extremist adherents to some secular ideology. A political threat, on the other hand, is the danger that some group will "take over"—by violent revolution or by subverting the ordinary political process—and impose some repressive and un-American system on our country—presumably with the support of at least a substantial minority of the population. An astonishing number of Americans seem convinced that Islamic extremists genuinely pose a *political* threat to the United States and to our Constitution—that Muslims are poised to "take over."

The danger that Christian Reconstructionists (or some other flavor of Christian theocrats) will take over the United States and succeed in destroying our Constitution and our way of life is about like the danger of being struck by lightning. Every year, a few dozen Americans are killed by lightning.[35] Any prudent person will take reasonable precautions against this threat—architects will make sure buildings have appropriate lightning-protection systems; fun-seekers will avoid playing golf or picnicking in thunderstorms. If we are foolish, the danger can be very great, but with a few simple steps, the danger can be made very remote. If we uphold our basic principles of separating government and religion and respecting the freedom of *everyone*, even those we disagree with, there will be no threat to our way of life.

For the president of Turkey or the king of Jordan, there might be a genuine concern about the possibility of a political takeover (initially peaceful or otherwise) by Islamic theocrats. But to worry about such a thing *in the United States* is sheer fantasy. Even in the countries of Western Europe (the authors can personally attest that there is a thriving Islamic subculture in the United Kingdom), the threat of an Islamic takeover or the imposition of Islamic law is extraordinarily unlikely. In the United States, fear of Muslims "taking over" is more like fearing that one will be hit on the head by a meteorite than it is like the fear of being struck by lightning. (In recorded human history, there have been perhaps a dozen cases of human beings being hit by meteorites or of meteorites causing noticeable property damage, with one possible fatality, to a seventeenth-century Italian monk, a number of injuries, mostly minor, and no other known fatalities beyond a horse in nineteenth-century Ohio and a dog in Egypt in 1911.)[36]

To walk around with a meteor-proof helmet on one's head would be absurdity; to take measures against the alleged threat of some Muslim "takeover" in the United States is not only absurd, it is an invitation to witch-hunts and political demagoguery far more dangerous to our liberties than the "threat" that is being guarded against. In the United States there has been major controversy over the so-called Ground Zero mosque, as well as considerable public opposition to the construction of a mosque in Murfreesboro, Tennessee.[37] In Switzerland, voters in 2009 approved a ban on the construction, not of mosques, but solely on the building of *minarets* (the distinctive towers found on many mosques, most prominently used for the call to prayer).[38] In former times, kings would sometimes resort to the mass expulsion of all members of a particular religion deemed threatening to the social order or spiritual health of a nation (as was done in Spain in the days of Ferdinand and Isabella[39]). Today, we have come to realize that no civilized society can resort to such measures. Yet not only are minaret bans and demagoguery on the construction of mosques inimical to the concept of religious liberty for all, it should be obvious they are less-than-useless half-measures. Rather than expelling all Muslims, such measures may merely serve to convince Muslims, still living in Switzerland or in Tennessee, that they can never be more than second-class citizens, that to "assimilate" and accept such "Western" values as constitutional democracy or freedom of religion is incompatible with maintaining the religion of their forefathers. There is the real risk that such demonization of religious minorities will in fact incite more of the extremism and even violence it is supposedly meant to prevent, inhibiting the assimilation of genuine American values by new immigrant groups and undermining the sort of police work truly needed to prevent security threats, which relies heavily on the cooperation of minority communities in voluntarily rooting out the would-be terrorists in their midst.

Not all Muslims believe in the death penalty for apostasy from Islam or blasphemy against it—but some (too many) certainly do. Not all Christians believe in the death penalty for apostasy from Christianity or blasphemy against it—but some (a few) certainly do. Within Islam there are the "Islamists," who wish to see their religion supported by the state (at the expense of other religions, such as Christianity). Within Christianity there are the "Christianists," who wish to see *their* religion supported by the state (at the expense of other religions, such as Islam—

atheists get the short end of the stick in either case, of course). There is certainly NOT an equivalence in power or popularity between the "Islamists" and the "Christianists." On the world stage, rather than here in the United States, at this point in human history the Islamists are far, far more likely to topple governments and change constitutions and establish new officially Islamic (and repressive) regimes. But there is a *moral* equivalence between those who seek an Islamic theocracy and those within our own country who seek a Christian theocracy. Americans should no more support politicians who demagogically talk of our laws being based on the Ten Commandments or of this being a Christian nation than they would support a politician who called for the American imposition of Sharia or for the United States to become an Islamic nation. Supporters of religious liberty (atheists and believers alike) must be vigilant against any attempt at imposing the beliefs of one religion or sect on all. At home, we must support the principles of our Constitution, regardless of who is trying to subvert them. Around the world, we must stand in solidarity with our fellow human beings who still live in areas where religion—any religion—still possesses political power and can therefore still be a force for evil.

An example of the extreme danger of allowing religious law to be treated as a direct basis for criminal law occurred in September 2012 in Mali.[40] Four men there were punished for robbery by having one foot and one hand each amputated while the men were tied, upside down, in a town center. A spokesperson explained, "It is not us who ordered this. It is God." A Mali government spokesman decried the punishment, calling it "Truly barbaric; not worthy of our civilization." The example happened to have come from an Islamic interpretation, but our purpose here is not to add to the irrational fears in America of the religion of Islam, but to emphasize the risk to liberty and civility from any identification of religious and criminal law. And, not incidentally, to show that once "God's law" is accepted as the sole basis for criminal law, argument against it can be difficult if not futile.

As we were completing an early version of this book, the news came of deadly terrorist attacks in Norway.[41] Someone had set off a car bomb in Oslo, followed by a horrific shooting attack in which scores of young people were murdered at a nearby youth camp. The coordinated and vicious nature of the attacks immediately led to speculation, from people of many different political stripes, that the attacks were the work of al Qaeda. In some quarters, there were the usual mocking references to "the religion of peace." But when an arrest was swiftly made, the man accused was one Anders Behring Breivik, a native-born Norwegian and avowed Christian whose manifesto proclaimed him to be a latter-day Crusader fighting to save Christian Europe from an unholy alliance of Muslim immigrants and "cultural Marxists."[42] The fanaticism of al Qaeda and other militant proponents of Islamic theocracy must certainly be opposed by all decent people. But the casual toleration of lies and bigotry in the name of fighting against some future Muslim takeover of the Western world has real consequences. Meeting fanaticism with fanaticism, Islamic demagoguery with anti-Islamic demagoguery, leads only to tragedy.

Although one hopes few Oklahomans (or Alabamians, Tennesseans, or South Carolinians) are full-bore Christian Reconstructionists, one cannot help but think that a ballot initiative or legislative measure barring the state's courts from considering "the Ten Commandments or biblical law" when deciding cases would not fare particularly well. In truth, Americans should see calls for Sharia and calls for laws based on the Bible as fundamentally similar, and equally wrong. What the followers of Rushdoony (however few of them there may be) want is just as bad and just as un-American as what the proponents of radical Islam are after. And at least *slightly* more likely to actually come to pass in Oklahoma.

Chapter 17.

Blasphemy and Heresy
Where Free Speech and
Freedom of Religion Must *Meet*

Blasphemy, in one sense, has probably been around as long as humans have had anything like religion. Heresy, a related "crime" or "sin," is equally old. Religions are better than most other human ideologies at developing cultural mechanisms to protect themselves from criticism or disagreement. (For another such mechanism religions have created, see chapter 15, "The Big Lie.") Blasphemy and heresy both are discussed, in a variety of contexts, in other chapters of this book. (See especially chapter 5, "History Is Not on the Side of the Angels" and chapter 16, "God's Law.") In this chapter the focus is on the stark conflict between secularism and any attempt to control blasphemy or heresy in society at large, as well as to comment briefly on attempts to control either within a religious organization. In this sense, blasphemy means saying or writing things that are considered to be irreverent toward or slanderous of any god(s) or religious ideas or institutions. And heresy means holding and especially publicly professing ideas that are contrary to those proclaimed as true by a particular religion or sect. In another sense, real blasphemy and real heresy do not exist, since—we argue—there are no gods available to defame, no "true" religions available to violate.

Among the many works on the subject, the two best are Leonard W. Levy's *Blasphemy: Verbal Offense against the Sacred, from Moses to Salman Rushdie* and Edwin F. Kagin's *Baubles of Blasphemy*, second edition. Levy's almost seven hundred pages provide a thoroughly comprehensive reference work on the subject, detailing every aspect from ancient Egypt to the burning at the stake of Michael Servetus for the crime in Geneva in the 1500s, to Thomas Jefferson's extensive opinions on the subject, and more. Levy writes as well extensively about heresy, including detailed discussions of the distinctions between *blasphemy* and *heresy*. The latter is, he notes, "not a Hebrew term at all, and no equivalent for it appears in the pre-Christian era."[1]

Kagin's book deals with many subjects, much of it satire, some of it likely to be considered blasphemy by some, and with blasphemy as one of his subjects: "Blasphemy is the crime of making fun of religious beliefs someone else holds sacred."[2]

Modern Americans are likely, thanks to taking for granted living under a Constitution and First Amendment that guarantee freedom of speech and of religion, to find the idea of blasphemy a little quaint, perhaps just a matter of being polite, or a matter for academics and historians to study, rather than a serious threat to liberty. But there are people in prison under the death penalty for blasphemy today in more than one part of the world:

> Even relatively progressive Islamic countries, such as Malaysia, retain and enforce blasphemy laws. The rigor with which blasphemy laws are enforced in these countries varies greatly, but prosecutions are frequent enough and penalties severe enough to present a grave danger to freedom of conscience. For example, since 1986, when its current blasphemy law was adopted, more than four thousand people have been accused of blasphemy in Pakistan. Some have been convicted and sentenced to death (although no death sentence has been carried out). Iran has the most intolerant regime, with hundreds of individuals convicted of blasphemy since the Khomeini revolution of 1979; dozens have been executed.[3]

Islamic religious law is supported by criminal law, in the name of avoiding blasphemy, in many parts of the world—and not, as Ronald A. Lindsay noted above, just in nations considered by some to be the most rigidly Islamic. Indonesia, for example, still sentences dissidents to prison terms for "promoting . . . a heretical interpretation of Islam."[4] Pakistan has recently arrested a Christian girl, Rimsha Masih, for allegedly burning the pages of "a religious textbook"; though predictions were that the charges would be dropped, in the meantime not only the girl and her family but her neighbors as well have been in fear of their lives.[5] Blasphemy laws, as clearly demonstrated in that case in Pakistan, endanger the lives and liberty of not only those who oppose a particular religious view but also any who can be accused of blasphemy, with or without real evidence to support the accusations. By making government officials protectors of the "true" religion and empowering those officials to use criminal laws to enforce orthodoxy, the free speech and freedom of everyone can be put at risk by opponents eager to manipulate or fabricate. Intimidation and exploitation are enhanced. Personal disputes can be (and are) transformed into offenses against God, with profoundly disruptive effects.[6]

Nor is it only Islamic religious law that the state is called on to reinforce. In Russia in 2012, members of a feminist punk-rock band, Pussy Riot, were charged (and later sentenced to two years in prison) for offending the Russian Orthodox Church and, not incidentally, the Russian government, by chanting a "punk prayer" at a cathedral.[7] Many contemporary examples show that serious threats to basic freedom are inevitable if the law is expected to protect religious sensibility. Even in the midst of the "Arab Spring," instances such as the 2012 conviction of Adel Imam, an Egyptian comic actor, for "insulting Islam,"[8] make it clear that satirizing religion is a crucial part of free speech. Fazil Say, famed Turkish classical and jazz pianist, was charged in Istanbul in June 2012 with "insulting Islamic values in Twitter® messages" and "faced up to 18 months in prison if convicted."[9] And there are still those who would like such satire criminalized in the United States. (For examples, see chapter 16, "God's Law.")

Accepting the possibility of blasphemy as a terrible practice, even if not as a crime, is dangerous to freedom as well. The riots and violence throughout the Middle East and beyond in fall 2012, sparked by an allegedly blasphemous anti-Islamic video, provide a clear example.[10] Those violent episodes demonstrated not only that believing in blasphemy is dangerous but also that not understanding American secularism exacerbates the danger. The quintessentially American ideal of religious liberty that puts any regulation of religious criticism or expression beyond the control of the law led to apparent confusion by many rioters. The protesters and rioters seemed not to appreciate that the US government could not prevent the production of a video offensive to Islam—or any religion or ideology—because of a profound, necessary restriction on government. As Secretary of State Hillary Clinton noted,

We've seen rage and violence directed at American embassies over an awful Internet video that we had nothing to do with. It is hard for the American people to make sense of that, because it is senseless. And it is totally unacceptable.[11]

According to Nicholas D. Kristof, a "Pakistani imam" once told him that President Bill Clinton had been responsible for executing blasphemers, citing the 1993 raid on David Koresh's compound in Waco, Texas.[12] Bill Keller, analyzing the riots in September 2012, reported approvingly that Salman Rushdie "would have liked a more robust White House defense of the rights that made the noxious video possible."[13] If the US government would proudly and consistently defend American secularism—the fact that "the government of the United States of America is not in any sense founded on the Christian religion" (see chapter 8 for details on the treaty quoted here)—against all sorts of theists who demand government protection for religious ideas, the global need for better understanding would be easier to achieve. As the language of that treaty went on to declare in its famous Article 11, the US government "has in itself no character of enmity against the laws, religion, or tranquility of" Islam—or of any other religion.

Why, from a religious perspective, is blasphemy considered so dangerous that it deserves the ultimate punishment, that it is even the one unforgivable sin according to the New Testament? ("And so I tell you, every kind of sin and slander can be forgiven, but blasphemy against the Spirit will not be forgiven." Matthew 12:31.) Christians differ, it should be noted, about the nuances of the biblical meaning of *blasphemy* and about whether it is in fact "unforgivable." Some theologians have even, with what seems to an outsider like tortured logic indeed, declared the particular unforgivable sin allegedly described by Jesus as in fact impossible to commit in the modern era.[14]

The justification offered by theologians such as John Calvin (the driving force behind Servetus's execution) is that blasphemy is poisonous, that it can lead others—especially young and innocent others—into errors that will cause them to be punished by God for all eternity.[15] Modern theists, especially Muslims, sometimes imply that blasphemy laws are needed to protect believers from being offended by all manner of acts—including, famously, depictions, even innocent ones, of

Mohammed. Satirical rather than innocent depictions are of course more likely to lead to rioting, but anger over depictions of Mohammed, while most uneven over Islamic history, is not at all new. For a thorough discussion (and for publication of some of the "offensive" cartoons) of recent (2005–2006) controversy and rioting over cartoon depictions of Mohammed, see Tom Flynn's essay "Islam and the Cartoons" in *Free Inquiry*.[16] For many illustrations and much more information on this subtopic of blasphemy, see the Mohammed Image Archive[17] on the Internet, which includes an extensive set of depictions, some controversial, others apparently not. Among those that have caused mild controversy is a depiction of Mohammed in the frieze in the main courtroom at the US Supreme Court Building in Washington, DC—a sculptural figure that has been there since the building opened in 1935.[18]

While devout believers may continue to see blasphemy as dangerous, as the worst of sins, there are thousands of examples of just how dangerous to human beings differences in religious understanding are. Montesquieu summed this up succinctly in 1721: "There never was a realm in which so many civil wars have broken out, as in the kingdom of Christ."[19]

Lest anyone misunderstand and think that blasphemy declarations and punishments have not in the past been extraordinarily dangerous and destructive, consider Leonard W. Levy's description:

> Sixteenth-century Europe was hostile to religious toleration. On both sides of the Reformation, political and religious leaders believed that the safety of the state and the preservation of the faith required the execution of obstinate and blasphemous heretics. They saw nothing unchristian in punishing capitally for a crime against the majesty of God. Had an epidemic among livestock annihilated as many pigs and sheep as the number of people slaughtered for their religious opinions, governments would have bemoaned the loss. But they would have thought themselves traitors to their faiths if they had not rid the world of its Servetuses.[20]

And read a description, though not if you are prone to nightmares, of the execution of one of the victims of a government intertwined with a religion and not restricted by secularism—for example, a description of the horrific death of Michael Servetus himself.[21] The declaration by governments of acts as "blasphemy" is a long-standing practice but not at all one restricted to the Old World or to other cultures. John Adams and Thomas Jefferson exchanged letters on the subject near the end of their lives (they both died on Independence Day, 1826). They agreed that attempts to regulate free speech and open criticism of religion by labeling these attempts "blasphemy" was dangerously wrong.[22] Jefferson had earlier (in 1814) famously declared in a letter to bookseller N. G. Dufief about attempts to outlaw a particular book as blasphemous (emphasis Jefferson's),

> I am really mortified to be told that, *in the United States of America*, a fact like this can become a subject of inquiry, and of criminal inquiry, too, as an offence against religion; that a question about the sale of a book can be carried before the civil magistrate. Is this then our freedom of religion? And are we to have a censor whose imprimatur shall say what books may be sold, and what we may buy? And who is thus to dogmatize religious opinions for our citizens? . . . Is a priest to be our inquisitor, or shall a layman, simple as ourselves, set up his reason as the rule for what we are to read, and what we must believe? It is an insult to our citizens to question whether they are rational beings or not, and blasphemy against religion to suppose it cannot stand the test of truth and reason.[23]

Jefferson's anger and mortification, which he emphasized as explicitly American anger with his italics, should be shared by all Americans.

Though our focus is primarily national, on the need for the federal government to be strictly secular, it is worth remembering that the Fourteenth Amendment, passed in 1868, protects the rights of all US citizens from infringement by state (and by extension, local) governments as well. Some states still have blasphemy laws on the books, but "once the Supreme Court began to apply the Bill of Rights to the states . . . blasphemy laws effectively became dead letters."[24]

Even those who may think religion deserves protection from offensive utterances or acts should oppose blasphemy laws. There is quite literally no way to know how far to take such laws. Shall this phrase or that word or that idea be included or excluded? Who shall decide? A Muslim might consider it blasphemous to assert that God can beget a son; a Christian might consider it blasphemous to deny it. If any government agent has, directly or indirectly, the power to enforce respect under law for any religious idea, then that agent has essentially unlimited and arbitrary power over anyone he comes across.

And, by the way, the prohibition against government agents trying to protect anyone from simply being offended extends to atheists, too. Under our secular form of government, under the First Amendment, ridiculing and satirizing atheism or atheists is—and must be—protected. The false idea that church-state separation is designed to protect atheists' sensitivities is often used to attack secularism. Atheists, like all other Americans, should of course be deeply offended if anyone is attempting to use the government to promote religion. But all ought also to be offended at parallel attempts to use governments to attack religion. And liberty, not protection from offense, is the purpose of separating government and religion.

There can be no meaningful freedom of religion *or* freedom of speech where blasphemy (or heresy) laws are in effect. Social customs, which change with time and situation, can be brought to bear to discourage speech or behavior that some consider rude or offensive. Religious bodies can regulate behavior among adherents with penalties up to expulsion from the group—though not with penalties for anyone not in the group. Penalties even within a group cannot, in a secular society, include depriving an individual of his civil rights. And law and government cannot be used to stop blasphemy or heresy, however defined, without trampling on liberty.

Chapter 18.

What in the Name of God?
*Why "God" Doesn't Belong
in America's Motto or in
Any Official Pledges of Allegiance*

Ronald Reagan, as president, made much of the importance of "In God We Trust" (hereafter "IGWT") on US currency and "under God" in the pledge. According to Richard J. Ellis, Reagan "deplored the efforts to remove religion from public life," specifically connecting this to lawsuits about the pledge and motto. Ellis quoted Reagan as saying in 1984 on the day he accepted the Republican nomination for reelection:

> politics and morality are inseparable. And as morality's foundation is religion, religion and politics are necessarily related. We need religion as a guide. We need it because we are imperfect, and our government needs the church, because only those humble enough to admit they're sinners can bring to democracy the tolerance it requires in order to survive. . . . Without God, there is no virtue, because there's no prompting of the conscience. . . . Without God, there is a coarsening of the society. And without God, democracy will not and cannot long endure. If we ever forget that we are a nation under God, we will be a nation gone under.[1]

Reagan's narrow understanding of tolerance and his stated conclusion that morality depends on religion are not new ideas. And neither his declarations on either matter nor his heavy piety necessarily tell us a great deal beyond what audience (in this specific case to a prayer breakfast in Texas—but likely to a broader spectrum of voters) he was pandering to. The long-standing but wrongheaded connection between morality and religion is discussed in chapter 15, "The Big Lie," and we analyze the meaning and importance of tolerance and toleration in chapter 10, "Tolerance, Toleration, and Liberty." But the pledge and motto deserve special attention in any case for American secularism.

Many anti-secularists declare that the motto, ubiquitous on all American coins and currency, on legislative and courtroom walls, and in federal legislation, as well as elsewhere, constitutes necessary and sufficient evidence that this is a Christian nation, that the United States is not and should not be secular. Those same critics frequently cite the pledge for the same reasons.

"IN GOD WE TRUST"

Most American atheists and many other secularists are offended by the religious motto printed on our money, but, whatever else it tells us, it says nothing about the intentions of the Founding Fathers, whose choice of a motto was *E pluribus unum* ("out of the many, one"). That thoroughly unchristian motto "was chosen by a committee appointed on July 4, 1776, by the Continental Congress 'to prepare a device for a Seal of the United States of America.' Committee member Benjamin Franklin proposed the motto 'Rebellion to Tyrants is Obedience to God,' but the phrase 'e pluribus unum' was chosen by the committee and officially adopted on June 20, 1782. The phrase—which was well known, having appeared for many years on the cover of the *Gentleman's Magazine*—is from 'Moretum,' attributed to Vergil."[2] It is interesting that our allegedly oh-so-pious and Christian Founding Fathers had an opportunity to choose a national motto with the word *God* in it and rejected it in favor of a secular one.

The religious (IGWT) motto was not printed on all US money until required under the McCarthy-inspired law enacting the IGWT motto as law in the 1950s. The courts have essentially held, by the way, that the motto is constitutional because it is *not* Christian or even really religious (just "ceremonial deism"). As Justice William Brennan summed it up in a 1984 dissenting opinion, "I would suggest that such practices as the designation of 'In God We Trust' as our national motto, or the references to God contained in the Pledge of Allegiance to the flag can best be understood, in Dean Rostow's apt phrase, as a form of 'ceremonial deism,' protected from Establishment Clause scrutiny chiefly because they have lost through rote repetition any significant religious content."[3] A later federal court ruling reaffirmed this idea.[4] We do not agree that the motto or the "under God" phrase added to the pledge are constitutional, largely because we understand them to be religious. Some Christians, including ardent advocates of the United States as a Christian nation like John W. Whitehead, agree with us that the motto and "under God" *should* be seen as deeply religious: "The Pledge of Allegiance . . . still contains the phrase 'Under God' only because a federal court said that the phrase has lost *any* religious significance through rote repetition and now amounts to 'ceremonial deism'"[5] (emphasis is Whitehead's). But if the motto or pledge language *is* interpreted as Christian, the courts would then necessarily interpret it as constitutionally impermissible.

The IGWT motto has, to be sure, apparently achieved *political* security even if it should not. Fearful politicians still blithely support it, we suspect most often as an easier path—easier because more people who care very much about it want to keep it than because it makes sense—than any to change it. State legislatures frequently pass laws or resolutions regarding IGWT, almost certainly for mostly political reasons. For example, the Georgia General Assembly has invested time and energy in arguing over whether "In God We Trust" stickers for Georgia automobile license plates should be available for free or at a charge of $1.00 each.[6]

When the US House passed a nonbinding resolution reaffirming the motto, 396 to 9, in November 2011, President Obama correctly called that "political posturing." But neither Obama nor any other prominent political leader from either party called then for eliminating the motto.[7]

E pluribus unum has appeared on most US coins, beginning in the late 1790s. The motto "In God We Trust" did not appear on *any* US coin until 1864, when "its presence on the new coin was due largely to the increased religious sentiment during the Civil War Crisis," according to R. S. Yeoman.[8]

PLEDGE OF ALLEGIANCE AND
ONE NATION "UNDER GOD"

Not only Ronald Reagan, but scores of leaders, political and religious, have, probably with widely varying degrees of sincerity, concluded that the short but inspiring declaration apparently agreed to by every patriotic American is strong evidence of our nonsecular status. After all, we seem to proudly include the words "under God" as a core part of our freedom and of our united indivisibility. If that's not a reference to Christianity, what could it possibly refer to?

Expressing fealty to any god, however vaguely, should not, we insist, be a condition of citizenship. Love of country is not, nor should it be, measured by a citizen's religious belief or lack thereof. Many atheists, freethinkers, secular humanists, and agnostics have laid down their lives for this country. Many other Americans object to false piety as a part of nationalism.

As noted by Princeton historian Kevin Kruse, the history of the phrase "under God" has had a checkered past:

> The concept of "one nation under God" has a noble lineage, originating in Abraham Lincoln's hope at Gettysburg that "this nation, under God, shall not perish from the earth." After Lincoln, however, the phrase disappeared from political discourse for decades. But it re-emerged in the mid-20th century, under a much different guise: corporate leaders and conservative clergymen deployed it to discredit Franklin D. Roosevelt's New Deal.[9]

Kruse went on to provide details of corporate financing of clergy as part of this effort and the heavily political intentions that led up to it being used as part of a campaign to tie capitalism closely to conservative Christianity, including being added to the Pledge of Allegiance. The US Congress added "under God" to the pledge—amazingly enough, actually *dividing* the phrase "One nation indivisible"—to insert it in 1954. The Ninth Circuit US Court ruled in 2002:

> In the context of the Pledge, the statement that the United States is a nation "under God" is an endorsement of religion. It is a profession of

a religious belief, namely, a belief in monotheism. The recitation that ours is a nation "under God" is not a mere acknowledgment that many Americans believe in a deity. Nor is it merely descriptive of the undeniable historical significance of religion in the founding of the Republic. Rather, the phrase "one nation under God" in the context of the Pledge is normative. To recite the Pledge is not to describe the United States; instead, it is to swear allegiance to the values for which the flag stands: unity, indivisibility, liberty, justice, and—since 1954—monotheism. The text of the official Pledge, codified in federal law, impermissibly takes a position with respect to the purely religious question of the existence and identity of God. A profession that we are a nation "under God" is identical, for Establishment Clause purposes, to a profession that we are a nation "under Jesus," a nation "under Vishnu," a nation "under Zeus," or a nation "under no god," because none of these professions can be neutral with respect to religion. [T]he government must pursue a course of complete neutrality toward religion (Wallace, 472 US at 60, 105 S.Ct. 2479). Furthermore, the school district's practice of teacher-led recitation of the Pledge aims to inculcate in students a respect for the ideals set forth in the Pledge, and thus amounts to state endorsement of these ideals. Although students cannot be forced to participate in recitation of the Pledge, the school district is nonetheless conveying a message of state endorsement of a religious belief when it requires public school teachers to recite, and lead the recitation of, the current form of the Pledge.[10]

While that ruling has since been overturned on technical grounds, it accurately describes why the phrase "under God" should never have been added by the US Congress to any official pledge of allegiance to this nation.

What Jefferson said in a letter to his friend Benjamin Rush in 1803 is still true today: "It behooves every man who values liberty of conscience for himself, to resist invasions of it in the case of others; or their case may, by change of circumstances, become his own."[11] Whoever is in the majority today, could, by next year or next century, find themselves in the minority. Minority rights therefore should matter and be preciously guarded by those now in the majority. Only by opposing a convergence between church and state, only by insisting on a religiously neutral pledge of allegiance and government, can we succeed in defending freedom of conscience for us all. For political leaders to pretend to have the power to act or speak "In the Name of God" is deeply un-American, unpatriotic at its core, and hypocritical quite directly in the sense conveyed in red-letter words in the Bible (Matthew 6:5)—"do not be like the hypocrites, for they love to pray standing in the synagogues and on the street corners to be seen by men. I tell you the truth, they have received their reward in full."

Chapter 19.

Questions

Frequent Questions or Claims by Christian-Nation Proponents with Specific Answers to the Claims

1. The Declaration of Independence famously and prominently invokes our Creator and refers to God in several places. What stronger evidence of the founders' devotion to God could you ask for?

This question is answered in detail in chapter 6, "The Unchristian Roots of the Fourth of July," but a short reply would include these points:

1. The Declaration, while quite important historically and emotionally for all Americans and many millions of others worldwide, is not our governing charter—which is the US Constitution, written and ratified over a decade later.
2. The Declaration, written primarily by Thomas Jefferson (probably not a Christian in any modern, orthodox sense) includes references only to a more deistic version of God; "Nature's God" or "Creator," and not to anything even remotely Christian.
3. The Declaration is directly contradictory to biblical principles as it declares rebellion against a Christian king, George III.

2. The Constitution specifically treats Sunday as a day set aside as important and not a workday. Since only Christians and not Muslims or Jews do that, isn't this prima facie evidence of the framers' understanding that this is a Christian nation?

This is another example of desperate supporters (of the idea that the Constitution is Christian) grasping at straws. (See chapter 7, "The Unchristian Nature of the Constitution," for far more.) As with other calendar-related items (see the chapter on the Constitution), not counting Sunday for some purposes was conventional practice at the time, not an indication of Christian piety. Perhaps the best evidence of this can be found in a popular report by US senator from Kentucky Richard M. Johnson in 1829 (he served later—from 1837 to 1840—as vice president of the United States) urging that Sunday mail delivery *be continued* on separation-of-church-and-state grounds.[1] Though eventually those on Johnson's side lost that battle, the reverence for Sunday was at best uneven in the early years of the American republic.

3. If this isn't a Christian nation, why did the legislators in the very beginning set aside land for churches in the Northwest Territory?

The Northwest Ordinance established the Northwest Territories, which later became Ohio, Michigan, Indiana, Illinois, Wisconsin, and part of Minnesota. It was groundbreaking legislation of great importance in American and even world history. But it was not created under the US Constitution—it was passed under the Articles of Confederation, one of the last important laws so established, in 1787.[2] Whatever the reasons for the set-aside of plots and endorsement of religion, this was not legislation passed under our current rules.

4. *We had prayer in school—Christian prayer—when my*
   parents were children. Doesn't that show that the Supreme
   Court justices—not the founders—are the ones who are
   anti-Christian? Given that in our public schools, separation
   of church and state means keeping Christian students from
   praying or saying grace before their lunches or from reading
   their Bibles in school, how can a Christian even consider
   supporting that?

For much more on these questions, see chapter 11, "Secular Schooling,"
and for a different aspect of it, see the question that follows this one. Many
public schools across the United States had unconstitutional government-
sponsored prayer and Bible reading before the court rulings of the 1960s,
but many others did not. As Rob Boston convincingly showed in his book
Why the Religious Right Is Wrong about Separation of Church and State, strife
and conflict, even rioting, especially between Catholics and Protestants,
was frequent as a result. One of the school systems involved in the 1960s
cases, Baltimore, had conflict at least as far back as 120 years before that.[3]
The necessary and sufficient reply is that the First Amendment (1791) and
the Fourteenth Amendment (1868), taken together, are the legal source of
individual rights that no government at any level can abridge. The courts
merely decreed what is obvious from those amendments. And that includes
the right to be free of government-imposed prayer.

The false idea that church-state separation denies individual religious expression is completely wrong. As the bumper sticker says, "As
long as there are algebra tests, there will be prayer in schools." Sincere
believers in prayer—all of them that we know, at least—deny that anyone
can keep anyone else from praying, especially if they pray in the way that
Matthew 6:5–6 reports that Jesus told followers to pray—privately. All
that is prohibited by separation is *forced* government-sponsored prayer.
The great American hero, civil rights martyr, and Protestant minister
Rev. Martin Luther King Jr., as he knelt in prayer awaiting arrest during
a protest in 1962, said of the Supreme Court school-prayer decision
(rendered a few weeks earlier), that it was "a sound and good decision,
reaffirming something that is basic in our Constitution, namely separation of church and state."[4]

5. *How can there be anything wrong with children being able to pray in school, as they could until Madalyn Murray O'Hair and the Supreme Court deprived them of that basic right. And hasn't the country suffered a great decline (lower morals, higher crime rates, even lower SAT scores) since we took prayer out of school? And why do atheists even care whether county-commission meetings start with a prayer?*

Some of this is answered in much greater detail in chapter 18, "What in the Name of God?" Questions like these are fraught with multiple errors: incorrect assumptions, historical facts distorted or completely misrepresented, and more. Part of this is an incorrect application of inferential statistics: Correlation is necessary but not sufficient to conclude causation. Or, if B occurs just after A, that is not enough reason to believe that A caused B. If it were, then adding "In God We Trust" to US paper money and "under God" to the Pledge of Allegiance—both changes made in the 1950s[5]—could be identified as causes of any great moral declines anyone perceives since the 1950s. Or, similarly, we could attribute the many improvements in life and morals that have occurred since the early 1960s (improved civil rights for minorities, medical advances, better status for women, etc.) to the school-prayer and Bible-reading decisions. Either is irrational—but just as rational as the attempt to blame various alleged declines on the prayer decisions.

The other problem the questions ignore is that government-sponsored religion in schools was not practiced uniformly before the court decisions, nor has the practice been uniformly ended. Many states and some school districts within states did not allow such forced prayer or Bible readings long before the 1960s decisions—and some (mostly Southern) schools still illegally allow such religious indoctrination, despite court decisions. (Such illegal practices will continue until someone with legal standing—probably someone with a child in the specific school—is willing and able to endure the social and perhaps the financial costs of bringing suit.) And none of this started in the 1960s, anyway. There was, for example, a legal brouhaha in Cincinnati in the 1860s over daily readings of the King James Bible.[6]

The declaration that there is obviously no harm in school religious exercises (or prayers before county-commission meetings) betrays a lack of awareness of the kind of facts and logic laid out in chapter 1, "Why Secularism?" and chapter 11, "Secular Schooling." The baseless presumption of the questioner is often that all atheists or freethinkers want others to be denied the right to pray and that the evil US Supreme Court has decreed that Americans should be so deprived.

The truth is that most of us atheists do think children or commissioners who pray are wasting their time, and many of us think there is real reason to believe that there may be ill effects, maybe even serious ones, from praying to imaginary supernatural creatures and the self-abasement that accompanies it. But we know very few atheists in the United States who want the government or the courts to deny anyone the right to pray. Few of us are so arrogant that we are willing to trample on the religious freedom of others, even when we are confident they are wrong and foolish.

The bottom line for many aggressive Christians on this issue is not really that they want their children to pray. After all, from age five to age eighteen the public schools have control of less than 15 percent of a child's time, with parents or guardians in control most of the rest of the time. What these folks really want is the power to force other people's children—or other citizens at a commission meeting—to pray. And what is wrong with that is that we atheists and our children deserve religious liberty as much as they and their children do.

6. Are you trying to deny that a solid majority of Americans are Christians? And, if you do admit this obvious fact, why not admit the corollary that it's a Christian nation unless Christianity is suppressed?

A much more detailed answer to this one can be found in the introduction and in chapter 1, "Why Secularism?" and chapter 5, "History Is Not on the Side of the Angels"), but the short answer is that we are certainly not denying that a majority of Americans are in one sense or another Christians. A solid majority, about three-fourths, of Americans are generally considered "white,"[7] but very few Americans would call this a "white nation" (or want to be associated with the racists who do want to).

A slight majority are women,[8] but no one suggests we call America a "female nation." Christianity, Judaism, Islam, and every other religion is available as a free choice to any American who wants to adopt one of these as his choice. And, happily for Christians and every other American, there is no government agent at any level who is empowered to decide what it means to be a Christian.

7. Explain, if this isn't a Christian nation, why the Judeo-Christian Bible is used in all our courts and government swearing ceremonies, and why all those who testify must swear, "So help me God."

The premise of this question is false. As is made clear in Article VI of the US Constitution, no one is required in the United States to swear to any God or to add "so help me God" to any oath of office—or to swear at all ("affirmation" may be substituted). Where such things do occur, including when the president of the United States is sworn in, religious oaths are sometimes added by tradition. But, for example, when Theodore Roosevelt was first sworn in as president, after the death by assassination of President William McKinley in Buffalo, New York, on September 14, 1901, Roosevelt was not sworn in using a Bible and he did not add "so help me God."[9]

One of the enduring conventional conclusions about George Washington and religion is that he was the American official who began the unofficial but supposedly consistent practice of adding "so help me God" after taking an oath of office. But that well-known and widely accepted story may be false:

> Washington is widely credited with first adding the words "so help me, God" after the presidential inaugural oath, but none of the detailed contemporaneous eyewitness accounts of the first inauguration supports this belief. These words are not part of the Constitutional oath. The first authors to state that Washington added the words were Rufus Wilmot Griswold in 1854 and Washington Irving in 1857, and neither cited a source.[10]

George Mason University Professor of History, Emeritus, Peter R. Henriques has weighed in on the side of those who say Washington likely did not add those words.[11] Those interested in this aspect of the George Washington story would do well to read the *American Atheist* article cited in our answer to question 9 on Washington and then to follow up on the sources cited there.

8. *Of course we have religious freedom in this country—but that means freedom* **of** *religion, not freedom* **from** *religion.*

If a citizen is free to choose among religions but not free to choose no religion, then that citizen is not free. Aside from that major question, to declare that we cannot as individuals choose to be irreligious, then the government (or the majority) must decide what counts as being "religious." Good sense and strong protection for religious liberty require that government be deprived of the power to make any religious decisions at all for individual citizens. This certainly does not imply a responsibility by government agents to eliminate religion from people's lives— only from government imposition into those aspects of our lives.

9. *George Washington—our first president, the father of our nation—is well known to have said, "It is impossible to govern the world without God and the Bible. Of all the dispositions and habits that lead to political prosperity, our religion and morality are the indispensable supporters. Let us with caution indulge the supposition that morality can be maintained without religion. Reason and experience both forbid us to expect that our national morality can prevail in exclusion of religious principle." Who are you to disagree with Washington?*

This comment was supposedly said by George Washington (according, at one time, to David Barton). Much of what should be said about this Washington "quotation" is the same as what we wrote (in chapter 18, "What in the Name of God?") about a Madison "quotation." No one can find this quote in Washington's papers, nor is it consistent with almost everything else we know about Washington.[12] Washington *did* make some pious official statements and did apparently accept what we call, in chapter 15, "The Big Lie" that religion and morality are causally related—or at least that it was politic to say so. There is at least one genuine 1784 Washington quotation that accepts atheists as honorable and moral (see chapter 2, "Atheists Are Not Un-American" for the quote). And George Washington was never known to argue that either the Bible or Christianity are required to be moral or to be a good American.

For more on George Washington and his support for secularism, please see the Fourth Quarter 2011 issue of *American Atheist*.[13]

There are many "Christian" quotations that claim to demonstrate that the founders intended to establish a Christian government. The gross insult to the founders that this suggests is usually overlooked—that they wanted to create a Christian government but were too stupid or careless to remember to actually provide for this in the documents they approved. What matters is not whether these founders or leaders were Christian, as indeed many were, but whether they wanted to create a Christian government. Some historical Americans really did want that— but they lost the fight, and for very good reasons. See chapter 5, "History Is Not on the Side of the Angels," for much more.

We must all be on guard not only against overzealous theists who fabricate (or accept false quotes as genuine) but also against overzealous freethinkers and atheists who accept too readily some quote we want to believe is accurate even if the evidence for it is weak or nonexistent.

10. *Why on earth do atheists, secular humanists, and freethinkers—a tiny minority of Americans by any reckoning—think they have the right to keep good Christians from praying and acknowledging our love of God Almighty?*

The First Amendment to the US Constitution guarantees the right to free religious expression (by denying the Congress the power to make laws "prohibiting the free exercise thereof"), and no atheist we know of is opposed to such expression by individuals. Nor do we oppose religious exercises by groups freely organized by individuals, including praying or acknowledging any deities anyone wants to acknowledge. What we and other supporters of secularism (religious and irreligious) oppose is governments at any level deciding for individuals what gods—if any—to pray to or acknowledge. Individual rights cannot be subjected to majority rule or to government control, or they are not in fact rights.

11. Isn't it true that "separation of church and state" appeared in the constitution of the Soviet Union, not the United States Constitution? Isn't "separation of church and state" a Communist idea, not an American one?

This red herring dates back at least to January 22, 1995, when, according to Robert S. Alley, Pat Robertson declared it—and probably back at least to 1982 when Robertson testified before a US Senate committee on the matter.[14]

The concept appeared in the US Constitution and Bill of Rights long before it appeared elsewhere. The exact words, "a wall of separation," come from a letter President Thomas Jefferson issued in 1802: "I contemplate with sovereign reverence that act of the whole American people which declared that their legislature should make no law respecting an establishment of religion, or prohibit the free exercise thereof, thus building a wall of separation between church and state."[15] Many constitutional concepts, including many that Americans most revere, are not called in the Constitution by the terms now most popular. The words "separation of church and state" are now used as a shorthand description for the idea that religious liberty can be protected only by excluding government from making any religious decisions for individuals. (See chapter 1, "Why Secularism?" for more details.)

12. But Christianity and the Bible are true—shouldn't our laws and system of government be based on the truth?

We—Americans but also human beings in general—do not agree on what constitutes religious truth. That universal lack of agreement will be the basis of endless discord, loss of individual liberty, and worse, in the absence of secularism. The American inventors of secularism—our Founding

Fathers—understood that determining truth in such matters cannot be the business of government (see chapter 1, "Why Secularism?" and chapter 5, "History Is Not on the Side of the Angels" for more details).

13. We are at war with radical Islam, and you can't beat something with nothing. Don't we need a firm Christian or Judeo-Christian foundation to defeat the fanatical followers of Islamofascism?

Secularism is most assuredly something, not "nothing." And it is the only something with any real chance of avoiding endless religious strife and war, because only secularism can secure respect for all religious and irreligious viewpoints without calling on the immense powers of governments to enforce any of them.

14. Why should we allow church-state separation when it is antireligious or anti-Christian, either by design or in effect?

This is almost the direct opposite of the truth: the secular, nonreligious government of the United States has stood the test of time, protecting religious liberty and the freely chosen religious beliefs of all Americans specifically by keeping the government out of the business of making religious decisions for any of America's citizens. Please see chapter 13, "He Who Is Not With Me . . . ," for more on this. The framers of the Constitution did not slam the door on mixing government and religion because they hated religion or Christianity (though some of them may have); they did not slam that door only because they feared that strife over religious differences could destroy the nation—though many did have such fears and the fears were well-founded, historically. What they most feared, because history repeatedly demonstrated to them the sound basis for fearing it, was that *liberty would be lost*, that power would become concentrated and individual liberty lost, that both the national government and religion would be corrupted, if the two were entangled. (Some states did have, until 1833, established churches and no separation. Massachusetts was the last state to have this but voted it out at last by an overwhelming majority;[16] the Fourteenth Amendment of 1868 makes the rights of US citizens more important and prohibits any future religious establishment by a state.) The framers were *not* anti-Christian or antireligious, and they did not produce an anti-Christian or antireligious Constitution—they were pro-freedom. And therefore this is a free country, for Christians and everyone else—and *not* a Christian nation.

15. Isn't the overwhelmingly Christian language found in the Mayflower Compact proof that this is a Christian nation?

The Mayflower Compact[17] was signed by forty-one men aboard the *Mayflower* on November 11, 1620, and it is an interesting and important historical document. (It was important in terms of setting a precedent as a mutually agreed-upon self-governing charter.) Newt Gingrich[18] and many others have claimed the Mayflower Compact as evidence that the much later Declaration of Independence and even the Constitution must as well be dependent on God and religious belief. (See chapter 7 on the Constitution for more on the Mayflower Compact.) But the *Mayflower* document remained in force only until 1691, when the Plymouth colony became part of the Massachusetts Bay Colony. It had not had any legal force for nearly a hundred years when the current governing charter of the United States, the Constitution, was approved.

Further, if the heavily Christian language from that charter "proves" we're a Christian nation, then we must also still be loyal subjects of the Crown of England. The Mayflower Compact signers began and ended their document with declarations of loyalty both to God and to their "dread sovereign lord, King James." The fundamental problem with the question is a thorough misunderstanding of just how revolutionary and unprecedented it was for the framers to write and get approved a godless Constitution for the United States in 1787–1789.

16. Are you calling all those good Christians, like my Aunt Sarah, fools or liars?

We had an aunt/great aunt (her name was not Sarah) who was a deeply religious Christian, and she was generally (except when religious ideas were uppermost in her mind) one of the nicest, most gracious, most decent people we knew—and we loved her dearly. She was certainly not a fool or a liar, and we try to remember how anything we say or write about Christianity would have sounded to this aunt before we say or write it. If every Christian were like her when she was not engaged in proselytizing, we would be much more content to live and let live.

It is rude and it is bad strategy to call any Christians fools or liars just for being Christians, but there is more to it than etiquette and tactics—it is often not true. Even good Christians, including those we love, are, we are convinced, profoundly mistaken in their beliefs. But we clearly cross the line into unwarranted arrogance if we claim that only our own beliefs and conclusions deserve respect.

All who want to convert either of us to their religion (or their philosophy or politics) deserve the full weight of our arguments against them. And the many Christians who use slander, illogic, and rudeness in their arguments deserve to have those shortcomings pointed out to them, forcefully when necessary. We have long advocated honesty and clarity in defending irreligion, and we know that some Christians take offense at such truth-telling. When they do, the problem is with them, not us.

But we should not say nor even think that others are fools or liars merely because they do not accept our conclusions.

17. *Don't atheists believe in the Golden Rule and in being good to people, and isn't that in the Bible? And that of course is the* **Christian** *basis for our morality and our laws—which we should not destroy just because atheists want to impose church-state separation.*

Of course atheists and freethinkers are at least as likely to believe in the Golden Rule as the members of any religious group. Of course many atheists and secular humanists learned at least some of the moral principles they consider crucial from relatives or other teachers who happen to be religious. But neither fact has anything to do with the truth of religion or of the idea that morality springs from a god. Any good anthropologist (like Marvin Harris or David Eller) can provide you with a coherent, logical explanation of how specific moral principles have evolved in specific cultures. And any competent anthropologist will assure you that moral ideas are specific to cultures—that what is considered abhorrent in one culture may be admired in another.[19]

The Golden Rule, "Do unto others as you would have them do unto you" or similar words, is not a Christian invention. Versions of it occur in the Old and New Testaments (see Matthew 7:12 for one version). But versions of it occur in many other places, including in texts that predate the New Testament and are not part of Judeo-Christian heritage. For example, Confucius is believed to have written, about five hundred years before the start of the Common/Christian Era, "Do to every man as thou would'st have him do to thee; and do not unto another what thou would'st not have done to thee."[20] And, according to *The Interpreter's Bible*, the Golden Rule "is not a new rule. Lao-tzu, Confucius, Plato, and the Old Testament all taught it in positive or negative forms."[21]

All the above plus chapter 15, "The Big Lie" (which, see) is a long answer to a theistic questioner, but the questions are among the most pervasive and pernicious we atheists face. The association of morality and religion is based on ideas that preachers and theologians have spent centuries drumming into the heads of believers, and it will take a while to counteract.

18. *No culture has ever been without a belief in some sort of god or higher power; surely everyone else can't be wrong and only a handful of atheists be right, can you? Why should we believe that atheists, a tiny minority, are right, and the great majority of people who do believe in God [or are Christians] are wrong?*

No religion on Earth is accepted by a majority of the population—Christians, the largest religious group, still make up no more than a third of the world population. Back in the 1970s there was a popular idea floating around that "75% of the people who have ever been born were alive at that time." In fact, various calculations show that there have probably been at least one hundred billion human beings who have ever lived on the planet Earth.[22] Countless tens of billions of human beings were born, lived, and died during the "BCE" eras, or in places (like the

Americas between the rise of Christianity but before Columbus) where they never had any opportunity to "hear the Gospel" (or the Qur'an or the collected works of L. Ron Hubbard, either). Of the tens of billions of humans who have ever lived, most did not agree with the authors of this book on religion or the meaning of life—but they did not agree with each other or very likely with the religious beliefs of anyone now alive. We are *all* members of religious minorities. Truth, of course, is not determined by a majority vote, anyway. In terms of the objective reality of the universe, one person with the true facts on her side is right, and everyone else is wrong, and persecuting or killing the one person who is right doesn't make the rest of us any less wrong.

19. Since the Supreme Court declared Secular Humanism a religion, doesn't teaching Secular Humanism in public schools violate church-state separation? Also, some Christians claim Christianity isn't a religion.

As we point out in chapter 11, "Secular Schooling," nontheistic belief systems should certainly be treated as "religions" (legally and constitutionally speaking) for some purposes. Although nontheistic belief systems are not, from a philosophical point of view, religions, we atheists and other nonbelievers nonetheless certainly insist that our beliefs (or lack of beliefs) are just as protected by the free-exercise clause of the First Amendment as are those of Christians, Muslims, Hindus, or Rastafarians. Conversely, public-school teachers should no more use their taxpayer-provided classrooms to teach students that there are no gods than they should to teach students that there is a Judeo-Christian God. However, if Secular Humanists accept the scientific facts about the age of the Earth, or that the sun is the center of the solar system, or for that matter that it is good to stay in school, study hard, and not cheat on one's schoolwork, that does not make those beliefs "religious." If everything is a religion, the concepts not only of separation of religion and government but also of freedom of religion become meaningless—which is precisely why the most totalitarian of the theocrats make such arguments at all.

Some Christians like to claim that Christianity is not a "religion," claiming that it is just a "personal relationship with the Lord" or words to that effect. So . . . does that mean we could outlaw having a personal relationship with this "Lord" (a foreigner from the Middle East with all sorts of dangerously radical ideas)? Of course not. To say *Christianity* is not a religion does violence to the English language, to the extent of making any rational discussion of the subject impossible.

20. Since Benjamin Franklin inspired the Constitutional Convention to begin sessions with a prayer and bring in preachers to advise them, doesn't that show that we're a God-fearing Christian nation? (I think it was then Speaker Newt Gingrich who pointed this out, and he's a brilliant professional historian, so it must be true.)

Gingrich is indeed one of the anti-secularists who has made this bogus claim, but it is bogus nevertheless. Benjamin Franklin did move that clergy be brought in to inspire the Constitutional Convention in 1787, but his motion was tabled and never voted on, much less enacted. The late Robert S. Alley debunked the hoax perpetrated by Gingrich (and others) quite thoroughly in 1995[23]—and the whole Alley article that analyzed this hoax is detailed, clear, and well documented. None of this, of course, kept Gingrich from continuing to use this false claim ten years later. See chapter 4 on Gingrich for Benjamin Franklin's own comment on the disinterest of the delegates in prayers.

21. How can you argue that the founders intended for this to be a secular nation when they held Christian worship services in the US Capitol—which Thomas Jefferson himself attended on many occasions?

To begin with, one must not—as James Madison said of military and legislative chaplainships—allow a "step beyond the landmarks of power [to] have the effect of a legitimate precedent."[24] That the Constitution does not allow Congress to make laws respecting establishments of religion and instead protects the free exercise thereof by *the individual citizen* is of greater importance than that there were religious lectures in the Capitol in nineteenth-century America. That Thomas Jefferson—a man noted for an insatiable and broad-ranging intellectual curiosity—attended religious services in which speakers from a variety of denominations held forth cannot negate his lifelong devotion to religious liberty and (in his own famous words) building up "a wall of separation between church and state."

Chris Rodda at the Talk to Action website has ably dissected this particular claim of the Christian-nation propagandists. The eyewitness reports of Mrs. Margaret Bayard Smith, a newspaper editor's wife, and the British diplomat Sir Augustus Foster, who actually attended these services, bear quoting at some length, first from Mrs. Smith:

> I have called these Sunday assemblies in the capitol, a *congregation*, but the almost exclusive appropriation of that word to religious assemblies, prevents its being a descriptive term as applied in the present case, since the gay company who thronged the H. R. looked very little like a religious assembly. The occasion presented for display was not only a novel, but a favourable one for the youth, beauty and fashion of the city, Georgetown and environs. The members of Congress, gladly gave up their seats for such fair auditors, and either lounged in the lobbies, or round the fire places, or stood beside the ladies of their acquaintance. This sabbathday-resort became so fashionable, that the floor of the house offered insufficient space, the platform behind the Speaker's chair, and every spot where a chair could be wedged in was crowded with ladies in their gayest costume and their attendant beaux and who led them to their seats with the same gallantry as is exhibited in a ball room. Smiles, nods, whispers, nay sometimes tittering marked their recognition of each other, and beguiled the tedium of the service. Often, when cold, a lady would leave her seat and led by her attending beau would make her way through the crowd to one of the fire-places where she could laugh and talk at her ease. One of the officers of the house, followed by his attendant with a great bag over his shoulder, precisely at 12 o'clock, would make his way through the hall to the depository of letters to put them in the mail-bag, which sometimes had a most ludicrous effect, and always diverted attention from the preacher. The musick was as little in union with devotional feelings, as the place. The marine-band, were the performers. Their scarlet uniform, their various instruments, made quite a dazzling appearance in the gallery. The marches they played were good and inspiring, but in their attempts to accompany the psalm-singing of the congregation, they completely failed and after a while, the practice was discontinued,—it was *too* ridiculous.[25]

[**Then from Foster:**] Church service can certainly never be called an amusement; but from the variety of persons who are allowed to preach in the House of Representatives, there was doubtless some alloy of curiosity in the motives which led one to go there. Though the regular Chaplain was a Presbyterian, sometimes a Methodist, a minister of the Church of England, or a Quaker, or sometimes even a woman took the speaker's chair; and I don't think that there was much devotion among the majority. The New Englanders, generally speaking, are very religious; though there are many exceptions, I cannot say so much for the Marylanders, and still less for the Virginians.[26]

From the descriptions given by Mrs. Smith and Sir Augustus of these observances, the truly devout should take no particular comfort in the prospect of politicians staging public worship services.

22. *How can you support secular government, or say secular government is better than a government grounded in religious ideas, given the horrors perpetrated by such twentieth-century atheistic regimes as Nazi Germany and Stalinist Russia?*

Nazi Germany was not atheistic, but askers of questions like this often claim it is. Gregory S. Paul has shown, in exhaustive detail, that Christians, Christianity, and the church played a major role in the rise of Nazism. Others have provided similar evidence and analysis.[27] That said, the various totalitarian Communist regimes of the twentieth century—Stalin's Russia, Mao's China, Pol Pot's Cambodia—were undeniably atheistic and hostile to traditional religion and to religious liberty. As we state in this book's introduction, although we are atheists, the authors of this book are in no way calling for an "atheistic government" in the sense of a government that promotes atheism over religious belief. We no more want atheistic repression of theism than we do theistic repression of atheism (or of competing theisms). What we (and the Founding Fathers, as they expressed in the US Constitution and First Amendment) demand is a government that is neutral between atheism and religious belief, as well as between different sorts of religious belief. Stalin was an atheist, and so are we; Osama bin Laden was a monotheist, and so was Mister

Rogers. Stalinism has about as much in common with the kind of secularism we are advocating as the Taliban does with mainstream American Protestantism.

Conclusion

The United States Is and Should Remain a Free Country and Not *a Christian Nation*

In any but a superficial sense, the United States is not and should not become a Christian nation. Atheists though we are, we do not think it is or should become an atheist nation, either. Atheists as individual citizens can argue against religion and work to reduce its power and influence; individual religious citizens can similarly argue for their religious views and freely promote those ideas—but not through government.

We do not argue that religion is merely a private matter nor do we say that religious ideas should not be brought into the public square or the marketplace of ideas. We only argue that any idea, religious or not, should not be brought into the public sphere unless criticism of it is welcome. Political ideals may certainly be rooted in religious beliefs, but in a democratic society, proponents of public policies must be prepared to defend those ideas in terms that go beyond mere assertions of God's alleged will. To put it another way, anyone seeking to change public policy must understand that in our secular government, saying "God says it should be this way" is never a sufficient basis for adopting or changing a policy, regardless of how deeply held and sincere the religious belief that underlies the statement. *Secular* means nonreligious, not antireligious, and a *government* that works to support or to undercut religious ideas or that urges its citizens to be religious or to avoid religiosity is dangerous to religious liberty for anyone.

American secularism is not, despite loud and fierce claims to the contrary, some sort of atheism-protection racket, an antireligion subterfuge, or a protect-the-feelings-of-overly-sensitive-atheists scheme. It is instead the *only* approach that can consistently secure religious liberty for all.

There really is no middle ground here: either governments have the power to make religious decisions for citizens, or governments lack that power. As noted and quoted above (in "Why Secularism?") James Madison, later to act as "the father of the Constitution," summed up nicely the core of the argument: "Who does not see that the same authority which can establish Christianity in exclusion of all other religions may establish, with the same ease, any particular sect of Christians in exclusion of all other sects?"[1]

Freedom, especially religious liberty, is worth having and protecting. This seems self-evident to most of us, regardless of our religious or irreligious beliefs. The American ideal is not, despite myths and misconceptions held by many, of all religious and political persuasions, pure majoritarian democracy. Nor is the core ideal that has made America strong, a beacon to individuals and nations everywhere, tied to any religious idea.

The evidence and logic are overwhelming: If you thought that America is or ought to be a Christian nation, then what you thought was wrong and you should change your mind, if only for selfish reasons. To guarantee your own religious liberty, you really do have to help protect everyone else's, too.

The secularism at the heart of American liberty, established by the authors of the US Constitution (including the First Amendment and extended by the Fourteenth Amendment) is compatible with a wide range of political philosophies, from doctrinaire libertarianism to democratic socialism, from true conservatism to left-of-center progressivism. It is compatible with most nonreligious viewpoints and most religions. If a religion requires its adherents to involve government in supporting the religion to any degree, to that degree American secularism will be unacceptable to its followers. Such secularism is not compatible with theocratic, statist, or other forms of absolutist, authoritarian government.

For all who agree with us that secularism is the only way forward, the only proper ideal for securing religious liberty and domestic tranquility in America, the question now is what must be done to protect secularism. The answers are multiple and depend in some cases on the individual's own political or religious preferences. All should support the work of national organizations such as Americans United for Separation of Church and State or the American Civil Liberties Union. Each nonreligious American should work within and support national organizations like American Atheists, the Council for Secular Humanism, the American Humanist Association, the Richard Dawkins Foundation, and the Freedom from Religion Foundation, and with local or regional groups as well. For secularists, especially those of the irreligious sort, support the strategic plan laid out in chapter 9 of Sean Faircloth's *Attack of the Theocrats*.[2] Religious Americans should work within the mainstream church that best matches their religious beliefs to insist on secularism and support for it.

Letters to editors of all sorts of publications will help, especially when false arguments or facts in need of correction appear in those publications. Knowing the facts, the history and the logic, that support secularism and then speaking up, cordially but firmly, in public debates (formal or just at the workplace water cooler) is essential. Silence will generally be assumed to be consent—and we must speak up. Lobbying steadfastly for real neutrality in government at all levels and in public schools must be continual, as must be pressure for accurate curricular materials in schools everywhere. National organizations like the Secular Coalition for America can help in this.

The quintessentially American ideal is not to trust in the government, nor in any party or religious authority, nor in any charter or document, but instead in a democratic republic, a society where no authority ultimately trumps the inalienable rights of every individual. Americans should not blindly trust in Washington, DC. We do not unthinkingly trust in the Declaration of Independence or even in the Constitution of the United States (including the Bill of Rights). And we do not rely on or, *as a nation*, call on or trust in any god. We rely instead on competing ideas and competing individuals, with careful safeguards for the rights of every individual, no matter what any of them think or say or believe. *E pluribus unum*—out of the many, one. In freedom we trust.

Acknowledgments

Two people—**Rob Boston** (a leader of Americans United for Separation of Church and State) and **Diane Buckner** (wife to Ed, mother to Michael)—stand out as especially important to the development of this book, but many, many others have contributed as well. Rob has researched and written on the subject at hand for many years, inspired us with his thorough and careful research and clear writing, and responded to an early version of the book with thoughtful, detailed suggestions—and to other requests since then. Diane read and reread nearly all the book and its many predecessor writings, with advice ranging across all the possibilities, from deleting commas to toning down sarcasm to recasting opaque sentences or paragraphs. She has long been a major supporter in both our lives and has also been crucial for this work.

We are also deeply grateful to the many people on the staff of Prometheus Books who have put in such effective work on behalf of this book. Leading these consummate professionals was our patient, expert, good-humored, and thorough editor, Jade Zora Ballard, but we benefited as well from efforts by Steven L. Mitchell, Catherine Roberts-Abel, Bruce Carle, Grace Conti-Zilsberger, Julia DeGraf, Meghan Quinn, Melissa Raé Shofner, Amy Vigrass, and others whose names we did not even learn.

We have both written on the subjects addressed in this book many times: in letters to editors, online, and in previously published material. Some of the material in this book is based on some of those earlier writings (or on talks or debates by Ed). We thank the many people involved, directly or indirectly, in those earlier efforts.

Some (not cited here but named in many cases in the text or bibliography) have contributed in a negative way with their literally incredible offerings, published and unpublished, in support of the idea that the United States is or should be a Christian nation. They taught us that education matters—that we should never take for granted what we know is true.

But even among the more credible and supportive people listed alphabetically below, none are responsible for any errors we have made, and certainly none should be presumed to have come to the same specific conclusions we have. Some gave us a key moment (offered just the right encouragement at the right time); some gave us hours; some helped us sharpen a point or find a source; some may not even know they helped.

We thank all who helped, especially: Dan Barker, Tim Binga, Claudia Bright, Ronald Bright, CCPLS (Cobb County [Georgia] Public Library System) staff, Robert Collins, Richard Dawkins, DeKalb County [Georgia] Public Library staff, Jan Eisler, Tom Flynn, Adam Friedstein, Oliver Halle, Kathleen Johnson, Edwin Kagin, Helen Kagin, Woody Kaplan, Robert Konopelski Sr., Paul Kurtz, Steven Lowe, Jay Lucas, Dwight Lyman, Jim MacIver, Dennis Martin, Jack McKinney, Dennis Middlebrooks, Michael Newdow, Matt Noll, Massimo Pigliucci, Joanne Robinson, Joseph Scrivner, Charles Shapiro, Dave Silverman, Herb Silverman, John C. "Chris" Snider, Lew Southern, Edward Tabash, Floyd Taylor, Sheila Tefft, Judy Thompson, James Underdown, US Library of Congress staff, Pamela Whissel, Steve Yothment, and Frank Zindler. We also thank the many members of the Bright-Brownson-Buckner-Noll-Smith clan who have given us love and support in general.

Appendix
Key Dates—A List of Important Dates Related to the History of a Secular United States

313—Emperor Constantine issues the Edict of Milan, legalizing the practice of Christianity in the Roman Empire

380—Emperor Theodosius issues the Edict of Thessalonica, making orthodox Christianity the state religion of the Roman Empire

389–391—Theodosian decrees outlaw the practice of paganism in the Roman Empire

1066—Norman invasion of England, Battle of Hastings

1209–1229—The Albigensian Crusade violently suppresses Catharism in southern France; it is during this religious war that the sentiment "Kill them all; the Lord will know his own" is supposedly first uttered (by a Catholic monk)

1215—Barons of King John issue the Magna Carta

1290—King Edward I of England issues an edict ordering that all Jews be expelled from the kingdom

1306—King Philip IV issues an edict ordering that all Jews be expelled from France

1415 (July 16)—Religious reformer Jan Hus is burned at the stake for heresy in Constance, Germany

1491—The Treaty of Granada provides guarantees of religious liberty to the Muslim inhabitants of Granada (the last Muslim state in what is now Spain) upon the conquest of that kingdom by Spain

1492—King Ferdinand and Queen Isabella of Spain order all Jews expelled from the kingdom and its dominions

1502—Following forced conversions of Muslims to Christianity and the burning of Islamic books, resulting in a Muslim uprising in Granada in 1499–1501, the Spanish monarchy voids the terms of the Treaty of Granada and orders all Muslims in the territory of the kingdom of Castile to convert to Christianity or be expelled from that kingdom;

in 1526, the Muslims of Aragon are also forced to convert or face exile

1517—Martin Luther publishes his Ninety-Five Theses calling for the reformation of the Catholic Church

1534—King Henry VIII is declared "supreme head" of the Church of England; this and other reforms lead to the excommunication of Henry by the pope in 1538 and the separation of the Church of England from the Roman Catholic Church

1536—English theologian and scholar William Tynedale, first to translate the Bible into ordinary English, is "strangled to death while tied at the stake, and then his dead body [is] burned"

1536—John Calvin publishes his *Institutes of the Christian Religion*

1543—English parliament makes it illegal for commoners "to read the New Testament in English"

1553–1558—Nearly three hundred Protestants are burned at the stake during the reign of Queen Mary I of England as part of her effort to reestablish the Catholic Church in that country

1553 (October 27)—Michael Servetus is burned at the stake for heresy in Calvinist Geneva

1572—St. Bartholomew's Day massacre; thousands of Huguenots (French Protestants) are killed in one of the most infamous incidents in the French Wars of Religion (1562–1598)

1598—Edict of Nantes is issued by King Henry IV of France, granting religious liberty to the Huguenots and ending the French Wars of Religion

1600 (February 17)—Giordano Bruno is burned at the stake for heresy in Catholic Rome

1609—The Moriscos (descendants of Muslims who had been converted to Christianity, many by force) are expelled from Spain on suspicion that many are still secretly practicing Islam

1618–1648—The Thirty Years' War, at least in part a religious conflict between Catholics and Protestants, devastates large areas of Germany, with some areas losing over half their population

1620 (November 11)—Mayflower Compact is agreed to in Massachusetts—important social compact, asserted allegiance to God/Christianity and to King James

1649 (April 21)—Maryland Toleration Act grants freedom of worship to all Christians (Catholic or Protestant) in that colony, while maintaining the death penalty for any person who denied the Christian doctrine of the Trinity

1685—Edict of Fontainebleau is issued by King Louis XIV of France, revoking the Edict of Nantes' guarantee of religious liberty for the Huguenots, hundreds of thousands of whom were driven out of France (to the economic loss of the kingdom, as those driven out included many skilled craftsmen in a variety of important industries)

1692–1693—Twenty people are put to death in Massachusetts during the Salem witch trials

1776 (July 2)—American Declaration of Independence is agreed upon

1776 (July 4)—American Independence is declared

1781 (September–October)—Battle of Yorktown, last major battle of Revolutionary War

1782–1784—Treaty of Paris is negotiated, agreed to, and ratified—officially ending the Revolutionary War

1785 (June 20)—"Memorial and Remonstrance against Religious Assessments," a petition written by James Madison and subscribed to by over ten thousand, is delivered to the Virginia General Assembly

1786—Virginia Statute for Religious Freedom is passed (Jefferson wrote it in 1779)

1786–1787 (winter)—Tripolitan ambassador to England meets with John Adams and Thomas Jefferson in London

1787 (May 25)—US Constitutional Convention is convened in Philadelphia

1787 (July 13)—Northwest Ordinance, adopted under the Articles of Confederation, establishes the Northwest Territory

1787 (September 17)—US Constitution is agreed to by delegates

1788 (June 21)—US Constitution is ratified (New Hampshire, the ninth state to do so, voted for ratification)

1789 (March 4)—First president (George Washington) and First Congress under the Constitution take office; start of the United States as now governed

1790 (May 29)—Rhode Island, last of the original states to ratify, voted for the Constitution (making it unanimous)

1791 (December 15)—Bill of Rights, including First Amendment, is ratified

1796 (November 4)—Treaty with Bey and People of Tripoli is agreed upon; included: "Article XI. As the government of the United States is not in any sense founded on the Christian religion . . ."

1797 (June 7)—Treaty with Tripoli is unanimously agreed to by US Senate

1797 (June 10)—Treaty with Tripoli is signed and proclaimed by President John Adams

1833—Massachusetts repeals, by a ten-to-one vote, the establishment of the Congregationalist Church in the state—thus ending the last establishment of religion in America (the Fourteenth Amendment eliminates the possibility of any future establishment)

1843—Rioting over which Bible to use in public schools in Philadelphia between Protestants and Catholics kills thirteen; homes and churches are burned

1864 (December 8)—Pope Pius IX promulgates the *Syllabus of Errors*, condemning many tenets of modernism and liberalism

1868 (July 9)—Fourteenth Amendment is ratified: "No State shall make or enforce any law which shall abridge the privileges or immunities of citizens of the United States"

2001 (September 11)—Members of the religious (Islamic) terrorist group al Qaeda mount the deadliest and most destructive terrorist attacks ever carried out on American soil

Notes

INTRODUCTION

1. See for example, Richard A. Oppel Jr. and Erik Eckholm, "Prominent Pastor Calls Romney's Church a Cult," *New York Times*, October 8, 2011; Harold Bloom, "Will This Election Be the Mormon Breakthrough?" *New York Times Sunday Review*, November 13, 2011; and Richard A. Oppel Jr., "Santorum Questions Education and Obama," *New York Times*, February 19, 2012.

2. James F. Simon, *What Kind of Nation* (New York: Simon & Schuster, 2002), p. 123.

3. Edward J. Larson, *A Magnificent Catastrophe: The Tumultuous Election of 1800, America's First Presidential Campaign* (New York: Free Press, 2007), p. 29.

4. David Gibson, "New Alabama Governor Says Non-Christians 'Not My Brother, Not My Sister,'" *Politics Daily*, January 18, 2011, http://www.politics-daily.com/2011/01/18/new-alabama-governor-says-non-christians-not-my-brother-not-my/print/ (accessed February 28, 2011).

5. "Inauguration Proclamation," *Bowie County* (TX) *Citizens Tribune*, January 5, 2011.

6. Lawrence D. Jones, "Rick Perry Invites US Governors to 'Prayer and Fasting Rally,'" *Christian Post*, June 6, 2011, http://www.christianpost.com/news/texas-gov-rick-perry-to-host-prayer-rally-to-solve-americas-problems-50897/ (accessed August 28, 2012).

7. Robert Wilonsky, "Rick Perry Wants You to Pray for Rain," April 21, 2011, Politics, *Dallas Observer Blogs*, http://blogs.dallasobserver.com/unfairpark/2011/04/rick_perry_wants_you_to_pray_f.php (accessed July 6, 2011).

8. Jones, "Rick Perry Invites US Governors to 'Prayer and Fasting Rally.'"

9. Ray Suarez, *The Holy Vote: The Politics of Faith in America* (New York: HarperCollins, 2006), pp. 262–63.

10. Bill O'Reilly, "Sarah Palin on National Day of Prayer Controversy," *The O'Reilly Factor*, May 7, 2010, http://www.foxnews.com/on-air/oreilly/2010/05/07/sarah-palin-national-day-prayer-controversy (accessed March 3, 2011). See also Sarah Palin, "Introduction," *America by Heart: Reflections on Family, Faith, and Flag* (New York: HarperCollins, 2010), pp. xvii–xviii.

11. Lee Fang, "Gingrich: Americans Surrounded by 'Paganism,'" *Think Progress*, June 6, 2009, http://thinkprogress.org/politics/2009/06/06/44283/

gingrich-paganism/ (accessed March 3, 2011).

12. Newt Gingrich, *To Save America: Stopping Obama's Secular-Socialist Machine* (Washington, DC: Regnery, 2010), p. 268.

13. Laurie Goodstein, "Omitting Clergy at 9/11 Ceremony Prompts Protests," *New York Times*, September 9, 2011.

14. Michael Medved, *The 10 Big Lies about America: Combating Destructive Distortions about Our Nation* (New York: Crown Forum, 2008), pp. 72–94.

15. John A. Stormer, *Betrayed by the Bench: How Judge-Made Law Has Transformed America's Constitution, Courts and Culture* (Florissant, MO: Liberty Bell, 2007), p. 41.

16. Melanie Phillips, *The World Turned Upside Down: The Global Battle over God, Truth, and Power* (Jackson, TN: Encounter Books, 2010), flap copy.

17. Mark Weldon Whitten, *The Myth of Christian America: What You Need to Know about the Separation of Church and State* (Macon, GA: Smyth and Helwys, 1999), p. 28.

18. Thomas Paine, *The Rights of Man* (1791; repr., New York: Heritage Press, 1961), p. 215.

19. Thomas Jefferson, *Writings: Autobiography; Notes on the State of Virginia; Public Papers; Addresses, Messages, and Replies; Miscellany; Letters*, ed. Merrill D. Peterson (New York: Library of America, 1984), p. 285.

20. James Madison, "Letter to Robert Walsh, March 2, 1819," in *The Complete Madison: His Basic Writings*, ed. Saul K. Padover (New York: Harper and Brothers, 1953; Kraus Reprint Co., 1971), pp. 309–10.

21. Gingrich, *To Save America*, p. 6.

22. Richard Cohen, "The Myth of American Exceptionalism," *Washington Post*, May 9, 2011.

23. Mark Landler, "A Moment for Obama to Savor, If Briefly," *New York Times*, August 23, 2011; and Sarah Wheaton, "News from Libya Pushes G.O.P. Candidates to Respond," *New York Times*, August 23, 2011.

24. Robert A. Slayton, "When a Catholic Terrified the Heartland," *New York Times*, December 11, 2011.

25. Display at the LBJ Library in Austin, Texas; photographed by author Ed Buckner on June 11, 2011.

26. John C. "Chris" Snider, personal communication with the author.

27. Cullen Murphy, "The Certainty of Doubt," *New York Times*, February 12, 2012.

28. J. Gordon Melton, *Melton's Encyclopedia of American Religions*, 8th ed. (Detroit, MI: Gale, 2009), p. 44.

29. Robert S. Alley, "Public Education and the Public Good," *William &*

Mary Bill of Rights Journal 4, no. 277 (1995): 315, http://scholarhip.law .wm.edu/wmborj/vol4/iss1/6 (accessed September 14, 2011).

30. Barack Obama, *The Audacity of Hope: Thoughts on Reclaiming the American Dream* (New York: Crown, 2006), p. 218.

31. Barack Obama, "Inaugural Address," January 20, 2009 (delivered), *White House Blog*, http://www.whitehouse.gov/blog/inauguraladdress, January 21, 2009 (posted) (accessed August 22, 2012).

32. Rob Boston, *Why the Religious Right Is Wrong about Separation of Church and State* (Amherst, NY: Prometheus Books, 1993), pp. 86–87.

33. *The Holy Bible, New International Version, NIV* (Grand Rapids, MI: Biblica, 1973, 1978, 1984, and 2011).

CHAPTER 1. WHY SECULARISM?

1. Mortimer J. Adler, ed., "The Declaration of Independence," in *The Annals of America*, vol. 2, *1755 –1783, Resistance and Revolution* (Chicago: Encyclopedia Britannica, 1968), p. 447.

2. Mortimer J. Adler, ed., "Article V, The Constitution of the United States," in *The Annals of America*, vol. 3, *1784 –1796, Organizing the New Nation* (Chicago: Encyclopedia Britannica, 1968), p. 129.

3. "Gender in the United States," *nationalatlas.gov*, http://nationalatlas .gov/articles/people/a_gender.html (accessed August 23, 2011).

4. Alice Duer Miller, "Why We Don't Want Men to Vote" (1915), quoted in Jone Johnson Lewis, "August 26, 1920: The Day the Suffrage Battle Was Won," About.com, Women's History, http://womenshistory.about.com/od/ suffrage1900/a/august_26_wed.htm (accessed August 28, 2011).

5. Mortimer J. Adler, ed., "Amendment XIII; Civil War Amendments to the Constitution," in *The Annals of America*, vol. 10, *1866 –1883, Reconstruction and Industrialization* (Chicago: Encyclopedia Britannica, 1968), p. 133.

6. Johnny H. Killian and George A. Costello, eds., "Amendments to the Constitution of the United States of America," in *The Constitution of the United States of America: Analysis and Interpretation* (Washington, DC: US Government Printing Office, 1996), p. 36.

7. Amir Shah, "Afghan Convert Freed from Prison," *Atlanta Journal-Constitution*, March 28, 2006.

8. Mortimer J. Adler, ed., "James Madison: Against Religious Assessments," in *The Annals of America*, vol. 3, *1784 –1796, Organizing the New Nation* (Chicago: Encyclopedia Britannica, 1968), p. 17.

9. Thomas Jefferson, "The Morals of Jesus; Letter to Dr. Benjamin Rush, with a Syllabus, Apr. 21, 1803," in *Writings: Autobiography; Notes on the State of Virginia; Public Papers; Addresses, Messages, and Replies; Miscellany; Letters*, ed. Merrill D. Peterson (New York: Library of America, 1984), p. 1123.

10. James Madison, *James Madison: A Biography in His Own Words*, vol. 1, ed. Merrill D. Peterson (New York: Newsweek, 1974), pp. 30–31.

11. Douglas Southall Freeman, *R. E. Lee: A Biography*, vol. 1 (New York: Charles Scribner's Sons, 1934), p. 373.

CHAPTER 2. ATHEISTS ARE NOT UN-AMERICAN

1. Louis Rabaut, *Congressional Record of the 83rd Congress, Second Session* (February 12, 1954), p. 1700.

2. Thomas Jefferson, "Letter to Thomas Law, June 13, 1814," in *Writings: Autobiography; Notes on the State of Virginia; Public Papers; Addresses, Messages, and Replies; Miscellany; Letters*, ed. Merrill D. Peterson (New York: Library of America, 1984), p. 1336.

3. George Washington, "Letter to Tench Tilghman, March 24, 1784," in *Writings*, ed. John Rhodehamel (New York: Library of America, 1997), pp. 555–56.

4. George Washington, "Letter to the Hebrew Congregation in Newport, Rhode Island," in *Writings*, p. 767.

5. Thomas Jefferson, "The Homage of Reason," "Letter to [Jefferson's nephew] Peter Carr, Aug. 10, 1787," in *Writings*, pp. 900–906.

6. Eric Foner, *Tom Paine and Revolutionary America* (London: Oxford University Press, 1976), p. 270.

7. Steven C. Lowe, "Platform Star: Robert G. Ingersoll in Washington," *White House History*, no. 31 (Summer 2012): 36–43.

8. Jon Krakauer, *Where Men Win Glory: The Odyssey of Pat Tillman* (New York: Doubleday, 2009), pp. 116, 143, 273–74, and 314–16. And C. T. Chivers, "10 Years into Afghan War, a Thunderous Duel," *New York Times*, October 8, 2011.

CHAPTER 3. RELIGION AND POLITICS NOW

1. Jennifer Burns, "Atlas Spurned," *New York Times*, August 14, 2012; and Paul Krugman, "Galt, Gold and God," *New York Times*, August 24, 2012.

2. Rachel Zoll, Associated Press, "A Catholic Connection: VP Choices Have Similar Religious Backgrounds," *Marietta* [GA] *Daily Journal*, August 25, 2012; Laurie Goodstein, "Invitation to Cardinal Shows G.O.P.'s Catholic Push," *New York Times*, August 25, 2012; and Sharon Otterman, "Dolan to Deliver Prayer at Democrats' Convention," *New York Times*, August 29, 2012.

3. Lisa Desjardins, "As Politicians Talk More about Faith, Voters Seem to Want Less," *CNN Belief Blog*, April 27, 2012, http://religion.blogs.cnn.com/2012/04/27/as-politicians-talk-more-about-faith-voters-seem-to-want-less/ (accessed April 27, 2012).

4. Cal Thomas, "Media's Obsession with Romney's Mormonism Latest Proof of Its Religion Deficit," *Marietta* [GA] *Daily Journal*, May 24, 2012.

5. T. M. Luhrmann, "Do as I Do, Not as I Say," *New York Times*, May 7, 2012.

6. Andrew Malcolm, "Poll Shows Rev. Jeremiah Wright Hurting Barack Obama," Top of the Ticket, *Los Angeles Times*, March 17, 2008, http://latimes-blogs.latimes.com/washington/2008/03/poll-shows-rev.html (accessed August 16, 2011).

7. Michael D. Shear, "Race and Religion Rear Their Heads: Political Memo," *New York Times*, May 19, 2012.

8. Greg Sargent, "Romney Stands by Invocation of Rev. Wright," *WP Opinions*, May 17, 2012, http://www.washingtonpost.com/blogs/plum-line/post/i-stand-by-what-i-said-whatever-it-was/2012/05/17/gIQADnyhWU_blog.html (accessed May 23, 2012).

9. Mark Oppenheimer, "A Campaign Pitch Rekindles the Question: Just What Is Liberation Theology?" Beliefs, *New York Times*, May 26, 2012.

10. Anthony Stevens-Arroyo, "Hagee and the 'Whore of Babylon,'" May 20, 2008, On Faith, Catholic America, *Washington Post*, http://newsweek.washingtonpost.com/onfaith/catholicamerica/2008/05/the_whore_of_babylon.html (accessed August 16, 2011).

11. Stephen Labaton, "Constitution Based in Christian Principles, McCain Says," *New York Times*, September 27, 2007, http://www.nytimes.com/2007/09/29/us/politics/29cnd-mccain.html?ref=politics (accessed August 16, 2011).

12. Richard Cohen, "The Myth of American Exceptionalism," *Washington Post*, May 9, 2011.

13. Barbara Ehrenreich, *Bright-Sided: How the Relentless Promotion of Positive*

Thinking Has Undermined America (New York: Metropolitan Books, 2009), pp. 6–7.

14. Kyle Mantyla, "Huckabee: Americans Should Be Forced, at Gunpoint, to Learn from David Barton," *Right Wing Watch*, March 25, 2011, http://www.rightwingwatch.org/content/huckabee-americans-should-be-forced-gunpoint-learn-david-barton (accessed August 16, 2011).

15. "Heather," "Rick Santorum Explains Right Wing Anger: Obama Wants to Change US from Being a Judeo-Christian Nation," *Crooks & Liars, Video Café*, April 11, 2010, http://videocafe.crooksandliars.com/heather/rick-santorum-explains-right-wing-anger-ob (accessed March 12, 2011).

16. Frank Bruni, "The Do-Over Derby," *New York Times*, February 14, 2012.

17. Amy Davidson, "Santorum Sees a Guillotine," Close Read, *New Yorker*, February 9, 2012, http://www.newyorker.com/online/blogs/closeread/2012/02/santorum-sees-a-guillotine.html (accessed February 14, 2012); and Eugene Robinson, "Drumming Up a Phony War on Religion," PostOpinions, *Washington Post*, February 14, 2012, http://www.washingtonpost.com/opinions/drumming-up-a-phony-war-on-religion/2012/02/14/gIQAdvpUER_story.html (accessed February 15, 2012).

18. Richard A. Oppel Jr., "Santorum Questions Education and Obama," *New York Times*, February 19, 2012.

19. Michael Barbaro, "Santorum Makes Case for Religion in Public Sphere," *New York Times*, February 27, 2012.

20. Maureen Dowd, "GOP Appears to Stand for Ghastly Outdated Party," *Atlanta Journal-Constitution*, February 26, 2012.

21. Andrew Sullivan, "How State Beat Church: Conservatives Gleefully Revived the Culture Wars—But They're Not Winning," *Newsweek*, February 20, 2012, p. 45.

22. Joe Nocera, "A Revolutionary Idea," *New York Times*, February 25, 2012; John M. Barry, "God, Government and Roger Williams' Big Idea," *Smithsonian*, January 2012, pp. 72–90; and John M. Barry, "Roger Williams: America's First Rebel," *Church & State* 65, no. 7 (July/August 2012): 11–12.

23. Charles M. Blow, "What Rick Santorum Wrought," *Campaign Stops* (blog), *New York Times*, April 11, 2012, http://campaignstops.blogs.nytimes.com/2012/04/11/what-rick-santorum-wrought/ (accessed April 11, 2012).

24. "dogemperor," "The *Other* Members of Hillary's 'Family' Cell," *Daily Kos*, April 7, 2008, http://www.dailykos.com/story/2008/04/07/491583/-The-*other*-members-of-Hillarys-Family-cell (accessed August 16, 2011).

25. Max Blumenthal, "The Witch Hunter Anoints Sarah Palin," *Huffington Post*, September 24, 2008, http://www.huffingtonpost.com/max-blumenthal/the-witch-hunter-anoints_b_128805.html (accessed August 17, 2011).

26. Scott Wong, "Eugene Robinson: Christine O'Donnell 'Looks Like She Might Be a Witch,'" *Politico*, October 5, 2010, http://www.politico.com/news/stories/1010/43137.html (accessed August 17, 2011).

27. Pamela Geller, *The Post-American Presidency: The Obama Administration's War on America* (New York: Threshhold Editions, 2010), p. 38.

28. Ibid., p. 59.

29. Ibid., p. 201.

30. Newt Gingrich, *Rediscovering God in America: Reflections on the Role of Faith in Our History* (Nashville, TN: Integrity House, 2006), p. 6.

31. Bill O'Reilly, "Sarah Palin on National Day of Prayer Controversy," *The O'Reilly Factor*, May 7, 2010, http://www.foxnews.com/on-air/oreilly/transcript/sarah-palin-national-day-prayer-controversy (accessed March 3, 2011).

32. Willoughby Mariano, "Cain Mistakes Declaration of Independence Language for Constitution," Georgia Truth-O-Meter/PolitiFact, *Atlanta Journal-Constitution*, May 25, 2011.

33. Eugene Robinson, "Stand Up to Herman Cain's Bigotry," Post-Opinions, *Washington Post*, July 18, 2011, http://www.washingtonpost.com/opinions/stand-up-to-herman-cains-bigotry/2011/07/18/gIQA5QChMI_story.html (accessed July 19, 2011).

34. Jeremy Redmon, "Cain Says God Told Him to Run," *Atlanta Journal-Constitution*, November 13, 2011.

35. Sarah Palin, *America by Heart: Reflections on Family, Faith, and Flag* (New York: HarperCollins, 2010), p. 195.

36. Ibid., p. 184.

37. Andrew Kruger, "Michele Bachmann on Gay Marriage: God Inspires Inequality," Chicago/Religion & Spirituality, *examiner.com*, April 18, 2011, http://www.examiner.com/freethought-in-chicago/michele-bachmann-on-gay-marriage-god-inspires-inequality (accessed July 17, 2011).

38. Sheryl Gay Stolberg, "Where God and Justice Were Once Intertwined: Bachmann's Years at Law School," *New York Times*, October 14, 2011.

39. Associated Press, "Last-Place Finisher Drops Bid," *Atlanta Journal-Constitution*, January 5, 2012.

40. Warren Throckmorton, "Ron Paul Touts Endorsement of Pastor Who Defends Death Penalty for Gays, Delinquent Children & Adultery," December 28, 2011, http://wthrockmorton.com/2011/12/28/kayserendorsemen/ (accessed January 2, 2012); also Pema Levy and Benjy Sarlin, "Death Penalty for Gays: Ron Paul Courts the Religious Fringe in Iowa," *Talking Points Memo*, December 28, 2011, http://2012.talkingpointsmemo.com/2011/12/ron-paul-hired-anti-gay-activist-to-run-iowa-campaign.php (accessed January 2, 2012). See Philip

G. Kayser, "Is the Death Penalty Just?" *Biblical Blueprints*, Revision 3, © 2011/2009/2007, http://www.biblicalblueprints.org/wp-content/uploads/2011/01/DeathPenalty.pdf (accessed October 8, 2012) for the actual text of Kayser's writings.

41. Danny Wilcox Frazier, "Romney's Mormon Question," *Time*, May 10, 2007, http://www.time.com/time/magazine/article/0,9171,1619552,00.html (accessed August 20, 2011); Richard A. Oppel Jr. and Erik Eckholm, "Prominent Pastor Calls Romney's Church a Cult," *New York Times*, October 8, 2011; and Laurie Goodstein, "The Theological Differences Behind Evangelical Unease with Romney," *New York Times*, January 15, 2012.

42. Kathleen Kennedy Townsend, "Sarah Palin Is Wrong about John F. Kennedy, Religion and Politics," Opinions, *Washington Post*, December 3, 2010, http://www.washingtonpost.com/wp-dyn/content/article/2010/12/03/AR2010120303209.html (accessed August 20, 2011).

43. Michael D. Shear, Erik Eckholm, and Ashley Parker, "Once Again, Social Issues Test Romney," *New York Times*, October 9, 2011; Bryan Fischer, "Islam and the First Amendment: Privileges but Not Rights," *Renew America*, March 24, 2011, http://www.renewamerica.com/columns/fischer/110324 (accessed October 9, 2011); and Kyle Mantyla, "Fischer: First Amendment Does Not Apply to Mormons," People for the American Way, *Right Wing Watch*, September 29, 2001, http://www.rightwingwatch.org/content/fischer-first-amendment-does-not-apply-mormons (accessed October 9, 2011).

44. Jane Mayer, "Letter from Tupelo: Bully Pulpit; An Evangelist Talk-Show Host's Campaign to Control the Republican Party," *New Yorker*, June 18, 2012, pp. 56–65.

45. J. Spencer Fluhman, "Why We Fear Mormons," *New York Times*, June 4, 2012.

46. David V. Mason, "I'm a Mormon, Not a Christian," *New York Times*, June 13, 2012.

47. Frank Rich, "Who in God's Name Is Mitt Romney? His Greatest Passion Is Something He's Determined to Keep Secret," *New York* magazine, January 29, 2012, http://nymag.com/news/frank-rich/mitt-romney-2012-2/ (accessed February 1, 2012).

48. Frank Bruni, "Mitt's Muffled Soul," *New York Times*, February 5, 2012.

49. Jodi Kantor, "Convention Voices Hope to Add Texture to Romney's Faith," *New York Times*, August 30, 2012; and Jeff Zeleny, "'Now Is the Moment': Romney Talks of Faith, Family—and Fixing US," *Atlanta Journal-Constitution*, August 31, 2012.

50. Glynnis MacNicol, "Romney: Anger over Wealth Distribution Is All about 'Envy,'" *Business Insider*, January 12, 2012, http://articles.businessinsider

.com/2012-01-12/politics/30618859_1_mitt-romney-envy-matt-lauer#ixzz1o SfIWfET (accessed March 7, 2012).

51. Forrest Wilder, "Rick Perry's Army of God," *Texas Observer*, August 13, 2011; see also Jon Meacham, "In God We Trust: Few in Number, Dominionists Believe the Bible Should Govern Society," Viewpoint, *Time*, September 26, 2011.

52. Kurt Andersen, "Our Politics Are Sick," *New York Times*, August 20, 2011.

53. Dana Milbank, "Rick Perry Is No Libertarian," PostOpinions, *Washington Post*, August 30, 2011, http://www.washingtonpost.com/opinions/rick -perry-is-no-libertarian/2011/08/30./glQA6lsbql_story.html (accessed September 2, 2011) .

54. Thomas Beaumont, "Republicans Seek Iowa Social Conservatives' Nod," *Marietta* [GA] *Daily Journal*, November 20, 2011.

55. Michael Gerson, "Two Parties Pray to the Same God, but Different Economists," *Washington Post*, August 4, 2011.

56. Michael Gerson, "Too Much Religion in Politics?" *Washington Post*, March 27, 2012.

57. Jennifer Steinhauer, "In God We Trust, with the House's Help," *New York Times*, November 2, 2011.

58. White House press release, "Remarks by the President at the University of Indonesia in Jakarta, Indonesia," November 10, 2010, http://www.white house.gov/the-press-office/2010/11/10/remarks-president-university -indonesia-jakarta-indonesia (accessed February 10, 2012).

59. Steinhauer, "In God We Trust"; and Andrew Taylor, "In God We Trust: Why Congress Reaffirmed the US Motto," Latest News Wires, *Christian Science Monitor*, http://www.csmonitor.com/USE/Latest-News_Wires/2011/ 1103/In-God-We-Trust-Why-Congress-reaffirmed-the-US-motto (accessed November 3, 2011).

60. Joel Siegel, "Obama Leaves God out of Thanksgiving Speech, Riles Critics," *ABC News*, November 25, 2011, http://abcnews.go.com/Politics/ obama-omits-god-thanksgiving-address-riles-critics/story?id=15028644 (accessed November 26, 2011).

61. Julie Pace, "'Faith and Values' Help Guide President," *Atlanta Journal-Constitution*, February 3, 2012.

62. Erick Erickson, "The Perversion of the Words of Our Lord Jesus Christ by the Sinner Barack H. Obama," Diary, *RedState*, February 5, 2012, http://www.redstate.com/erick/2012/02/05/the-perversion-of-the-words-of -our-lord-jesus-christ-by-the-sinner-barack-h-obama/ (accessed February 6, 2012).

63. Cal Thomas, "'Spinning' the Bible: Obama Misusing Scripture to Push for Higher Taxes," *Marietta* [GA] *Daily Journal*, February 7, 2012.

64. Martin Schram, "A Case of Classic 'Gingrichian Deceit by Distortion,'" *Marietta* [GA] *Daily Journal*, February 2, 2012.

65. Gail Collins, "Tales from the Kitchen Table," *New York Times*, February 10, 2012; Gail Collins, "The Battle behind the Fight," *New York Times*, February 11, 2012.

66. Kathleen Parker, "Contraception Rule an Assault on Liberty," *Atlanta Journal-Constitution*, February 8, 2012.

67. Kevin Drum, "Why I'm Feeling So Hard-Nosed over the Contraception Affair," Politics, Reproductive Rights, Sex and Gender, Top Stories, *Mother Jones*, February 10, 2012, http://motherjones.com/kevin-drum/2012/02/why-im-so-hardnosed-over-contraception-affair (accessed February 11, 2012).

68. Stephanie Mencimer, "What War on Religion?" *Mother Jones*, February 16, 2012, http://motherjones.com/politics/2012/02/what-war-on-religion-obama-catholic-charities (accessed February 21, 2012).

69. Laurie Goodstein, "Bishops Say Rules on Gay Parents Limit Freedom of Religion," *New York Times*, December 28, 2011, http://www.nytimes.com/2011/12/29/us/for-bishops-a-battle-over-whose-rights-prevail.html?pagewanted=all (accessed February 27, 2012).

70. "Catholic Charities: At a Glance," *Catholic Charities USA*, 2010, http://www.catholiccharitiesusa.org/document.doc?id=2853 (accessed February 27, 2012).

71. Rachel Zoll, "Catholic Groups Sue over Obama Mandate," *Atlanta Journal-Constitution*, May 22, 2012; ("Most Rev.") John J. Myers, Archbishop of Newark, "Religious Freedom: An American Bishop's View," Letters, *New York Times*, May 26, 2012; Laurie Goodstein, "Bishops Say They Won't Second-Guess Campaign against Obama's Policies," *New York Times*, June 14, 2012; and Ricardo Alonso-Zaldivar, "Catholic Hospitals Reject Deal," *Atlanta Journal-Constitution*, June 16, 2012.

72. Nicholas D. Kristof, "Beyond Pelvic Politics," *New York Times*, February 12, 2012.

73. Trip Gabriel, "Ryan Says Prayer in Schools Is a State Issue," *The Caucus: The Politics and Government Blog of the Times*, September 5, 2012, http://thecaucus.blogs.nytimes.com/2012/09/05/ryan-says-prayer-in-schools-in-a-state-issue/ (accessed September 8, 2012).

74. Mark Landler, "Pushed by Obama, Democrats Alter Platform over Jerusalem," *New York Times*, September 6, 2012.

75. Ashley Parker, "In Romney's Hands, Pledge of Allegiance Is Framework for Criticism," *New York Times*, September 9, 2012.

CHAPTER 4. WHY NEWT GINGRICH'S ABUSE OF LANGUAGE MATTERS TO THE DEFENSE OF SECULARISM

1. "Words Gingrich Governed By," Politics, *New York Times*, January 27, 2012, http://www.nytimes.com/interactive/2012/01/27/us/politics/27gingrich -text.html (accessed February 6, 2012).

2. Newt Gingrich with Joe DeSantis, *To Save America: Stopping Obama's Secular-Socialist Machine* (Washington, DC: Regnery, 2010), p. 4.

3. James Salzer, "Gingrich's Language Set New Course," *Atlanta Journal-Constitution*, January 29, 2012.

4. Newt Gingrich, *Winning the Future: A 21st Century Contract with America* (Washington, DC: Regnery, 2005), pp. 47–48.

5. Max Farrand, ed., *The Records of the Federal Convention of 1787*, vol. 1, rev. ed. (New Haven, CT: Yale University Press), p. 452 (footnote).

6. Abe Levy, "Gingrich Calls for Return to Religious Roots," MySA, *San Antonio Express-News*, March 27, 2011, http://www.mysanantonio.com/news/ local_news/article/Gingrich-Back-to-religiousroots-1309996.php#ixzz1IBYNS FiT (accessed May 5, 2011).

7. Kendra Marr, "Newt Gingrich Talks Faith—Not Affairs—at Corner-stone Church in Texas," *Politico*, March 27, 2011, http://www.politico.com/ news/stories/0311/52023.html (accessed May 5, 2011).

8. Brian Montopoli, "Newt Gingrich Warns US at Risk of Atheism and Radical Islam," Political Hotsheet, *CBS News*, March 29, 2011, http://www.cbs news.com/8301-503544_162-20048494-503544.html (accessed May 5, 2011).

9. "Watch the Full Iowa Thanksgiving Family Forum," 2012 Election Central video, 2:58:10 (Gingrich statement, 48:12 to 49:00), from a forum moderated by Frank Lutz and participated in by Gingrich, Bachmann, Perry, Paul, Cain, and Santorum, November 19, 2011, http://www.2012presidentialelection news.com/2011/11/video-watch-the-full-iowa-thanksgiving-family-forum/ (accessed August 31, 2012); and Jay Bookman, "Gingrich's Priority: Politics, Not Religion," *Atlanta Journal-Constitution*, November 23, 2011.

10. Ross Douthat, "Critics Saw This Kind of Overreach Coming," *Atlanta Journal-Constitution*, February 1, 2012; and Michele Malkin, "Obama's Health Care 'Reforms': First, They Came for the Catholics," *Marietta* [GA] *Daily Journal*, February 2, 2012.

11. Martin Schram, "A Case of Classic 'Gingrichian Deceit by Distortion,'" *Marietta* [GA] *Daily Journal*, February 2, 2012.

12. Daniel Malloy, "Religious Conservatives Rallying to Romney," *Atlanta Journal-Constitution*, June 16, 2012.

CHAPTER 5. HISTORY IS NOT ON THE SIDE OF THE ANGELS

1. William H. McNeill, *History of Western Civilization: A Handbook*, 6th ed. (Chicago: University of Chicago Press, 1986), p. 191.

2. F. L. Cross and E. A. Livingstone, eds., "Albigenses," in *Oxford Dictionary of the Christian Church*, 3rd ed. (Oxford: Oxford University Press, 1997), p. 35.

3. William H. McNeill, "Reformation and Religious Wars, 1500–1660," in McNeill, *History of Western Civilization*, pp. 372–17.

4. E. S. Gaustad, "Religion," in *Thomas Jefferson: A Reference Biography*, ed. Merrill D. Peterson (New York: Charles Scribner's Sons, 1986), p. 291.

5. F. L. Cross and E. A. Livingstone, eds., "Servetus, Michael (c. 1511–1553)," in *Oxford Dictionary of the Christian Church*, p. 1487; and Lawrence Goldstone and Nancy Goldstone, *Out of the Flames: The Remarkable Story of a Fearless Scholar, a Fatal Heresy, and One of the Rarest Books in the World* (New York: Broadway Books, 2002), pp. 3–4.

6. Joseph Telushkin, "Expulsion of Jews from England, 1290," in *Jewish Literacy: The Most Important Things to Know about the Jewish Religion, Its People, and Its History* (New York: William Morrow, 2001), pp. 194–95.

7. Bernhard Blumenkranz, "Philip IV the Fair," in *Encyclopedia Judaica*, vol. 16, ed. Fred Skolnik and Michael Berenbaum (Detroit: Macmillan Reference USA, 2007), p. 48.

8. Joseph Telushkin, "The Spanish Expulsion," in Telushkin, *Jewish Literacy*, pp. 199–201.

9. Joseph Telushkin, "Crusades," "Fourth Lateran Council Yellow Badge," and "Blood Libel, Also Known as Ritual Murder," in Telushkin, *Jewish Literacy*, pp. 189–90, 510–12.

10. Leonard W. Levy, *Blasphemy: Verbal Offense against the Sacred, from Moses to Salman Rushdie* (New York: Alfred A. Knopf, 1993), pp. 255–57.

11. Samuel Eliot Morison, Henry Steele Commager, and William E. Leuchtenburg, "Time of Troubles in Virginia and New England 1675–92," in *A Concise History of the American Republic* (New York: Oxford University Press, 1977), pp. 39–41.

12. Levy, *Blasphemy*, pp. 241–42.

13. Ibid., pp. 238–71.

14. Ibid., p. 265.

15. Lester J. Cappon, *The Adams–Jefferson Letters: The Complete Correspondence between Thomas Jefferson and Abigail and John Adams* (1959; repr., Chapel Hill: University of North Carolina Press, 1988), pp. 607–608.

16. "Massachusetts Laws," "General Laws," "Title I: Crimes and Punishments," "Chapter 272, Crimes against Chastity, Morality, Decency and Good Order," and "Section 36, Blasphemy," *The Commonwealth of Massachusetts*, http://www.malegislature.gov/Laws/GeneralLaws/PartIV/TitleI/Chapter272/Section36 (accessed September 8, 2011).

17. Dan Graves, "Forced Religion Sinful and Tyrannical," Church History Timeline, January 16, 1768, *Christianity.com*, http://www.christianity.com/ChurchHistory/11630274 (accessed September 10, 2011); and John Richard Alden, *The South in the Revolution 1763–1789* (*A History of the South, Volume III*) (n.p.: Louisiana State University Press, 1957), pp. 320–21.

18. Kenneth W. Boyd, "Damascus Baptist Church" and "Falling Creek Baptist Church," in *The Historical Markers of North Georgia: The Complete Text and Location of the Various State and Non-state Historical Markers Located throughout Forty-Four North Georgia Counties* (Atlanta, GA: Cherokee, 1993), pp. 56 and 68, respectively.

19. Roger Williams, "The Hireling Ministry—None of Christ's," in *The Annals of America*, vol. 1, *1493 – 1754, Discovering a New World*, ed. Mortimer J. Adler (Chicago: Encyclopedia Britannica, 1968), pp. 213–16.

20. Samuel Eliot Morison, *Oxford History of the American People* (New York: Oxford University Press, 1965), pp. 126–33.

21. David L. Holmes, *The Faiths of the Founding Fathers* (Oxford: Oxford University Press, 2006), p. 21; and Alden, *South in the Revolution*, p. 319.

22. Goldwin Smith, *A History of England*, 3rd ed. (New York: Charles Scribner's Sons, 1966), pp. 352–55, 413–16, and 571–73.

23. Mortimer J. Adler, ed., "The Declaration of Independence," in *The Annals of America*, vol. 2, *1755–1783, Resistance and Revolution* (Chicago: Encyclopedia Britannica, 1968), p. 447.

24. Mortimer J. Adler, ed., "The Constitution of the United States," in *The Annals of America*, vol. 3, *1784–1796, Organizing the New Nation* (Chicago: Encyclopedia Britannica, 1968), p. 129.

25. Pauline Maier, *Ratification: The People Debate the Constitution, 1787–1788* (New York: Simon & Schuster, 2010), p. 170.

26. Robert S. Alley, "Public Education and the Public Good," *William & Mary Bill of Rights Journal* 4, no. 277 (1995), http://scholarhip.law.wm.edu/wmborj/vol4/iss1/6 (accessed September 14, 2011), pp. 315–16.

27. Richard Beeman, *Plain, Honest Men: The Making of the American Constitution* (New York: Random House, 2009), pp. 178–81; and Max Farrand, ed., *The Records of the Federal Convention of 1787*, rev. ed., vol. 1 (New Haven, CT: Yale University Press), p. 452 (footnote).

28. Benjamin Franklin, "Religious Tests: Letter to Richard Price, Oct. 9,

1780," in *Writings*, ed. J. A. Leo Lemay (New York: Library of America, 1987), p. 1031.

29. Morison, *Oxford History of the American People*, pp. 84–85.

30. George Washington, *Writings*, ed. John Rhodehamel (New York: Library of America, 1997), p. 767.

31. "XVII. Religious Liberty," in *The Baptist Faith and Message: A Statement Adopted by the Southern Baptist Convention* (Nashville, TN: Sunday School Board of the Southern Baptist Convention, 1963), p. 19; and, according to "the official website of the Southern Baptist Convention," no changes were made to that section when the statement was reissued in 2000, "Comparison of 1925, 1963 and 2000 Baptist Faith and Message," *SBC.net*, http://www.sbc.net/bfm/bfm comparison.asp (accessed September 9, 2011).

32. Mortimer J. Adler, ed., "James Madison: Against Religious Assessments," in *The Annals of America*, vol. 3, *1784–1796, Organizing the New Nation* (Chicago: Encyclopedia Britannica, 1968), p. 17.

33. John Adams, preface to *A Defence of the Constitutions of Government of the United States of America*, vol. 1 (1787–1788; repr., New York: Da Capo, 1971), pp. xiv–xvi.

34. Ibid., pp. xvii–xviii.

35. David L. Holmes, *The Faiths of the Founding Fathers* (Oxford: Oxford University Press, 2006), pp. 50–51.

36. James Madison, "Letter to Edward Livingston, July 10, 1822," in James Madison, *The Complete Madison: His Basic Writings*, ed. Saul K. Padover (New York: Harper and Brothers, 1953), pp. 308–309. Reprinted by Kraus Reprint, 1971. Citations are to the 1971 edition.

37. Hunter Miller, ed., "Treaty of Peace and Friendship between the United States and the Bey and Subjects of Tripoli of Barbary," *Treaties and Other International Acts of the United States of America*, vol. 2, *Documents 1–40: 1776–1818* (Washington, DC: US Government Printing Office, 1931), pp. 349–85.

38. Rob Boston, *Why the Religious Right Is Wrong about Separation of Church and State* (Amherst, NY: Prometheus Books, 1993), pp. 86–87.

39. Merrill D. Peterson, *Thomas Jefferson and the New Nation: A Biography* (London: Oxford University Press, 1970), p. 988.

40. Pauline Maier, *American Scripture: Making the Declaration of Independence* (New York: Alfred A. Knopf, 1997), p. 186.

41. Beeman, *Plain, Honest Men*, p. 28.

42. David Goldfield, "Evangelicals, Republicans, and the Civil War," *Opinionator* (blog), *New York Times*, July 7, 2011, http://opinionator.blogs.nytimes.com/2011/07/07/evangelicals-republicans-and-the-civil-war/ (accessed August 25, 2011).

43. Ryan Lizza, "Leap of Faith: The Making of a Republican Front-runner," *New Yorker*, August 15 and 22, 2011, p. 63.

44. Eric Foner, *Tom Paine and Revolutionary America* (London: Oxford University Press, 1976), pp. 253–70.

45. Jackie Hogan, "Lincoln's Party Would Nix Him," *Atlanta-Journal Constitution*, February 11, 2012.

46. *Congressional Record*, vol. 4, pt. 7, p. 175, according to George Seldes, comp., ed., *The Great Quotations* (Secaucus, NJ: Citadel, 1983), p. 288.

47. Susan Jacoby, *Freethinkers, A History of American Secularism* (New York: Metropolitan Books, 2004), pp. 165–66.

48. Steven C. Lowe, "Platform Star: Robert G. Ingersoll in Washington," *White House History*, no 31 (Summer 2012): 36–43.

49. Lee Stein and Elizabeth J. Kruschek, Cain v. Horne, *Arizona Court of Appeals*, Brief of *Amicus Curiae*, National School Boards Association, February 7, 2008, http://www.nsba.org/SchoolLaw/AmicusBriefs/CainvHorneArizCtApp.PDF (accessed September 10, 2011).

50. Pope Pius IX, *The Syllabus of Errors*, Eternal Word Television Network Global Catholic Network, http://www.ewtn.com/library/PAPALDOC/P9SYLL.HTM, condemned propositions 63, 55, 47, 77, 79, and 80 (accessed September 18, 2011).

51. *Congressional Record*, 2 [6]: 5384 [H.R., June 22, 1874], according to Philip Hamburger, *Separation of Church and State* (Cambridge, MA: Harvard University Press, 2002), p. 336 (footnote).

52. Seldes, *Great Quotations*, p. 288.

53. West Virginia State Board of Education v. Barnette, 319 U.S. 624 (1943), http://caselaw.lp.findlaw.com/scripts/getcase.pl?court=us&vol=319&invol=624 (accessed September 18, 2011).

CHAPTER 6. THE UNCHRISTIAN ROOTS OF THE FOURTH OF JULY

1. Mortimer J. Adler, ed., "The Constitution of the United States," in *The Annals of America*, vol. 3, *1784–1796, Organizing the New Nation* (Chicago: Encyclopedia Britannica, 1968), pp. 122–29.

2. Mortimer J. Adler, ed., "The Declaration of Independence," in *The Annals of America*, vol. 2, *1755–1783, Resistance and Revolution* (Chicago: Encyclopedia Britannica, 1968), pp. 447–49.

3. Thomas Jefferson, "The Morals of Jesus; Letter to Dr. Benjamin Rush,

with a Syllabus, Apr. 21, 1803," in *Writings: Autobiography; Notes on the State of Virginia; Public Papers; Addresses, Messages, and Replies; Miscellany; Letters*, ed. Merrill D. Peterson (New York: Library of America, 1984), p. 1122.

4. Thomas Jefferson, "I Too Am an Epicurean, Letter to William Short, October 31, 1819," in Peterson, *Writings*, p. 1431.

5. George Seldes, comp., ed., *The Great Quotations* (Secaucus, NJ: Citadel Press, 1983), p. 373.

6. Thomas Jefferson, "A Declaration by the Representatives of the United States of America, in General Congress Assembled," in Peterson, *Writings*, p. 22. ("CHRISTIAN" shown in all capital letters in cited source.)

7. Pauline Maier, *American Scripture: Making the Declaration of Independence* (New York: Alfred A. Knopf, 1997), p. xix.

8. Mortimer J. Adler, "Preamble, The Constitution of the United States," in *Annals of America*, 3:122.

9. James Madison, "Letter to Edward Livingston, July 10, 1822," in *The Complete Madison: His Basic Writings*, ed. Saul K. Padover (New York: Harper and Brothers, 1953; Kraus Reprint, 1971), pp. 308–309. Citations are to the 1971 edition.

10. John Adams, preface to *A Defence of the Constitutions of Government of the United States of America*, vol. 1 (1787–1788; repr., New York: Da Capo, 1971).

CHAPTER 7. THE UNCHRISTIAN NATURE OF THE US CONSTITUTION

1. Avalon Project, "Articles of Confederation—March 1, 1781," Yale Law School, Lillian Goldman Law Library, http://avalon.law.yale.edu/18th _century/artconf.asp (accessed February 13, 2012).

2. "United States Constitution" (Preamble) in *Roots of the Republic: American Founding Documents Interpreted*, ed. Stephen L. Schechter, Richard B. Bernstein, and Donald S. Lutz (Madison, WI: Madison House, 1990), p. 277.

3. George Washington, "Letter to the Hebrew Congregation in Newport, Rhode Island," in *Writings*, ed. John Rhodehamel (New York: Library of America, 1997), p. 767.

4. Richard Beeman, *Plain, Honest Men: The Making of the American Constitution* (New York: Random House, 2009), p. 180.

5. Ibid., p. 181.

6. Avalon Project, "Mayflower Compact—1620," Yale Law School, Lil-

lian Goldman Law Library, http://avalon.law.yale.edu/17th_century/mayflower
.asp (accessed February 13, 2012).

7. Donald S. Lutz, "The Fundamental Orders of Connecticut, 1639, Commentary," in Schechter, Bernstein, and Lutz, *Roots of the Republic*, p. 24.

8. "The Fundamental Orders of Connecticut, 1639," in *Roots of the Republic*, p. 29.

9. Avalon Project, "The First Charter of Virginia; April 10, 1606," Yale Law School, Lillian Goldman Law Library, http://avalon.law.yale.edu/17th _century/va01.asp (accessed February 13, 2012).

10. Avalon Project, "The Second Charter of Virginia; May 23, 1609," Yale Law School, Lillian Goldman Law Library, http://avalon.law.yale.edu/17th _century/va02.asp (accessed February 13, 2012).

11. Avalon Project, "The Charter of Maryland : 1632," Yale Law School, Lillian Goldman Law Library, http://avalon.law.yale.edu/17th_century/ma01 .asp (accessed February 13, 2012).

12. Avalon Project, "Maryland Toleration Act; September 21, 1649—An Act concerning Religion," Yale Law School, Lillian Goldman Law Library, http://avalon.law.yale.edu/18th_century/maryland_toleration.asp (accessed February 13, 2012).

13. Avalon Project, "Charter of Rhode Island and Providence Planta- tions—July 15, 1663," Yale Law School, Lillian Goldman Law Library, http:// avalon.law.yale.edu/17th_century/ri04.asp (accessed February 13, 2012). All spelling is true to the original source.

14. Avalon Project, "Constitution of New Jersey; 1776," Yale Law School, Lillian Goldman Law Library, http://avalon.law.yale.edu/18th_century/nj15.asp (accessed February 13, 2012); and "The Constitution of the State of Georgia," revised January 2009, http://www.sos.ga.gov/elections/GAConstitution.pdf (accessed February 13, 2012).

15. Graham Dolan, "The Names of the Months" and "Day Names," in *The Greenwich Guide to Measuring Time* (Chicago: Heinmann Library, 2001), pp. 12–15.

16. Rob Boston, *Why the Religious Right Is Wrong about Separation of Church and State* (Amherst, NY: Prometheus Books, 1993), pp. 86–87.

17. Nelson Price, "Mendacity Knows No Bounds on Founders' Religion," *Marietta* [GA] *Daily Journal*, July 3, 2011.

18. Charles de Secondat, Baron de Montesquieu, *The Spirit of the Laws* (1748), trans. Thomas Nugent, http://www.constitution.org/cm/sol.txt (ac- cessed September 25, 2011).

19. Johnny H. Killian and George A. Costello, eds., "Constitution of the United States of America," in *The Constitution of the United States of America:*

Analysis and Interpretation (Washington, DC: US Government Printing Office, 1996), p. 36, footnote 11.

20. Annie Laurie Gaylor, "Elizabeth Cady Stanton," in *Women without Superstition: "No Gods—No Masters": The Collected Writings of the Women Free-thinkers of the Nineteenth & Twentieth Centuries* (Madison, WI: Freedom from Religion Foundation, 1997), p. 103.

21. Ibid., p. 130.

22. Ibid., p. 103.

23. Joseph Morecraft III, "Women Civil Magistrates?" *Chalcedon Presbyterian Church*, http://www.chalcedon.org/articles-print.php?id=7 (accessed June 25, 2011); archived at http://web.archive.org/web/20081001185306/http://www.chalcedon.org/articles?id=7 (accessed September 18, 2011).

24. John Hanna, "Women's Suffrage Called 'Mistake' by Conservative Kansas Politician," Nation and World, *Seattle Times*, September 29, 2001, http://web.archive.org/web/20011001040711/http://seattletimes.nwsource.com/html/nationworld/134347570_woman29.html (accessed February 25, 2012).

25. "Constitution of 1819, Article VI, 'Slaves,' Sec. 3," http://www.legislature.state.al.us/misc/history/constitutions/1819/1819_6.html#slaves (accessed February 25, 2012).

26. Avalon Project, "Confederate States of America—A Declaration of the Causes Which Impel the State of Texas to Secede from the Federal Union," Yale Law School, Lillian Goldman Law Library, http://avalon.law.yale.edu/19th_century/csa_texsec.asp (accessed February 25, 2012).

27. Killian and Costello, "Constitution of the United States of America," pp. 32–33.

28. Damon Linker, "Church, Temple, Mosque," a review of *The New Religious Intolerance* (Belknap Press/Harvard University Press) in *New York Times Book Review*, July 22, 2012, p. 18.

29. John Locke, "A Letter concerning Toleration" (1689) in Robert Maynard Hutchins, *Great Books of the Western World*, vol. 35, ed. Charles L. Sherman (Chicago: Encyclopedia Britannica, 1987), pp. 15–18.

CHAPTER 8. FROM THE SHORES
OF TRIPOLI

1. Christi Parsons, "Slain Americans Returned Home," *Atlanta Journal-Constitution*, September 15, 2012; and David D. Kirkpatrick, Suliman Ali Zway,

and Kareem Fahim, "Attack by Fringe Group Highlights the Problem of Libya's Militias," *New York Times*, September 16, 2012.

2. Hunter Miller, ed., "Treaty of Peace and Friendship between the United States and the Bey and Subjects of Tripoli of Barbary," *Treaties and Other International Acts of the United States of America*, vol. 2, *Documents 1–40: 1776–1818* (Washington, DC: US Government Printing Office, 1931), p. 365.

3. Paul F. Boller, *George Washington & Religion* (Dallas, TX: Southern Methodist University Press, 1963), pp. 87–88.

4. Joseph Wheelan, *Jefferson's War: America's First War on Terror 1801–1805* (New York: Carroll & Graf, 2003), p. 37.

5. Frederick Leiner, *The End of Barbary Terror* (New York: Oxford University Press, 2006), pp. 17–18. The quotation is from a letter written by Thomas Jefferson to John Jay recounting what the ambassador told him.

6. Ibid., p. 2.

7. Ibid., p. 20.

8. Miller, "Treaty of Peace and Friendship," p. 367.

9. *Wikipedia*, s.v. "Richard Stockton (US Senator)," http://en.wikipedia.org/wiki/Richard_Stockton_(U.S._Senator) (accessed August 23, 2011).

10. "About the Signers," *ConstitutionFacts.com*, http://www.constitutionfacts.com/?section=constitution&page=aboutTheSigners.cfm (accessed August 23, 2011).

11. Miller, "Treaty of Peace and Friendship," p. 384.

12. Ibid., p. 377.

13. Martin P. Claussen, ed., *The Journal of the Senate, including the Journal of the Executive Proceedings of the Senate, John Adams Administration, 1797–1801*, vol. 1, *Fifth Congress, First Session; March–July, 1797* (Wilmington, DE: Michael Glazier, 1977), p. 160.

14. Ibid.

15. Ibid.

16. Miller, "Treaty of Peace and Friendship," p. 383.

17. Ed Buckner, "Barlow, Joel (1754–1812)," in *The New Encyclopedia of Unbelief*, ed. Thomas W. Flynn (Amherst, NY: Prometheus Books, 2007), p. 106; and *Wikipedia*, s.v. "Joel Barlow," http://en.wikipedia.org/wiki/Joel_Barlow (accessed August 23, 2011).

18. Buckner, "Barlow, Joel," p. 106.

19. Ibid.

20. Bruce A. Ragdale and Kathryn Allamong Jacob, eds., *Biographical Directory of the United States Congress, 1774–1989* (Washington, DC: US Government Printing Office, 1989), p. 623 (William Bingham)—also available for download online: http://ir.library.oregonstate.edu/xmlui/handle/1957/12276 (accessed

August 24, 2011); p. 634 (Timothy Bloodworth); p. 635 (William Blount); p. 657 (William Bradford); p. 683 (John Brown); p. 801 (William Cocke); pp. 1020–21 (Theodore Foster); p. 1073 (Benjamin Goodhue); p. 1189 (James Hillhouse); p. 1218 (John Eager Howard); p. 1340 (John Langdon); pp. 1379–80 (Samuel Livermore); p. 1427 (Alexander Martin); p. 1606 (Elijah Paine); p. 1697 (Jacob Read); p. 1787 (Theodore Sedgwick); p. 1880 (Richard Stockton); p. 1919 (Henry Tazewell); p. 1912 (Josiah Tattnall); p. 1940 (Isaac Tichenor); and p. 1951 (Tracy Uriah).

21. Ibid., p. 1787.

22. *Wikipedia*, s.v. "Kyra Sedgwick," en.wikipedia.org/wiki/Kyra_Sedgwick (accessed June 26, 2012); and "Finding Your Roots with Henry Louis Gates: Kyra Sedwick and Kevin Bacon," *PBS Video*, video.pbs.org/video/2220828439 (aired April 8, 2012; accessed June 26, 2012).

23. Ragdale and Jacob, *Biographical Directory*, p. 1940.

24. Ibid., p. 1912; and James A. Crutchfield, ed., "County Name Origins," *Georgia Almanac and Book of Facts, 1989–1990* (Nashville, TN: Rutledge Hill, 1988), p. 104.

CHAPTER 9. TEN COMMANDMENTS

1. Ray Henry, "Bill: 10 Commandments OK in Public Buildings," *Marietta* [GA] *Daily Journal*, February 29, 2002.

2. Barry W. Lynn, "Guest Column: Religious Code Not the Basis of Our Laws," *Atlanta Journal-Constitution*, March 8, 2012.

3. Thomas Jefferson, "The Morals of Jesus; Letter to Dr. Benjamin Rush, with a Syllabus, Apr. 21, 1803," in *Writings: Autobiography; Notes on the State of Virginia; Public Papers; Addresses, Messages, and Replies; Miscellany; Letters*, ed. Merrill D. Peterson (New York: Library of America, 1984), p. 1123.

4. The authors visited the US Supreme Court Building in November 1993 and took photos of the inside and outside of the building, including of the depiction of Mohammed. Sources for information about the building include an unpublished, undated, and unpaginated copy of the docent's notes (21 pages in all; discussion of the friezes and Mohammed on the fifteenth and sixteenth pages); a visitor's brochure from the gift shop: *The Supreme Court of the United States* (undated; no author given except "Prepared by the Supreme Court of the United States, and published with the cooperation of the Supreme Court Historical Society"); and "The United States Supreme Court Building: Letter from the Architect of the Capitol," June 22, 1939 (Washington, DC: US Government Printing Office, 1939).

5. *Wikipedia*, s.v. "Roy Moore," http://en.wikipedia.org/wiki/Roy_Moore (accessed February 27, 2012); and "Ten Commandments Judge Removed from Office," *CNN Justice*, http://articles.cnn.com/2003-11-13/justice/moore.ten commandments_1_ethics-panel-state-supreme-court-building-ethics-charges ?_s=PM:LAW (accessed February 27, 2012).

6. Roy Moore, with John Perry, "Can the State Acknowledge God?" in *So Help Me God: The Ten Commandments, Judicial Tyranny, and the Battle for Religious Freedom* (Nashville, TN: Broadman & Holman, 2005), p. 3.

7. Lynn, "Guest Column."

8. "Exploratory 2012 Republican Presidential Candidate Former Chief Justice of the Alabama Supreme Court Roy Moore," *Presidential Candidates*, http://2012.presidential-candidates.org/Moore (accessed February 28, 2012).

9. Kevin Derby, "Roy Moore to Run for His Old Job—Not the White House," *Sunshine State News*, November 23, 2011, http://www.sunshinestate news.com/story/roy-moore-run-his-old-job-not-whitehouse (accessed February 28, 2012).

10. Robert S. Alley, "Public Education and the Public Good," *William & Mary Bill of Rights Journal* 4, no. 277 (1995), http://scholarhip.law.wm.edu/ wmborj/vol4/iss1/6 (accessed September 14, 2011), pp. 316–18.

11. Thom Hartmann, "Moses Didn't Write the Constitution," *Common Dreams*, March 3, 2005, http://www.commondreams.org/views05/0303-30.htm (accessed February 19, 2012).

12. Thomas Jefferson, "Most Honourable to Human Nature," Jefferson to Adams, January 24, 1814, in *The Adams–Jefferson Letters: The Complete Correspondence between Thomas Jefferson and Abigail and John Adams*, ed. Lester J. Cappon (1959; repr., Chapel Hill: University of North Carolina Press, 1988), p. 421. Citations are to the 1988 edition.

13. Ibid., p. 423.

CHAPTER 10. TOLERANCE, TOLERATION, AND LIBERTY

1. Merrill D. Peterson, *Thomas Jefferson and the New Nation: A Biography* (London: Oxford University Press, 1970), pp. 722–23.

2. John Leland, "An Excerpt from *The Virginia Chronicle*," Tripod.com, http://classicliberal.tripod.com/misc/vchronicle.html (accessed August 23, 2011).

3. "Tolerance is not enough . . . ," posted May 6, 2008, *Faith of the Free*,

http://faithofthefree.informe.com/forum/previous-quotes-early-2008-dt1052 -90.html (accessed August 5, 2011).

4. David L. Holmes, *The Faiths of the Founding Fathers* (Oxford: Oxford University Press, 2006), p. 21.

5. John Locke, "A Letter Concerning Toleration," 1689, in *Great Books of the Western World*, vol. 35, ed. Robert Maynard Hutchins and Charles L. Sherman (Chicago: Encyclopedia Britannica, 1987), pp. 1–22.

6. Thomas Paine, *The Rights of Man* (1791; repr., New York: Heritage, 1961), p. 55. Citations are to the 1961 edition.

7. George Washington, *Writings*, ed. John Rhodehamel (New York: Library of America, 1997), p. 767.

8. John Adams, "Letter to Francis van der Kemp," in *The Founders on Religion: A Book of Quotations*, ed. James H. Hutson (Princeton, NJ: Princeton University Press, 2005), p. 134.

9. Thomas Jefferson, *The Complete Jefferson: Containing His Major Writings, Published and Unpublished, Except His Letters*, ed. Saul K. Padover (New York: Duell, Sloan and Pearce, 1943; Freeport, NY: Books for Libraries Press, 1969), p. 945.

10. John T. Noonan Jr., *The Lustre of Our Country: The American Religious Experience of Religious Freedom* (Berkeley: University of California Press, 1998), p. 4.

11. Ibid.

CHAPTER 11. SECULAR SCHOOLING

1. William Ellery Channing, "Self Culture: An Address Introductory to the Franklin Lectures, delivered at Boston, Sept 1838," *American Unitarian Conference*, http://www.americanunitarian.org/selfculture.htm (accessed September 11, 2011).

2. Mortimer J. Adler, ed., "Amendment XIV; Civil War Amendments to the Constitution," in *The Annals of America*, vol. 10, *1866–1883, Reconstruction and Industrialization* (Chicago: Encyclopedia Britannica, 1968), pp. 133–34.

3. Sarah Palermo, "Bills Aim to Roll Back Teaching Evolution," *Concord Monitor*, December 29, 2011, http://www.concordmonitor.com/article/300905/ bills-aim-to-roll-back-teaching-evolution (accessed December 29, 2011).

4. John E. Jones III, "Memorandum Opinion," *Kitzmiller v. Dover Area School District*, December 20, 2005, Case 4:04-cv-02688-JEJ, p. 89, http://www .pamd.uscourts.gov/kitzmiller/kitzmiller_342.pdf (accessed September 11, 2011).

5. Kevin Drum, "Why I'm Feeling So Hard-Nosed Over the Contraception Affair," *Mother Jones*, February 10, 2012, http://motherjones.com/kevin-drum/2012/02/why-im-so-hardnosed-over-contraception-affair (accessed February 11, 2012).

6. Mortimer J. Adler, ed., "James Madison: Against Religious Assessments," in *The Annals of America*, vol. 3, *1784–1796, Organizing the New Nation* (Chicago: Encyclopedia Britannica, 1968), p. 17.

7. John Young, "Unholy Hoaxes," *Atlanta Journal/Constitution*, August 29, 1995.

8. Americans United for Separation of Church and State, http://www.au.org (accessed September 1, 2011).

CHAPTER 12. HOLY DAYS AND HOLIDAYS IN A SECULAR SOCIETY

1. B. A. Robinson, "Easter: Its Pagan Origins," Religious Tolerance, Ontario Consultants on Religious Tolerance, December 26, 2009, http://www.religioustolerance.org/easter1.htm (accessed February 27, 2012).

2. Rob Boston, "Mandatory Sunday-Closing Laws," in *Why the Religious Right Is Wrong about Separation of Church and State* (Amherst, NY: Prometheus Books, 1993), pp. 164–67.

3. "What Adventists Believe," *Seventh-Day Adventists*, http://www.adventist.org/beliefs/index.html (accessed February 27, 2012).

4. "Sabbath," *Seventh Day Baptists*, http://www.seventhdaybaptist.org/content/sabbath (accessed February 27, 2012).

CHAPTER 13. HE WHO IS NOT WITH ME IS AGAINST ME

1. Cullen Murphy, "The Certainty of Doubt," *New York Times*, February 12, 2012.

2. Benjamin Franklin, "Religious Tests: Letter to Richard Price, Oct. 9, 1780," in *Writings*, ed. J. A. Leo Lemay (New York: Library of America, 1987), p. 1031.

3. "Religion, Partisan Politics and Tax Exemption—What Federal Law Requires and Why," Americans United for Separation of Church and State,

http://www.au.org/resources/publications/religion-partisan-politics-and-tax
-exemption (accessed February 13, 2012).

4. Ed Buckner, "Who Gains or Loses if Churches Are Taxed?" *Henry County Herald*, July 27, 1994.

CHAPTER 14. THE NAKED PUBLIC SQUARE?

1. "Falwell Apologizes to Gays, Feminists, Lesbians," World Trade Center, September 14, 2001, CNN, http://articles.cnn.com/2001-09-14/us/Falwell.apology_1_thomas-road-baptist-church-jerry-falwell-feminists?_s=PM:US (accessed on September 11, 2011).

2. Barack Obama, "Faith," in *The Audacity of Hope: Thoughts on Reclaiming the American Dream* (New York: Crown, 2006), pp. 218–19.

3. GA. Code Ann. §16–1–3 (West).

4. *Internal Revenue Manual*, 4.76.3, "Public Charities," http://www.irs.gov/irm/part4/irm_04-076-003.html (accessed September 27, 2012).

5. *Wikipedia*, s.v. "Public Sphere," http://en.wikipedia.org/wiki/Public_sphere (accessed November 25, 2011).

6. Phillip E. Hammond, *With Liberty for All: Freedom of Religion in the United States* (Louisville, KY: Westminster John Knox Press, 1998), pp. 106–107.

7. Joseph L. Conn, "On Guard for Religious Liberty," *Liberty Magazine*, January/February 2007, http://www.libertymagazine.org/index.php?id=1175 (accessed September 1, 2011).

CHAPTER 15. THE BIG LIE

1. Billy Graham, "A Father's Sins Are Not Passed to Next Generation," *Marietta* [GA] *Daily Journal*, October 22, 2011.

2. Jerry A. Coyne, "As Atheists Know, You Can Be Good without God," *USA Today*, August 1, 2011.

3. Melanie Phillips, *The World Turned Upside Down: The Global Battle over God, Truth, and Power* (Jackson, TN: Encounter Books, 2010), pp. 142–43.

4. Nicholas Kristof and Sheryl WuDunn, *Half the Sky: Turning Oppression into Opportunity for Women Worldwide* (New York: Vintage Books, 2010), p. 234.

5. Douglas A. Blackmon, *Slavery by Another Name: The Re-Enslavement of Black Americans from the Civil War to World War II* (New York: Doubleday, 2008), p. 13.

6. Patricia Bradley, *Slavery, Propaganda, and the American Revolution* (Jackson: University Press of Mississippi, 1998), pp. 119–31.

7. Ibid., p. 16.

8. C. S. Lewis, *Mere Christianity* (New York: Macmillan Publishing, 1952), pp. 3–25.

9. Dan Barker, *Losing Faith in Faith* (Madison, WI: FFRF, 1992), p. 223.

10. Paul Kurtz, "Secular Humanism and Eupraxophy," in *The Question of Humanism*, ed. David Goicoechea, John Luik, and Tim Madigan (Amherst, NY: Prometheus Books, 1991), p. 318.

11. For the Hitler quotation, Ronald Hilton, "Hitler: Hitler's Religion," http://wais.stanford.edu/Germany/germany_hitler03102004.htm (accessed August 1, 2011); and Gregory S. Paul, "The Great Scandal: Christianity's Role in the Rise of the Nazis," 2 pts., *Free Inquiry* 23, no. 4 (October/November 2003) and *Free Inquiry* 24, no. 1 (December 2003/January 2004). Paul's essay is also available on the web: part 1, http://www.secularhumanism.org/index.php?section=library&page=paul_24_1; and part 2, http://www.secularhumanism.org/index.php?section=library&page=paul_23_4 (accessed February 11, 2012).

12. Louis Menand "Permanent Fatal Errors: Did the Voters Send a Message?" *New Yorker*, December 6, 2004.

13. James Wood, "Is That All There Is? Secularism and Its Discontents," *New Yorker*, August 15 and 22, 2011, p. 91. Wood's essay is a review of George Levine, ed., *The Joy of Secularism: 11 Essays for How We Live Now* (Princeton, NJ: Princeton University Press, 2011).

CHAPTER 16. GOD'S LAW

1. Bill Mears, "Judge Issues Permanent Injunction on Oklahoma Sharia Law Ban," November 29, 2010, CNN, http://articles.cnn.com/2010-11-29/us/oklahoma.sharia.law_1_sharia-law-state-courts-international-law?_s=PM:US (accessed September 18, 2011).

2. Bill Raftery, National Center for State Courts, "Bans on Court Use of Sharia/International Law: ABA House of Delegates Opposes 'Blanket Prohibitions,' State Legislatures out of Session," Gavel to Gavel: A Review of State Legislation Affecting the Courts, August 8, 2011, http://gaveltogavel.us/site/2011/08/08/bans-on-court-use-of-shariainternational-law-aba-house-of-delegates-opposes-blanket-prohibitions-state-legislatures-out-of-session/ (accessed September 18, 2011).

3. "Enrolled House Joint Resolution," https://www.sos.ok.gov/documents/questions/755.pdf (accessed September 18, 2011).

4. *Daily Mail* reporter, "Sharia Law Banned: Oklahoma to Become the First US State to Veto Use of Islamic Code," *Daily Mail Online*, November 2, 2010, http://www.dailymail.co.uk/news/article-1325986/Sharia-law-banned -Oklahoma-US-state-veto-Islamic-code.html (accessed August 25, 2011).

5. Amy Sullivan, "Sharia Myth Sweeps America," *USA Today*, June 13, 2011.

6. Eliyahu Stern, "Don't Fear Islamic Law in America," *New York Times*, September 3, 2011.

7. *Lawrence et al. v. Texas*, certiorari to the Court of Appeals of Texas, Fourteenth District, No. 02-102, argued March 26, 2003—decided June 26, 2003. "LAWRENCE et al. v. TEXAS," FindLaw, http://laws.findlaw.com/ us/539/558.html (accessed September 18, 2011).

8. Sheikh Muhammed Salih Al-Munajjid, "Punishment of the One Who Leaves Islaam [*sic*]," Islam Question and Answer, http://www.islamqa.com/ en/ref/696 (accessed August 25, 2011); Shaykh Ibn Baaz, "The Ruling concerning Neglecting to Fast," Fatwa-Online.com, http://www.fatwa-online.com/fataawa/ worship/fasting/fas002/9991120_1.htm (accessed August 25, 2011)—both of the previous are Salafist or "Wahhabite" websites; and Sayyid Muhammad Rizvi, "Apostasy (*Irtidād*) in Islam," 'Aalim Network QR, December 9, 1997, http:// www.al-islam.org/organizations/AalimNetwork/msg00613.html (accessed August 25, 2011)—the last website is a Shi'ite (Twelver) website.

9. David D. Kirkpatrick, "In Egypt Race, Battle Is Joined on Islam Role; 2 Muslim Rivals Differ on Place of Religion," *New York Times*, April 24, 2012; Kareem Fahim, "As Hopes Fade in Bahrain, Protesters Turn Anger on United States," *New York Times*, June 24, 2012; and David D. Kirkpatrick, "Libya Democracy Clashes with Fervor for Jihad," *New York Times*, June 24, 2012.

10. Maggie Michael and Sarah El Deeb, Associated Press, "Election Could Deepen Rifts," *Atlanta Journal-Constitution*, May 25, 2012; David D. Kirkpatrick and Kareem Fahim, "Egypt Race Pits Aide to Mubarak against Islamist," *New York Times*, May 26, 2012; Aya Batrawy, Associated Press, "Egyptians Rally against Former PM," *Atlanta Journal-Constitution*, June 2, 2012; Hamza Hendawi and Sarah El Deeb, Associated Press, "Egypt Votes for Mubarak's Successor in Runoff," *Marietta* [GA] *Daily Journal*, June 17, 2012; David D. Kirkpatrick, "As Tension Mounts, Egypt Delays Declaring Winner of Presidential Election," *New York Times*, June 21, 2012; David D. Kirkpatrick, "Panel to Name Egypt's President on Sunday as Rumors Swirl of Secret Talks," *New York Times*, June 24, 2012; David D. Kirkpatrick, "Named Egypt's Winner, Islamist Makes History," *New York Times*, June 25, 2012; Kareem Fahim, "Challenges Multiply for Victor in Egypt," *New York Times*, June 25, 2012; and Eric Schmitt and Helene Cooper, "After Election Announcement in Cairo, White House Is Relieved but Watchful," *New York Times*, June 25, 2012.

11. Bill O'Reilly, "Sarah Palin on National Day of Prayer Controversy," *The O'Reilly Factor*, May 7, 2010, http://www.foxnews.com/on-air/oreilly/2010/05/07/sarah-palin-national-day-prayer-controversy (accessed August 25, 2011).

12. Kenyn Cureton, "The Ten Commandments: Foundation of American Society," Family Research Council, http://www.frc.org/booklet/the-ten-commandments-foundation-of-american-society- (accessed September 18, 2011).

13. "Briefs Filed in *McCreary County v. ACLU of Kentucky*," Liberty Counsel, http://www.lc.org/ten/briefs.htm (accessed September 18, 2011).

14. Barry C. Hodge and Steven W. Fitschen, "Brief *Amicus Curiae* of Wall-builders, Inc.," http://www.lc.org/attachments/TenCommAmicus_Wallbuilders_NLF.pdf (accessed September 18, 2011).

15. R. J. Rushdoony, *The Institutes of Biblical Law* (Nutley, NJ: Craig Press, 1973), pp. 38–39.

16. R. J. Rushdoony, "Idolatry and the Law," *The Institutes of Biblical Law*, vol. 2, *Law and Society* (Vallecito, CA: Ross House Books, 1982), pp. 466–69.

17. R. J. Rushdoony, "The Idolatry of Testing God," *Law and Society*, p. 460.

18. R. J. Rushdoony, "Idolatry and the Sabbath," *Law and Society*, p. 458.

19. Gary North, *Political Polytheism: The Myth of Pluralism* (Tyler, TX: Institute for Christian Economics, 1989), p. 87.

20. Joseph Morecraft III, "Women Civil Magistrates?" Chalcedon Presbyterian Church, http://www.chalcedon.org/articles-print.php?id=7 (accessed June 25, 2011); archived at http://web.archive.org/web/20081001185306/http://www.chalcedon.org/articles?id=7 (accessed September 18, 2011).

21. Gary North, *The Sinai Strategy: Economics and the Ten Commandments* (Tyler, TX: Institute for Christian Economics, 1986), pp. 122–24.

22. "Al-Taqiyya/Dissimulation (Part III)," *A Shi'ite Encyclopedia*, Ahlul Bayt Digital Islamic Library, http://www.al-islam.org/encyclopedia/chapter6b/ 3.html (accessed September 18, 2011)—explanation of the doctrine of *taqiyya* from a Shi'ite point of view; and Warner MacKenzie, "Understanding Taqiyya—Islamic Principle of Lying for the Sake of Allah," Islam Watch, April 30, 2007, http://www.islam-watch.org/Warner/Taqiyya-Islamic-Principle-Lying-for-Allah.htm (accessed September 18, 2011)—discussion of *taqiyya* from an anti-Islamic site.

23. Rushdoony, *Institutes of Biblical Law*, pp. 542–49.

24. Gary North, "The Intellectual Schizophrenia of the New Christian Right," in *The Failure of the American Baptist Culture* (Tyler, TX: Geneva Divinity School Press, 1982), pp. 24–25.

25. George Grant, *The Changing of the Guard: Biblical Principles for Political Action* (Ft. Worth, TX: Dominion, 1987), pp. 50–51 and 145–60.

26. David Chilton, "Appendix A: The Eschatology of Dominion; A Summary," *Paradise Restored: A Biblical Theology of Dominion* (Tyler, TX: Dominion, 1994), p. 226.

27. Bob Enyart, "Quotes on Government," March 6, 2005, archived at http://web.archive.org/web/20050306141202/http://www.enyart.com/features/quotes/government.shtml (accessed September 18, 2011); Bob Enyart, "Day One," pt. 1 of *The First Five Days: How Would Christians Govern America?* April 5, 2005, archived at http://web.archive.org/web/20050405180043/http://www.enyart.com/features/writings/dayone.shtml (accessed September 18, 2011).

28. David James King, *Creating a Nation under God: Rebuilding America with Biblical Principles* (Lafayette, LA: Prescott, 2000), pp. 550–51.

29. William H. McNeill, *History of Western Civilization: A Handbook*, 6th ed. (Chicago: University of Chicago Press, 1986), p. 191.

30. Ryan Lizza, "Leap of Faith: The Making of a Republican Front-Runner," The Political Scene, *New Yorker*, August 15 and 22, 2011, pp. 54–63; Tim Murphy, "Crazy Like a Fox: The Method to Michele Bachmann's Madness," *Mother Jones*, September/October 2011, pp. 27–29 and 66–67; and Frank Bruni, "The Divine Miss M," *New York Times*, July 24, 2012.

31. Murphy, "Crazy Like a Fox," p. 66.

32. Lizza, "Leap of Faith," p. 56.

33. Ibid., p. 59.

34. John L. Esposito, ed., *Oxford Dictionary of Islam* (Oxford: Oxford University Press, 2003), p. 147.

35. Mary Ann Cooper, "Medical Aspects of Lightning," National Weather Service, http://www.lightningsafety.noaa.gov/medical.htm (accessed September 18, 2011).

36. Guy Worthey, "Meteor Near-Misses and Strikes," Astronomy Resources, Department of Physics, Washington State University, http://astro.wsu.edu/worthey/astro/html/im-meteor/strikes.html (accessed September 18, 2011).

37. Scott Broden, "Judge Upholds Ruling for Murfreesboro Mosque," August 31, 2011, *Tennessean*, http://www.tennessean.com/article/20110831/NEWS01/308310117/Judge-upholds-ruling-Murfreesboro-mosque (accessed September 18, 2011).

38. "Swiss Voters Back Ban on Minarets," November 29, 2009, *BBC News*, http://news.bbc.co.uk/2/hi/8385069.stm (accessed September 18, 2011).

39. Joseph Telushkin, "The Spanish Expulsion," *Jewish Literacy: The Most Important Things to Know about the Jewish Religion, Its People, and Its History* (New York: William Morrow, 2001), pp. 199–201.

40. Adam Nossiter, "Amputations and Killings Shake an Embattled Mali," *New York Times*, September 11, 2012.

41. "Norway Police Say 85 Killed in Island Youth Camp Attack," July 23, 2011, *BBC News*, http://www.bbc.co.uk/news/world-europe-14259356 (accessed September 18, 2011).

42. Steven Erlanger and Scott Shane, "Oslo Suspect Wrote of Fear of Islam and Plan for War," July 23, 2011, *New York Times*, http://www.nytimes.com/2011/07/24/world/europe/24oslo.html?_r=2&hp (accessed September 18, 2011).

CHAPTER 17. BLASPHEMY AND HERESY

1. Leonard W. Levy, *Blasphemy: Verbal Offense against the Sacred, from Moses to Salman Rushdie* (New York: Alfred A. Knopf, 1993), p. 11.

2. Edwin F. Kagin, *Baubles of Blasphemy*, 2nd ed., ed. Ed Buckner (Cranford, NJ: American Atheist Press, 2009), p. v.

3. Ronald A. Lindsay, "Blasphemy," in *The New Encyclopedia of Unbelief*, ed. Tom Flynn (Amherst, NY: Prometheus Books, 2007), p. 148.

4. Sara Schonhardt, "As Religious Tensions Rise in Indonesia, Officials Largely Turn a Blind Eye," *New York Times*, July 22, 2012.

5. Declan Walsh and Salman Masood, "Christian Girl's Blasphemy Arrest Incites a Furor in Pakistan," *New York Times*, August 21, 2012; Declan Walsh, "Lawyers Seek the Release of a Christian Girl Charged with Blasphemy in Pakistan," *New York Times*, August 29, 2012; and Salman Masood, "Blasphemy Arrest Highlights Tensions in Pakistan," *New York Times*, September 1, 2012.

6. Rebecca Santana and Zarar Khan, Associated Press, "Accusor Arrested in Pakistani Christian Blasphemy Case," *Marietta* [GA] *Daily Journal*, September 3, 2012; Salman Masood, "Pakistani Blasphemy Case Shifts as Cleric Is Arrested," *New York Times*, September 3, 2012; and Declan Walsh and Salman Masood, "Bail for Girl in Pakistan Facing Charge of Blasphemy," *New York Times*, September 8, 2012.

7. David M. Herszenhorn, "Mixed Feelings on Jailed Punk Rock Band," *New York Times*, August 3, 2012; David M. Herszenhorn, "In Russia, Madonna Defends a Band's Anti-Putin Stunt," *New York Times*, August 8, 2012; and David M. Herszenhorn, "Anti-Putin Stunt Earns Punk Band Two Years in Jail," *New York Times*, August 18, 2012.

8. David D. Kirkpatrick, "Egyptian Actor Insulted Islam, a Court Finds," *New York Times*, April 25, 2012.

9. Sebnem Arsu and Daniel J. Wakin, "Turkish Pianist Accused of Insulting Religion," *New York Times,* June 2, 2012.

10. Rick Gladstone, "Anti-American Protests Flare beyond the Mideast," *New York Times,* September 15, 2012.

11. Christi Parsons, "Slain Americans Returned Home," *Atlanta Journal-Constitution,* September 15, 2012.

12. Nicholas D. Kristof, "Exploiting the Prophet," *New York Times,* September 23, 2012.

13. Bill Keller, "The Satanic Video," *New York Times,* September 24, 2012.

14. Kyle Butt, "Blasphemy against the Holy Spirit—The 'Unpardonable Sin,'" *Apologetics Press,* http://www.apologeticspress.org/apcontent.aspx?category=11&article=1218 (accessed February 26, 2012).

15. Lawrence Goldstone and Nancy Goldstone, *Out of the Flames: The Remarkable Story of a Fearless Scholar, a Fatal Heresy, and One of the Rarest Books in the World* (New York: Broadway Books, 2002), pp. 200–10.

16. Tom Flynn, "Islam and the Cartoons," *Free Inquiry,* April/May 2006, pp. 8–11.

17. "Mohammed Image Archive: Depictions of Mohammed throughout History," http://zombietime.com/mohammed_image_archive/ (accessed May 23, 2011).

18. The authors visited the US Supreme Court Building in November 1993 and took photos of the inside and outside of the building, including of the depiction of Mohammed. Sources for information about the building include an unpublished, untitled, undated, and unpaginated copy of the docent's notes (21 pages in all; discussion of the friezes and Mohammed on the fifteenth and sixteenth pages); a visitor's brochure from the gift shop: *The Supreme Court of the United States* (undated; no author given except "Prepared by the Supreme Court of the United States, and published with the cooperation of the Supreme Court Historical Society"); and "The United States Supreme Court Building: Letter from the Architect of the Capitol," June 22, 1939 (Washington, DC: US Government Printing Office, 1939).

19. Montesquieu, *Persian Letters,* ed. and trans. John Davidson (1721; repr., London: Gibbons, 1899), available online at http://rbsche.people.wm.edu/teaching/plp/index.html and http://rbsche.people.wm.edu/teaching/plp/letter29.html (accessed September 25, 2011).

20. Levy, *Blasphemy,* pp. 66–67.

21. Goldstone and Goldstone, *Out of the Flames,* pp. 1–4.

22. Lester J. Cappon, *The Adams–Jefferson Letters: The Complete Correspondence between Thomas Jefferson and Abigail and John Adams* (1959; repr., Chapel Hill: University of North Carolina Press, 1988), pp. 607–10.

23. Thomas Jefferson, "The Censorship of Books, Letter to N. G. Dufief, April 19, 1814," in *Writings: Autobiography; Notes on the State of Virginia; Public Papers; Addresses, Messages, and Replies; Miscellany; Letters*, ed. Merrill D. Peterson (New York: Library of America, 1984), p. 1334.

24. Lindsay, "Blasphemy," p. 147.

CHAPTER 18. WHAT IN THE NAME OF GOD?

1. Richard J. Ellis, "One Nation . . . Indivisible," in *To the Flag: The Unlikely History of the Pledge of Allegiance* (Lawrence: University Press of Kansas), pp. 175–76.

2. *Wikipedia*, s.v. "Great Seal of the United States," http://en.wikipedia .org/wiki/Great_Seal_of_the_United_States (accessed September 15, 2011).

3. William Brennan, dissenting, in *Lynch v. Donnelly*, 465 US 668 (1984), http://caselaw.lp.findlaw.com/scripts/getcase.pl?court=us&vol=465&invol=668 (accessed September 19, 2011).

4. *Sherman v. Community Consolidated School District 21 of Wheeling Township*, 980 F.2d 437, 447 (7th Cir. 1992), No. 91-1684.

5. John W. Whitehead, *Religious Apartheid: The Separation of Religion from American Public Life* (Chicago: Moody, 1994), pp. 145–46.

6. Kristina Torres, "'In God' Stickers Would Be Free," *Atlanta Journal-Constitution*, February 29, 2012.

7. Jennifer Steinhauer, "In God We Trust, with the House's Help," *New York Times*, November 2, 2011; and Andrew Taylor, "In God We Trust: Why Congress Reaffirmed the US Motto," Latest News Wires, *Christian Science Monitor*, http://www.csmonitor.com/USE/Latest-News_Wires/2011/1103/In-God-We -Trust-Why-Congress-reaffirmed-the-US-motto (accessed November 3, 2011).

8. R. S. Yeoman, *A Guide Book of United States Coins (The Official Red Book)*, ed. Kenneth Bressett, 62nd ed. (Atlanta, GA: Whitman, 2008), p. 122.

9. Kevin M. Kruse, "For God So Loved the 1 Percent . . . ," *New York Times*, January 18, 2012.

10. "For Publication, United States Court of Appeals for the Ninth Circuit," http://www.constitution.org/usfc/9/newdow_v_us.htm (accessed September 27, 2012).

11. Thomas Jefferson, "The Morals of Jesus; Letter to Dr. Benjamin Rush, with a Syllabus, Apr. 21, 1803," in *Writings: Autobiography; Notes on the State of Virginia; Public Papers; Addresses, Messages, and Replies; Miscellany; Letters*, ed. Merrill D. Peterson (New York: Library of America, 1984), p. 1123.

CHAPTER 19. QUESTIONS

1. Isaac Kramnick and R. Laurence Moore, *The Godless Constitution: The Case against Religious Correctness* (New York: W. W. Norton, 1996), pp. 138–42.

2. Samuel Eliot Morison, *Oxford History of the American People* (New York: Oxford University Press, 1965), p. 300.

3. Rob Boston, *Why the Religious Right Is Wrong about Separation of Church and State* (Amherst, NY: Prometheus Books, 1993), pp. 97–100.

4. As quoted by Leo Pfeffer, "Prayer in Public Schools: The Court's Decisions," in "Church and State," special issue, *National Forum: Phi Kappa Phi Journal* (Winter 1988): 26.

5. Frank R. Zindler, "Prayer of Allegiance to Continue," in *Through Atheist Eyes: Scenes from a World that Won't Reason*, vol. 4 Omnium–Gatherum (Cranford, NJ: American Atheist Press, 2011), pp. 421–22.

6. The Board of Education of the City of Cincinnati et al., "Against Religious Exercises in Public Schools," in *The Annals of America*, vol. 10, *1866–1883, Reconstruction and Industrialization*, ed. Mortimer J. Adler (Chicago: Encyclopedia Britannica, 1968), pp. 214–16.

7. "Overview of Race and Hispanic Origin," nationalatlas.gov, http://www.nationalatlas.gov/articles/people/a_race.html (accessed September 15, 2011).

8. "Gender in the United States," nationalatlas.gov, http://national atlas.gov/articles/people/a_gender.html (accessed August 23, 2011).

9. "Theodore Roosevelt Inaugural," National Park Service, nps.gov, http://www.nps.gov/thri/index.htm (accessed September 16, 2011); and information volunteered by National Park Service docents to author Ed Buckner at the inauguration site, 641 Delaware Avenue, Buffalo, New York, June 21, 2003.

10. Ed Buckner and Michael Buckner, "George Washington: Atheist Hero?" in *American Atheist* 49, no. 4 (4th qtr. 2011).

11. Peter R. Henriques, "'So Help Me, God': A George Washington Myth That Should Be Discarded," George Mason University's History News Network, http://hnn.us/articles/59548.html (accessed November 10, 2011).

12. "Quotes That Never Were: Forged Religious Quotations: A Cottage Industry," Religious Tolerance, http://www.religioustolerance.org/badquotes.htm (accessed September 1, 2011); and *Wikiquote*, s.v. "George Washington," http://en.wikiquote.org/wiki/George_Washington (accessed September 1, 2011).

13. Buckner and Buckner, "George Washington," p. 5.

14. Robert S. Alley, "Public Education and the Public Good," *William &*

Mary Bill of Rights Journal 4, no. 277 (1995), http://scholarhip.law.wm.edu/wmborj/vol4/iss1/6 (accessed September 14, 2011), p. 309.

15. Thomas Jefferson, "To Messrs. Nehemiah Dodge and Others, a Committee of the Danbury Baptist Association, in the State of Connecticut," January 1, 1802, in *Writings: Autobiography; Notes on the State of Virginia; Public Papers; Addresses, Messages, and Replies; Miscellany; Letters*, ed. Merrill D. Peterson (New York: Library of America, 1984), p. 510.

16. Edwin S. Gaustad, *Sworn on the Altar of God: A Religious Biography of Thomas Jefferson* (Grand Rapids, MI: William B. Eerdmans, 1996), p. 194.

17. Mortimer J. Adler, ed., *The Annals of America*, vol. 1, *1493–1754, Discovering a New World* (Chicago: Encyclopedia Britannica, 1968), p. 64.

18. Newt Gingrich, *To Save America: Stopping Obama's Secular-Socialist Machine* (Washington, DC: Regnery, 2010), pp. 265–66.

19. Marvin Harris, *Our Kind: Who We Are, Where We Came From, Where We Are Going* (New York: Harper and Row, 1989); see especially the chapters "Why We Became Religious" and "The Evolution of the Spirit World," pp. 397–407, and the chapters that follow those.

20. George Seldes, comp., ed., *The Great Quotations* (Secaucus, NJ: Citadel, 1983), p. 174.

21. George Arthur Buttrick, ed., *The Interpreter's Bible: The Holy Scriptures in the King James and Revised Standard Versions with General Articles and Introduction, Exegesis, Exposition for Each Book of the Bible, in Twelve Volumes*, vol. 7 (New York: Abingdon-Cokesbury, 1951), p. 329.

22. "How Many People Have Ever Lived? Keyfitz's Calculation Updated (done June 18, 1999)," http://www.math.hawaii.edu/~ramsey/People.html (accessed September 13, 2011); and "Estimating the Number of People That Have Ever Lived," http://www.faculty.rsu.edu/users/f/felwell/www/Ecology/The%20Number%20of%20People%20That%20Have%20Ever%20Lived.htm (accessed September 13, 2011).

23. Alley, "Public Education and the Public Good," pp. 315–16.

24. James Madison, "Detached Memoranda," Document 64, Amendment 1 (Religion), *The Founders' Constitution*, http://press-pubs.uchicago.edu/founders/documents/amendI_religions64.html Madison's Detached Memoranda (accessed February 20, 2012).

25. Chris Rodda, "More Historical Revisionism from the Christmas Wars: Religion in the American Public Square," Talk to Action, February 20, 2007, http://www.talk2action.org/story/2007/2/20/171052/068 (accessed February 20, 2012).

26. Chris Rodda, "Stephen Mansfield's 'Ten Tortured Words'—A Book Review (Part 3)," Talk to Action, August 25, 2007, http://www.talk2action.org/story/2007/8/25/23580/0933 (accessed February 20, 2012).

27. Gregory S. Paul, "The Great Scandal: Christianity's Role in the Rise of the Nazis," 2 pts., *Free Inquiry* 23, no. 4 (October/November 2003) and *Free Inquiry* 24, no. 1 (December 2003/January 2004). Also available on the web: part 1, http://www.secularhumanism.org/index.php?section=library&page=paul_24_1; and part 2, http://www.secularhumanism.org/index.php?section=library&page=paul_23_4 (accessed February 11, 2012); and Ronald Hilton, "Hitler: Hitler's Religion," http://wais.stanford.edu/Germany/germany_hitler0310 2004.htm (accessed August 1, 2011).

CONCLUSION

1. Mortimer J. Adler, ed., "James Madison: Against Religious Assessments," in *The Annals of America*, vol. 3, *1784–1796, Organizing the New Nation* (Chicago: Encyclopedia Britannica, 1968), p. 17.

2. Sean Faircloth, "Our Secular Decade: A Strategic Plan," chap. 9 in *Attack of the Theocrats: How the Religious Right Harms Us All—and What We Can Do about It* (Charlottesville, VA: Pitchstone, 2012), pp. 119–32.

Glossary

agnosticism/agnostic—Agnosticism is the idea that it is not possible to know with certainty whether supernatural beings, including any gods, exist. Agnostics may have beliefs that make them in some sense theists, or they may have no such beliefs, hence qualifying as atheists.

atheism/atheist—Atheism is a conclusion or a statement about a lack of religious beliefs. Atheists may hold that the existence of any specifically defined god is impossible, but the term does not imply that an atheist claims to be able to prove that nothing considered a "god" can exist.

blasphemy—Saying or writing things that are considered to be irreverent toward or slanderous of a god or religious ideas or institutions. We agree with the unknown wag who said, "blasphemy is a victimless crime," and we insist that neither blasphemy nor heresy should be any part of the civil or criminal law.

Christianity/Christian—Contrary to the writings of Thomas Jefferson, we—like most modern Americans—would not consider someone a Christian unless that person believes that Jesus Christ was the divine "Son of God" and that Jesus died to expatiate human believers who accept him of their sins.

deism/deist—Deism varies somewhat according to which follower or critic is defining it, but it usually refers to a set of beliefs that include an ultimate, original, supernatural creator and lawgiver but that usually does not accept miracles that violate the laws of nature or mysticism. Deism does not therefore include a god who interferes in the workings of the natural world or can be led to interfere by prayers or entreaties.

Enlightenment, the—A movement primarily among European intellectuals of the eighteenth century (many of them known personally to men like Jefferson, Paine, Adams, and Franklin) that emphasized reason and science and downplayed received truth based on authority (especially religious authority—books or organizations). The roots of the Enlightenment, as its leaders themselves noted, go well back in time to ancient Greece and Rome and, especially, to the Renaissance humanists of the fourteenth and fifteenth centuries. The Enlightenment had major influence on American intellectuals and the Founding Fathers.

freedom of (or rights of) conscience—Freedom of conscience means (necessarily implies) that government has no right to require citizens to declare any religious idea to be true or untrue, and that neither government nor the majority of citizens have a right of inquiry regarding any individual's beliefs.

freethinker—Freethought is the general idea that opinions about life in general and religion in particular should be formed based on reason and the evidence of our senses, independently of tradition, authority, or established belief. Historically in the United States most—but not all and not by definition—people known as freethinkers have been atheists or agnostics.

heresy—Holding and especially publicly professing ideas that are contrary to those proclaimed as true by a particular religion or sect.

secular humanism—Secular humanism is a philosophy based on reason and science that concludes that human beings must and should work to find human solutions to human problems without relying on any supernatural sources.

secularism—Secularism is a basic idea related to government, an idea—primarily invented and developed by the Founding Fathers of the United States though now widely adopted elsewhere as well—frequently referred to as "separation of church and state." Under secularism, a government cannot rely on any god or religious principle as it acts for the common good; all agents of the government must, as governmental agents, remain neutral regarding religious ideas.

theism/theist—Theisms come in a bewildering variety, with little in common with each other except a conclusion that there are one or more gods in existence in the universe. Theists believe that there are supernatural powers behind nature, human origins, human morality, and so forth. Not all religions, however, are theistic—some attribute powers and effects not to gods but to forces or entities from another supernatural realm. Both the variety and the unprovable nature and existence of all the gods conceived of by man make secularism desirable if not required for human happiness and progress.

Selected Bibliography
Sources and Related Writing regarding Secularism and Religious Liberty

Abrahamson, Brant, and Frederick C. Smith. *The Decalogue: Bible Scholarship for Use Today*. Brookfield, IL: Teachers' Press, 2000.

Adams, John. *A Defence of the Constitutions of Government of the United States of America*. Vol. 1. 1787–1788. Reprint, New York: Da Capo, 1971.

———. *The Founding Fathers: John Adams; A Biography in His Own Words*. Edited by James Bishop Peabody. New York: Newsweek, 1973.

Adler, Mortimer J., ed. *The Annals of America*. Vols. 1–18. Chicago: Encyclopedia Britannica, 1968.

———. *Great Issues in American Life: A Conspectus*. Vols. 1–2. Chicago: Encyclopedia Britannica, 1968.

———. *Six Great Ideas*. New York: Macmillan, 1981.

———. *We Hold These Truths: Understanding the Ideas and Ideals of the Constitution*. New York: Macmillan, 1987.

Alden, John. *A History of the South*. Vol. 3, *The South in the Revolution 1763–1789*. N.p.: Louisiana State University Press, 1957.

Alley, Robert S. *James Madison on Religious Liberty*. Amherst, NY: Prometheus Books, 1985.

Barker, Dan. *Godless*. Berkeley, CA: Ulysses, 2008.

———. *Losing Faith in Faith*. Madison, WI: FFRF, 1992.

Barlow, Joel. "Preface and Postscript to *The Columbiad*." In *The Annals of America*. Vol. 4, *1797–1820: Domestic Expansion and Foreign Entanglements*. Chicago: Encyclopedia Britannica, 1968, pp. 227–32.

Beeman, Richard. *Plain, Honest Men: The Making of the American Constitution*. New York: Random House, 2009.

Bible, The Holy, New International Version, NIV. Grand Rapids, MI: Biblica, 1973, 1978, 1984, and 2011.

Blackmon, Douglas A. *Slavery by Another Name: The Re-Enslavement of Black Americans from the Civil War to World War II*. New York: Doubleday, 2008.

Blaker, Kimberly, ed. *The Fundamentals of Extremism: The Christian Right in America*. New Boston, MI: New Boston Books, 2003.

Boller, Paul F. *George Washington & Religion*. Dallas: Southern Methodist University Press, 1963.

Boston, Rob. "A Tangled Tale of Pirates, a Poet and the True Meaning of the First Amendment." *Church & State* 50, no. 6, June 1997, pp. 11–14.

———. *Why the Religious Right Is Wrong about Separation of Church & State*. Amherst, NY: Prometheus Books, 1993.

Boyd, Kenneth W. *The Historical Markers of North Georgia: The Complete Text and Location of the Various State and Non-state Historical Markers Located Throughout Forty-Four North Georgia Counties*. Atlanta: Cherokee, 1993.

Bradley, Patricia. *Slavery, Propaganda, and the American Revolution*. Jackson: University Press of Mississippi, 1998.

Buckner, Edward M., and Michael E. Buckner, eds. *Quotations That Support the Separation of State and Church*. 2nd ed. Smyrna, GA: Freethought (Atlanta Freethought Society), 1995.

Buttrick, George Arthur, ed. *The Interpreter's Bible: The Holy Scriptures in the King James and Revised Standard Versions with General Articles and Introduction, Exegesis, Exposition for Each Book of the Bible, in Twelve Volumes*. New York: Abingdon-Cokesbury, 1951.

Cappon, Lester J. *The Adams–Jefferson Letters: The Complete Correspondence between Thomas Jefferson and Abigail and John Adams*. 1959. Reprint, Chapel Hill: University of North Carolina Press, 1988.

Chilton, David. "Appendix A: The Eschatology of Dominion: A Summary," in *Paradise Restored: A Biblical Theology of Dominion*. Tyler, TX: Dominion, 1994.

Claussen, Martin P., ed. *The Journal of the Senate, including the Journal of the Executive Proceedings of the Senate, John Adams Administration, 1797–1801*. Vol. 1, *Fifth Congress, First Session; March–July, 1797*. Wilmington, DE: Michael Glazier, 1977.

Cohen, Richard. "The Myth of American Exceptionalism," *Washington Post*, May 9, 2011.

Collins, Robert. *100 Bible Math Mistakes*. Birmingham, AL: Freethinkers' Books, 2010.

Coyne, Jerry A., "As Atheists Know, You Can Be Good without God," *USA Today*, August 1, 2011.

Cross, F. L., and E. A. Livingstone, eds. *The Oxford Dictionary of the Christian Church*. 3rd ed. Oxford: Oxford University Press, 1997.

Crutchfield, James A., ed. *The Georgia Almanac and Book of Facts, 1989–1990*. Nashville, TN: Rutledge Hill, 1988.

Dacey, Austin. *The Secular Conscience: Why Belief Belongs in Public Life*. Amherst, NY: Prometheus Books, 2008.

Dawkins, Richard. *The God Delusion*. Boston: Houghton Mifflin, 2006. Paperback edition published 2007.

———. *The Greatest Show on Earth: The Evidence for Evolution*. New York: Free Press, 2009.

Dennett, Daniel C. *Breaking the Spell: Religion as a Natural Phenomenon*. New York: Penguin Books, 2006.

Dolan, Graham. *The Greenwich Guide to Measuring Time*. Chicago: Heinmann Library, 2001.

Dudley, William, ed. *Religion in America: Opposing Viewpoints*. San Diego: Greenhaven, 2002.

Ehrenreich, Barbara. *Bright-Sided: How the Relentless Promotion of Positive Thinking Has Undermined America*. New York: Metropolitan Books, 2009.

Ehrman, Bart D. *God's Problem: How the Bible Fails to Answer Our Most Important Question—Why We Suffer*. New York: HarperOne, 2008.

Eller, David. *Atheism Advanced: Further Thoughts of a Freethinker*. Edited by Frank R. Zindler. Cranford, NJ: American Atheist Press, 2007.

Ellis, Joseph. *American Creation: Triumphs and Tragedies at the Founding of the Republic*. New York: Alfred A. Knopf, 2007.

Ellis, Richard J. *To the Flag: The Unlikely History of the Pledge of Allegiance*. Lawrence: University Press of Kansas, 2005.

Esposito, John L., ed. *The Oxford Dictionary of Islam*. Oxford: Oxford University Press, 2003.

Faircloth, Sean. *Attack of the Theocrats: How the Religious Right Harms Us All—and What We Can Do about It*. Charlottesville, VA: Pitchstone, 2012.

Farrand, Max, ed. *The Records of the Federal Convention of 1787*. Rev. ed. 4 vols. Vol. 1. 1937. Reprint, New Haven, CT: Yale University Press, 1966.

Fea, John. *Was America Founded as a Christian Nation?* Louisville: Westminster John Knox Press, 2011.

Flynn, Thomas W. *The New Encyclopedia of Unbelief*. Amherst, NY: Prometheus Books, 2007.

———. *The Trouble with Christmas*. Amherst, NY: Prometheus Books, 1993.

Foner, Eric. *Tom Paine and Revolutionary America*. New York: Oxford University Press, 1976.

Frankel, Marvin E. *Faith and Freedom: Religious Liberty in America*. New York: Hill & Wang, 1994.

Franklin, Benjamin. *Writings*. Edited by J. A. Leo Lemay. New York: Library of America, 1987.

Freeman, Douglas Southall. *R. E. Lee: A Biography*. Vol. 1. New York: Charles Scribner's Sons, 1934.

Gaustad, Edwin S. *Sworn on the Altar of God: A Religious Biography of Thomas Jefferson*. Grand Rapids, MI: William B. Eerdmans, 1996.

Gaylor, Annie Laurie. *Woe to the Women: For the Bible Tells Me So*. Madison, WI: Freedom from Religion Foundation, 1981.

————, ed. *Women without Superstition: "No Gods—No Masters": The Collected Writings of Women Freethinkers of the Nineteenth & Twentieth Centuries*. Madison, WI: Freedom from Religion Foundation, 1997.

Geller, Pamela. *The Post-American Presidency: The Obama Administration's War on America*. New York: Threshhold Editions, 2010.

Gingrich, Newt. *A Nation Like No Other: Why American Exceptionalism Matters*. With Vince Hailey. Washington, DC: Regnery, 2011.

————. *Rediscovering God in America: Reflections on the Role of Faith in Our History*. Nashville, TN: Integrity House, 2006.

————. *To Save America: Stopping Obama's Secular-Socialist Machine*. With Joe DeSantis. Washington, DC: Regnery, 2010.

————. *Winning the Future: A 21st Century Contract with America*. Washington, DC: Regnery, 2005.

Goicoechea, David, John Luik, and Tim Madigan, eds. *The Question of Humanism*. Amherst, NY: Prometheus Books, 1991.

Goldstone, Lawrence, and Nancy Goldstone. *Out of the Flames: The Remarkable Story of a Fearless Scholar, a Fatal Heresy, and One of the Rarest Books in the World*. New York: Broadway Books, 2002.

Grant, George. *The Changing of the Guard: Biblical Principles for Political Action*. Ft. Worth, TX: Dominion, 1987.

Grant, R. G. *Slavery: Real People and Their Stories of Enslavement*. London: DK, 2009.

Hamburger, Philip. *Separation of Church and State*. Cambridge, MA: Harvard University Press, 2002.

Hammond, Phillip E. *With Liberty for All: Freedom of Religion in the United States*. Louisville, KY: Westminster John Knox Press, 1998.

Harris, Marvin. *Our Kind: Who We Are, Where We Came from, Where We Are Going*. New York: Harper and Row, 1989.

Harris, Sam. *The End of Faith: Religion, Terror, and the Future of Reason*. New York: W. W. Norton, 2005.

————. *Letter to a Christian Nation*. New York: Alfred A. Knopf, 2006.

————. *The Moral Landscape: How Science Can Determine Human Values*. New York: Free Press, 2010.

Harrison, Guy. *50 Reasons People Give for Believing in a God*. Amherst, NY: Prometheus Books, 2008.

Hitchens, Christopher. *God Is Not Great: How Religion Poisons Everything*. New York: Twelve, 2007.

Hoffman, R. Joseph, and Gerald A. Larue, eds. *Biblical v. Secular Ethics: The Conflict*. Amherst, NY: Prometheus Books, 1988.

Holmes, David L. *The Faiths of the Founding Fathers*. Oxford: Oxford University Press, 2006.

Hume, David. *Dialogues concerning Natural Religion*. Edited by Robert M. Baird. 1779. Reprint, Amherst, NY: Prometheus Books, 1989.

Hutson, James H., ed. *The Founders on Religion: A Book of Quotations*. Princeton, NJ: Princeton University Press, 2005.

Ingersoll, Robert G. Almost any essay, lecture, or book you can find by him.

Jacoby, Susan. *Freethinkers, A History of American Secularism*. New York: Metropolitan Books, 2004.

Jefferson, Thomas. *The Complete Jefferson: Containing His Major Writings, Published and Unpublished, Except His Letters*. Edited by Saul K. Padover. New York: Books for Libraries Press, 1969. First published Duell, Sloan and Pearce, 1943.

———. *Writings: Autobiography; Notes on the State of Virginia; Public Papers; Addresses, Messages, and Replies; Miscellany; Letters*. Edited by Merrill D. Peterson. New York: Library of America, 1984.

Kagin, Edwin F. *Baubles of Blasphemy*. 2nd ed. Edited by Ed Buckner. Cranford, NJ: American Atheist Press, 2009.

Kick, Russ, ed. *Everything You Know about God Is Wrong: The Disinformation Guide to Religion*. New York: Disinformation, 2007.

King, David James. *Creating a Nation under God: Rebuilding America with Biblical Principles*. Lafayette, LA: Prescott, 2000.

Koch, Adrienne, ed. *The American Enlightenment: The Shaping of the America Experiment and a Free Society*. New York: George Braziller, 1965.

Krakauer, Jon. *Where Men Win Glory: The Odyssey of Pat Tillman*. New York: Doubleday, 2009.

Kramnick, Isaac, and R. Laurence Moore. *The Godless Constitution: The Case against Religious Correctness*. New York: W. W. Norton, 1996.

Kristof, Nicholas D., and Sheryl WuDunn. *Half the Sky: Turning Oppression into Opportunity for Women Worldwide*. New York: Vintage Books, 2010.

Krueger, Douglas E. *What Is Atheism? A Short Introduction*. Amherst, NY: Prometheus Books, 1998.

Kurtz, Paul. *Embracing the Power of Humanism*. Lanham, MD: Rowman & Littlefield, 2000.

———. *Living without Religion: Eupraxophy*. Amherst, NY: Prometheus Books, 1994.

————. *The Transcendental Temptation: A Critique of Religion and the Paranormal.* Amherst, NY: Prometheus Books, 1985.

Larson, Edward J. *A Magnificent Catastrophe: The Tumultuous Election of 1800, America's First Presidential Campaign.* New York: Free Press, 2007.

Leiner, Frederick C. *The End of Barbary Terror: America's 1815 War against the Pirates of North Africa.* New York: Oxford University Press, 2006.

Levy, Leonard W. *Blasphemy: Verbal Offense against the Sacred, from Moses to Salman Rushdie.* New York: Alfred A. Knopf, 1993.

Lewis, C. S. *Mere Christianity.* New York: Macmillan, 1952.

Limbaugh, David. *Persecution: How Liberals Are Waging War against Christianity.* Washington, DC: Regnery, 2003.

Lizza, Ryan. "Leap of Faith: The Making of a Republican Front-Runner." *New Yorker*, August 15 and 22, 2011.

Locke, John. "A Letter concerning Toleration." 1689. Edited by Robert Maynard Hutchins and Charles L. Sherman. *Great Books of the Western World.* Vol. 35. Chicago: Encyclopedia Britannica, 1987, pp. 1–22.

Luhrmann, T. M. *When God Talks Back: Understanding the American Evangelical Relationship with God.* New York: Alfred A. Knopf, 2012.

Madison, James. *The Complete Madison: His Basic Writings.* Edited by Saul K. Padover. New York: Kraus Reprint, 1971. Originally published by Harper and Brothers, 1953.

————. *James Madison: A Biography in His Own Words.* Vols. 1 and 2. Edited by Merrill D. Peterson. New York: Newsweek, 1974.

Maier, Pauline. *Ratification: The People Debate the Constitution, 1787–1788.* New York: Simon & Schuster, 2010.

Martin, Michael. *The Big Domino in the Sky, and Other Atheistic Tales.* Amherst, NY: Prometheus Books, 1996.

————. *The Case against Christianity.* Philadelphia: Temple University Press, 1991.

McGowan, Dale. *Atheism for Dummies.* Hoboken, NJ: John Wiley & Sons, forthcoming 2013.

————. ed. *Parenting beyond Belief: On Raising Ethical, Caring Kids without Religion.* New York: AMACOM, 2007.

McNeill, William H. *History of Western Civilization: A Handbook.* 6th ed. Chicago: University of Chicago Press, 1986.

Medved, Michael. *The 10 Big Lies about America: Combating Destructive Distortions about Our Nation.* New York: Crown Forum, 2008.

Melton, J. Gordon. *Melton's Encyclopedia of American Religions.* 8th ed. Detroit: Gale, 2009.

Miller, Hunter, ed. "Treaty of Peace and Friendship between the United States and the Bey and Subjects of Tripoli of Barbary." In *Treaties and Other Interna-*

tional Acts of the United States of America. Vol. 2, *Documents 1–40: 1776–1818*. Washington, DC: US Government Printing Office, 1931, pp. 349–85.

Mills, David. *Atheist Universe: The Thinking Person's Answer to Christian Fundamentalism*. Berkeley, CA: Ulysses, 2006.

Moore, Roy. *So Help Me God: The Ten Commandments, Judicial Tyranny, and the Battle for Religious Freedom*. With John Perry. Nashville, TN: Broadman & Holman, 2005.

Morison, Samuel Eliot. *Oxford History of the American People*. New York: Oxford University Press, 1965.

Morison, Samuel Eliot, Henry Steele Commager, and William E. Leuchtenburg. *A Concise History of the American Republic*. New York: Oxford University Press, 1977.

Murphy, Tim. "Crazy Like a Fox: The Method to Michele Bachmann's Madness." *Mother Jones*, September/October 2011, pp. 27–29 and 66–67.

Neuhaus, Richard John. *The Naked Public Square; Religion and Democracy in America*. 2nd ed. Grand Rapids, MI: William B. Eerdmans, 1988.

Noonan, John T., Jr. *The Lustre of Our Country: The American Experience of Religious Freedom*. Berkeley: University of California Press, 1998.

North, Gary. "The Intellectual Schizophrenia of the New Christian Right." In *The Failure of the American Baptist Culture*. Tyler, TX: Geneva Divinity School Press, 1982.

———. *Political Polytheism: The Myth of Pluralism*. Tyler, TX: Institute for Christian Economics, 1989.

———. *The Sinai Strategy: Economics and the Ten Commandments*. Tyler, TX: Institute for Christian Economics, 1986.

Obama, Barack. *The Audacity of Hope: Thoughts on Reclaiming the American Dream*. New York: Crown, 2006.

Paine, Thomas. *The Rights of Man*. 1791. Reprint, New York: Heritage, 1961.

Palin, Sarah. *America by Heart: Reflections on Family, Faith, and Flag*. New York: HarperCollins, 2010.

Parker, Richard B. *Uncle Sam in Barbary: A Diplomatic History*. Gainesville: University Press of Florida, 2004.

Parsons, Keith. *Why I Am Not a Christian*. Edited by Ed Buckner. Smyrna, GA: Freethought (Atlanta Freethought Society), 2000.

Paulos, John Allen. *Irreligion: A Mathematician Explains Why the Arguments for God Just Don't Add Up*. New York: Hill & Wang, 2007.

Peterson, Merrill D. *Thomas Jefferson: A Biography*. London: Oxford University Press, 1970.

———, ed. *Thomas Jefferson: A Reference Biography*. New York: Charles Scribner's Sons, 1986.

Phillips, Melanie. *The World Turned Upside Down: The Global Battle over God, Truth, and Power*. Jackson, TN: Encounter Books, 2010.

Pigliucci, Massimo. *Tales of the Rational*. Edited by Ed Buckner. Smyrna, GA: Freethought (Atlanta Freethought Society), 2000.

Ragdale, Bruce A., and Kathryn Allamong Jacob, eds. *Biographical Directory of the United States Congress, 1774–1989*. Washington, DC: US Government Printing Office, 1989.

Rakove, Jack N., ed. *The Annotated U.S. Constitution and Declaration of Independence*. Cambridge, MA: Belknap Press of Harvard University, 2009.

Ray, Darrel W. *The God Virus: How Religion Infects Our Lives and Culture*. Bonner Springs, KS: IPC, 2009.

Rushdoony, Rousas John. *The Institutes of Biblical Law: A Chalcedon Study with Three Appendices by Gary North*. Nutley, NJ: Presbyterian and Reformed Publishing, 1973.

———. *The Institutes of Biblical Law: With a Special Supplement by Herbert W. Titus*. Vol. 2, *Law and Society*. Vallecito, CA: Ross House Books, 1982.

Russell, Bertrand. *Why I Am Not a Christian, and Other Essays on Religion and Related Subjects*. New York: Touchstone/Simon & Schuster, 1957.

Seldes, George, comp. and ed. *The Great Quotations*. Secaucus, NJ: Citadel, 1983.

Shanks, Niall. *God, the Devil, and Darwin: A Critique of Intelligent Design Theory*. Oxford: Oxford University Press, 2004.

Sharlet, Jeff. *C Street: The Fundamentalist Threat to American Democracy*. New York: Little, Brown, 2010.

———. *The Family: The Secret Fundamentalism at the Heart of American Power*. New York: Harper Perennial, 2009.

Shermer, Michael. *Why Darwin Matters: The Case against Intelligent Design*. New York: Henry Holt/Times Books, 2006.

Simon, James F. *What Kind of Nation*. New York: Simon & Schuster, 2002.

Singer, Peter, ed. *Ethics*. Oxford: Oxford University Press, 1994.

Skolnik, Fred, and Michael Berenbaum, eds. *Encyclopedia Judaica*. 2nd ed. Detroit: Macmillan Reference USA, 2007.

Smith, George H. *Atheism: The Case against God*. Amherst, NY: Prometheus Books, 1979.

Smith, Goldwin. *A History of England*. 3rd ed. New York: Charles Scribner's Sons, 1966.

Stein, Gordon, ed. *An Anthology of Atheism and Rationalism*. Amherst, NY: Prometheus Books, 1980.

———. *A Second Anthology of Atheism and Rationalism*. Amherst, NY: Prometheus Books, 1988.

Stenger, Victor J. *God: The Failed Hypothesis*. Amherst, NY: Prometheus Books, 2008.

Stormer, John A. *Betrayed by the Bench: How Judge-Made Law Has Transformed America's Constitution, Courts and Culture*. Florissant, MO: Liberty Bell, 2007.

Suarez, Ray. *The Holy Vote: The Politics of Faith in America*. New York: Harper-Collins, 2006.

Sullivan, Amy. *The Party Faithful: How and Why Democrats Are Closing the God Gap*. New York: Scribner, 2008.

Telushkin, Joseph. *Jewish Literacy: The Most Important Things to Know about the Jewish Religion, Its People, and Its History*. New York: William Morrow, 2001.

Thomson, J. Anderson, Jr. *Why We Believe in God(s): A Concise Guide to the Science of Faith*. With Clare Aukofer. Charlottesville, VA: Pitchstone, 2011.

Tyler, Alice Felt. *Freedom's Ferment: Phases of American Social History to 1860*. Minneapolis: University of Minnesota Press, 1944.

Walker, Jim. "Little-Known US Document Signed by President Adams Proclaims America's Government Is Secular." In *Early America Review* 2, no. 1 (Summer 1997).

Washington, George. *Writings*. Edited by John Rhodehamel. New York: Library of America, 1997.

Wheelan, Joseph. *Jefferson's War: America's First War on Terror 1801–1805*. New York: Carroll & Graf, 2003.

Whitehead, John W. *Religious Apartheid: The Separation of Religion from American Public Life*. Chicago: Moody, 1994.

Whitten, Mark Weldon. *The Myth of Christian America: What You Need to Know about the Separation of Church and State*. Macon, GA: Smyth & Helwys, 1999.

Wilson, James Q. *The Moral Sense*. New York: Free Press, 1993.

Woodress, James. *A Yankee's Odyssey: The Life of Joel Barlow*. Philadelphia: Lippincott, 1958.

Wright, Robert. *The Evolution of God*. New York: Back Bay Books, 2010.

Zindler, Frank R. *Through Atheist Eyes*. 4 vols. (vol. 5 forthcoming). Cranford, NJ: American Atheist Press, 2011.

Index